Hirsute Scribe Press

LET
NO STRANGER
WAIT
OUTSIDE
YOUR
DOOR

Lou Kief

We Two Boys
Together Clinging

We two boys together clinging
one the other never leaving
up and down the roads going,
north and south excursions making,
over enjoying, elbows stretching, fingers clutching,
arm'd and fearless, eating, drinking, sleeping, loving,
no law less than ourselves owning, sailing, soldering,
thieving, threatening,
misers, menials, priests alarming, air breathing, water
drinking, on the turf or the sea-breach dancing,
cities wrenching, ease scorning, statues mocking,
feebleness chasing, fulfilling our foray.

Walt Whitman
from Calamus
written in or
before 1859

In 1882 Oscar Wilde
Visits San Francisco

In his novel, "The Picture of Dorian Gray" (1891), Wilde writes, "It's an odd thing, but everyone who disappears is said to be seen in San Francisco. It must be a delightful city, and possesses all the attractions of the next world."

For Gene, who saw
in his wife's brother a
young man he knew would
never be happy in the
confinement of a normal
life, and encouraged him to
follow his dreams.

For Ann, a mother filled with unconditional abounding love and dedication, who taught her children the lessons they needed to be good human beings.

For George Cory and Douglass Cross, two gay men who, in 1954 wrote the song Tony Bennett immortalized: "I Left My Heart in San Francisco."

And for generations of gay men and women who lived their lives in fear and lies.

Awakening

This book is being written for my younger gay brothers and lesbian sisters who weren't alive during the 1960s and 70s, and for anyone who wants to understand the significance of the period and how it changed - for the better - the lives of gay men and women all over the United States and around the world.

It's time to write this. I'm getting older, and disappointed that as I do, the details of the wild and crazy good times are starting to fade, and my brain has begun to bury the devastating and sad times even deeper so they won't hurt as much. Someday, someone will dump a box of ashes among the plants and trees in the AIDS Memorial Redwood Grove in Golden Gate Park, and I'll be home again with all my friends who died so young. Too many have been lost. Too many lives have been lived too briefly and forgotten. They deserve more than that. They deserve a chance to be remembered by you.

"*Let No Stranger Wait Outside Your Door*" shares what it was like to be gay at a time when society, including our own families, chose to deny our existence, ignored or ridiculed us. It's a story about a sudden, great migration of men and women, who like pioneers a century before, found themselves bound for California and San Francisco where happy, exuberant people filled with hope discovered they didn't need anyone's approval to live their lives in the open. If you are gay, it was a time you need to know about and embrace. It was a time of which you can be very proud. Hopefully this memoir/novel will give you an historical reference and a greater understanding for some of the gay people who preceded you. If you aren't gay, I hope it will help you better understand your gay friends or children.

Forward

Before the 1970's America believed every gay person was a drag queen or a cross-dresser. Straight people typecasted us as hairdressers, florists, interior decorators or fashion designers, graciously conceding these professions to "the gays". Even though they depended on how our talents made their lives better, most of them considered us an embarrassment to their friends and families. They refused to acknowledge the millions of us, some of whom they were married to. They worked with us, played with us and shared our lives. We built their homes, educated their children, operated on them when they were sick, defended them in courts and even buried them when they died. They didn't see us in the faces of their own children and when they did, they denied it.

It was a time when we were more comfortable being invisible. It made life easier, albeit lonely and depressing for us. We were deep in our closets. It was safe there, but it condemned us to a life of lies told to the people we loved the most.

As much as being about San Francisco in the 1970's, this book is about what my life was like before I had the courage to head out west. It speaks of a time before cell phones, email, personal computers and the Internet, when gay people had few options to find self-respect or one another.

Gay bars in America were always in the worst part of town. Most were marked with just a street number and maybe a small light over a door in an alley or parking lot. They were our only form of socialization, and were frequently raided by the police. If you had a profession or family to protect, you dared not go for fear of being seen. Most of us were timid, frightened men and women living a lie. It was a damn hopeless life.

The gay awakening of the 1970's was the moment - call it a window in time that opened for some unexplained reason - maybe we just had enough! It was when our lot in life began to change dramatically. A part of this book tells the story about a small group of people that took a foothold in an old, declining San Francisco neighborhood and for the first time were able to concentrate all their imagination and creative talents on one small community for their own benefit. The results were nothing short of spectacular.

The book shares the story of the forces that made me drop everything and run to California. It speaks of what it was like to be there during that time of freedom and change, and how one of us was changed because of it. It's only my story, but I'm sure one that is similar to thousands of others. I hope it will make you laugh and cry, and think. If you are gay, I hope it makes you appreciate the lives thousands of others have lived to make it possible for you to live your life proudly, openly and honestly. I'll do my best as a witness to make it come alive for you and take you on an adventure that gave my life meaning.

"Gay people,
we will not win our rights
by staying quietly in our closets.
We are coming out to fight the lies,
the myths, the distortions.
We are coming out to tell the truths
about gays, for I am tired of
the conspiracy of silence,
so I'm going to talk about it.
And I want you to talk about it.
You must come out."

- *Harvey Milk*

I Left My Heart In San Francisco

"The loveliness of Paris
Seems somehow sadly gay
The glory that was Rome
Is of another day
I've been terribly alone
And forgotten in Manhattan
I'm going home to my city by the bay.

I left my heart in San Francisco
High on a hill, it calls to me.
To be where little cable cars
Climb halfway to the stars!
The morning fog may chill the air
I don't care.
My love waits there in San Francisco
Above the blue and windy sea
When I come home to you, San Francisco,
Your golden sun will shine for me!"

- George Cory & Douglass Cross

Contents

PART ONE
I've been terribly alone

PART TWO
I'm going home to my city by the bay

PART THREE
Above the blue and windy sea

Appendix

PART ONE

I've been terribly alone

1

Brown Leather Jacket

Every weekday at three-forty-five I would stand at the window in our living room. I don't know how I knew what time it was, but my internal clock faithfully led my feet to this spot. The window sill came up to my neck. The white sheer curtains had heavy hems. I can tell you they smelled of must and cigarette smoke and were almost opaque. They tasted acidic and old. When pushed aside there was a spot on the glass in the lower right corner with many nose prints. I'd pull the heavy curtains over my head and disappear behind them into my private space. It was here I would stand and wait faithfully. And then, just as every weekday before, he would appear. As soon as I saw him I could feel my tiny penis become erect and push against my pants. My heart would beat faster and I'd lean into the glass, touching it with my nose again so I could be as close to him as possible. He had dark brown hair, a moustache and always wore the same clothes: a pair of pressed khakis, well-worn work boots and a brown, weather-beaten leather flight jacket. It was here, on this piece of worn, floral axminister carpet, against the Kemtone Chinese Red walls and chipped white enamel window sill that I realized I wanted him more than anything else in the world.

I was in love.

I was four.

So anyone who tells you that being gay is a lifestyle choice is full of shit.

There could be a case made for environmental conditions affecting my sexuality. My father was a weekend alcoholic with a nasty streak when he drank, and my mother protected us from him. When he would get violent and hurt her, I'd run onto our front porch and scream for someone, anyone, to come help us. No one ever came. When he dragged the five-gallon can of gasoline he kept outside for his boat into the house and threatened to burn it down, she bundled us up in our warmest clothes and led us many blocks through ankle-deep snow to see "Mary Queen of Scotts" at a late night movie. We didn't return home until she was sure he would be asleep. She sent me and my sisters to tap dance classes, encouraged us to play musical instruments, brought us classical records recorded for children, took us to museums and generally made sure we were schooled in etiquette and the arts. She did all of this and kept us clothed and fed on my father's sixty-five dollar a week carpenter's salary. She had an eighth-grade education, five kids, never learned how to drive and was trapped in a marriage with an alcoholic husband who for years would verbally and sometimes physically make her life a living hell. To keep her sanity, she read incessantly, joined Al-Anon, and when my father would rip into her during his weekend binges, accusing her of having a lesbian relationship with someone named Claire, one of the women in her support group, she didn't deny it. I never knew if this was true, and if it was, I certainly couldn't blame her for seeking love and affection anyplace she could find it.

When my father died I finally told her I was gay. Instead of being surprised, she told me she had always known. Then, without emotion, she told me she thought my father might have been too.

She died too young at sixty-six, only two years after my dad. The bookshelves in the house were full of her reading. She was self-educated and wise beyond her years. She longed for a more romantic life. This was evidenced by her love of Fred Astaire and her copy of Margaret Mitchell's "*Gone with the Wind*," whose worn pages were warped and stained from her tears.

I can still hear the sound of the tumblers clicking into place in the lock on her front door as I closed it behind me. She was gone and the house was dead. I was leaving home for the last time. Soon her name would disappear from the phone book and the number would be reassigned to someone else. There would be no more "home," no one to call, no birthday or mother's day cards to send.

As I walked down the steps, the realization swept over me like a flood and I wept. At thirty-four I was an orphan, and it devastated me.

2

I'll Cut Your Ears Off

Everybody knows where Detroit, Michigan is so there's no need to start with the French missionaries who came down the river in 1670, discovered a stone idol venerated by the native Indians and destroyed it with an axe. Today Detroit lies in ruins, a ghost of what it was. The house where I was born is a collapsing, burned out shell. But that's not the Detroit of my memories. In the 1940's this racially-mixed city had 1.8 million black and white, hardworking

family people. The Twin Pines dairyman left milk on our porch in glass bottles with paper stoppers. The dry cleaners picked up and delivered. There were old trucks overflowing with vegetables and fresh fruits shaded by big canvas awnings, their Italian drivers sing-shouting what they had for sale from watermelons to ripe strawberries as they crept down the street. And if you were pregnant, you probably put out brown glass gallon bottles of your urine on the porch that Parke-Davis would pick up and use to make drugs.

During summer vacation we played baseball and rode our bikes in the street and pretty much did whatever we wanted with only a few rules, the most important was being home before dark in time for dinner. The neighbors kept an eye on everyone's kids - kids from all over the world: Italy, Germany, Poland, you name it. Depending on which house you were visiting, the language could be different, and everybody got along just fine. There was a season for flying kites, baseball cards, yo-yos and marbles, and whoa be the penalty if you didn't follow the calendar. Old Mrs. Adams next door would call us in on a hot Saturday afternoon with a special treat of popcorn, or lard mixed with granulated sugar she served from her chipped, white enamel dishpan. And in the early fall we were invited to bring paper sacks and allowed to climb a huge cherry tree down the alley to pick and eat as many as we wanted. We walked everywhere - to shop, to school, to the movies. Mom would take us downtown on the streetcar to J.L. Hudson's and at Christmas time Santa Claus would always be there waiting for us.

The city of my birth was a magical place for a kid growing up. Our doors were only locked when we went to bed, and the only thing between us and someone standing on the front porch was an eye-and-hook latch on an old wooden screen door. I remember one day when the garbage man came to the door to see if my mother had anything to be hauled away. He was as dark as night and I must have stared very hard at him because at one point he bent down, put his nose against the screen and instead of saying "Boo," jokingly said, "I'll cut your ears off!" My mother slammed the door in his face and consoled me. I was never aware of the racial tensions that were always just below the surface. As kids in those days, unfortunately we were raised with horrible prejudices. Later in life, I found that these prejudices were nothing more than fear and misunderstanding, but many people never realized that.

3

Hold Your Nose

On very special summer weekends when my father wasn't drinking, he and my mother would load us all in the car and head out of the city to visit my aunt. We could always smell Mount Clemens before we got there and made sure, no matter how hot it was, that all the car windows were rolled up. Even with the windows closed, there was an overwhelming stench of rotten eggs and we would all hold our noses. My dad was the only person who would inhale deeply and tell us we were being silly and missing the healing powers of the smell. Then one Saturday, instead of zipping through town, he parked the car right in the middle of it. "Don't stop!" we all cried, wanting to get away from the horrible smell. "Don't worry, you're going to like this," he assured us. "We're going to have lunch someplace special." At the door to Litwalk's Delicatessen a jolly, rotund old man in a white apron rushed to greet my Dad like an old friend and led us to a booth. He was prepared to take our order, but my father said: "Tell them the story, Nate." At first he looked surprised, and then turned to see if his customers were taken care of before pulling up a chair to join us.

"You should like this," he said in a thick Yiddish accent, putting his order pad and pencil back into his pocket. "I'm going to tell you about this magical place." He saw we hated the odor. "Dat smell has a lot of history and made lots of people well again." He went into a tale about a man who, during the Civil War in 1862, tried to drill an oil well but came up with only stinky brown water. Disappointed, he capped his well and left his tanks rusting in a farmer's field. A Frenchman who lived nearby had worked an old horse so much that he had to turn the old nag out to pasture. Taking shelter from the sun, the animal wandered under one of the leaking, abandoned tanks. The farmer later visited his rheumatic old horse and found it galloping around the fields, playing like a young colt.

Meanwhile, another man arrived in town suffering from a skin problem. After hearing the story about the horse, he tried using the dark brown, smelly water and soaked himself. His skin got better and he gave credit to the water for healing him. "And dats how Mount Clemens got to be known as da Bath City of America and became very famous." He noticed we weren't paying attention to the smell any more. "See, there's more magic!" He reached across the table touching each of us on our noses.

Intrigued by the number tattooed on his arm, I started to ask about it, but got a look from my dad telling me not to. My mother ordered for everyone and in a few minutes Nate returned with sandwiches on dark brown rye bread piled high with corned beef, pastrami, coleslaw, and his special Russian dressing.

The story of the healing but odorous waters in Mount Clemens spread around the world. Wealthy Jewish business people began flocking to experience the healing powers, many deciding to stay and open their own spas, hotels and restaurants. Babe Ruth, Clark Gable, Mae West, William Randolph Hearst, George Jessel and Eddie Cantor all made pilgrimages, and special railroad sidings were built to hold the elegant, private cars of industrial barons like the Vanderbilts.

THE MEDEA HOTEL

"What happened?" I asked my dad, finishing the last bite of my sandwich.

"The depression and penicillin happened. Then everyone started buying cars and that was the end. The hotels started to close, and now the smell only comes from The Medea Hotel, next door to where we're sitting." He went to the cash register to pay the bill and thank Nate for educating his children about a place they would soon be living.

By the time my father and mother moved our family to Mount Clemens and built their dream home, the last bathhouse was a pile of rubble, the last of the mineral wells had been capped off, and the smell we had hated as children was gone, but unfortunately so was an incredible amount of history, much of it worth saving.

4

The Magic Milton Show

Frigid morning air hung above the vehicles, covering them with water vapor. The ceiling was almost high enough to let clouds form. Below, a long line of ambulances and tow trucks all painted cream and coral stretched the length of the building. In the mist a short, heavy-set, balding man shuffled across the oil-stained concrete in his slippers, his breath visible as he flapped his arms against his well-worn, plaid wool jacket to stay warm. He made his way toward a hole in the cement floor and a narrow set of rickety wood stairs that led down into a tiny basement room filled with a huge old boiler that was large enough to power a locomotive. The gas main coming into it was at least four inches in diameter. He turned the wheel to open it, struck a match and tossed it inside the cast iron door. There was a loud "woof" sound that pushed against his chest as it pulled air from the tiny room into the boiler, igniting it. Milt climbed back up the stairs and headed toward the ready room.

The table along the wall was full of telephones. A line of red wall phones were mounted above on a sheet of plywood. In the center, at the top, was mounted a huge klaxon horn, like those used for dive warnings on submarines, its wires hanging down behind the telephones terminating in some unknown place. Milt eased himself onto a threadbare sofa with the morning paper. He watched the steam rise from his cup of coffee and rubbed his bald head wishing he had put on a hat. In a small adjacent room four snoring men in two sets of metal bunk beds were finishing up the last of their dreams. At seven-thirty they began to stir, and like the walking dead, found their way to either the coffee pot or bathroom. Faint strains of "*I wanna go back to my little grass shack*" began to be pounded out on a tiny five-octave upright piano upstairs, the tune was definitely upbeat for this time of day. It was Hazel's way of telling Milt that breakfast was ready.

The five-foot-two woman had orange hair that put Lucille Ball to shame. She was the mother of four grown kids, and her stern, no-nonsense exterior shell gave strangers pause. But inside she was one of the most vulnerable, loving people I had ever known. Hazel usually had a piece of gum in her mouth. She had decided long ago that the bat-winged glasses she wore were perfect for her personality, and indeed they were. She knew her husband had a wandering eye so she kept a self-reliant and independent attitude. Hazel was a vision of power with just a hint of Dallas-style nouveau riche when behind the wheel of her three-year-old Chrysler Imperial.

"Morning, Milt," I mumbled, shuffling back to the bunk room in my underwear to get dressed. He pulled me aside and invited me to come upstairs with him for breakfast. It was an honor not offered to strangers, but only to family, and I was flattered.

"Hurry up and get dressed, she's got food on the table."

I first met him when working rotating shifts in a small hospital emergency room and pharmacy during my senior year of high school. After graduating I tried college but wasn't prepared. Coming back home to lick my wounds, it wasn't long before I found myself back at the hospital during the day and working for Milt evenings and weekends. It seemed strangely predestined. It was a way to escape living at home and continually having to hide my sexuality from my parents. After weeks of emergency first aid classes and with my daily emergency room skills expanding, I naively felt ready for anything the world could throw my way.

Formerly the city's Greyhound bus station, the old brick building was large enough for a steady stream of busses to pull in and back up to park so they could load and unload passengers. There was little architectural detail except for its tan brick exterior. The former glory, if there had been any, was long gone. The plate-glass windows were cracked and dirty. Where passengers once waited for buses, several sheets of plywood, hinged at the top into easels, stood covered with photos of car accidents. Many were vividly graphic. The monotone black and white made

blood appear gray. People on the sidewalk would stop to
view the ever-changing variety of gore and death through
the dirty windows, usually turning away in disgust only to
return a moment later for another, longer look. Tim Farr's
business card was clipped to the board. The ambulance-
chasing accident photographer was a pushy, small man
with a face cratered by horrific acne scars. Most afternoons
would find him hanging around the garage. The evenings
were spent in his tiny downtown office decorated with
heavy velvet drapes like a whorehouse, which is exactly
how it was used. There was a police scanner constantly
hissing and chattering with conversations that killed any
atmosphere the horny, cratered bachelor tried to create
while he entertained any semi-attractive woman he could
snare off the street. His passions were taking pictures and
fucking, and he tried to be sure everyone knew how good
he was at both.

The ticket office in the waiting room was now the
domain of Lillian Moore, the company's office manager,
accountant, bill collector and morality cop, all rolled into
one. The skinny woman looked fifty but was only in her
late thirties and had gotten the job years earlier. Her work
outfit had never changed: bobby sox and white sneakers,
a pleated, short skirt that hung over pencil legs, a white
blouse with a lace collar that needed pressing, and a
button-up sweater. There was always a cup of coffee in one
hand and a box of Kleenex in the other. Her pink nose was
constantly running.

Behind the front office was a room where few were
invited. It contained a well-stocked bar and its card table

was always ready for a poker game. What happened in this room was never a topic for discussion on the other side of the door. If the owner came to collect the building payment he was taken here to meet in private, most times leaving empty-handed or with only a partial payment. When a select few of the police came on *official business,* they too met in here, leaving leisurely after thirty or forty minutes, always jovial and smelling like Jack Daniels and breath mints. And when the gas company came to shut off the service, the bearer of bad news was quickly escorted here to listen to Milt's pleading for more time to pay the bill. On one cold January day I can remember Milt convincing him that he would not be disconnecting the service while ushering him out of the building in front of a loaded carbine he kept mounted on the wall above his collection of deer heads.

From the waiting room there was a large opening into the back of the building where the vehicles were parked. Peeling paint on huge steel roof trusses covered in years of dust and soot stood watch over the activities below.

Milt was no ordinary guy. He was a mixture of dreamer, inventor, mechanical genius, and wannabe doctor with a heavy dose of P.T. Barnum. He was the first person to custom fit a tow truck with the special equipment needed to free trapped passengers in auto accidents. He used his "rescue wrecker" and his ambulances to save hundreds of lives. As a part of his design, he took the small hydraulic jacks auto body repair shops use to straighten damaged cars and re-purposed them to make tools that first responders could carry to free people trapped inside cars. He never realized a cent from his inventions, but his ideas went on to become the Porta-Power and Jaws of Life equipment carried today by every fire department and emergency vehicle responding to accidents today.

Milt was the first in the country to abandon the heavy, difficult-to-maneuver Cadillac ambulances and to begin to refit vans that had more room and more power to take their place. He adapted many medical machines to operate on twelve volts so he could include items never before carried by rescue equipment to help medics and doctors keep people alive on their way to trauma centers. His outgoing personality made people feel like they had known him all their lives. His round face, sparkling eyes and wry wit were always ready to unleash just the right words to calm the most chaotic situation. His tough, no-nonsense façade hid a tremendously touching heart. In spite of being a highly respected business owner, there was never enough money for a real salary for him and Hazel. Friday payrolls were always a struggle. He would give you anything he had if you asked. He was a father figure not only to his sons who worked there, but to the rest of us as well. Our love and trust of one another, knowing that in many situations we faced death together, bound us with unbreakable ties.

5

A Sense of Duty

Like sailors, we stood watches. Weekdays a team did 24 on and 24 off. That was enough to get an ambulance on the street quickly. If two ambulances were needed, Milt and anyone else in the building would come in the second one. Weekends were a different story. 48 on was the rule, backed up by second and third crews. We slept, ate and lived together waiting for a phone to ring. If it was a desk phone, it would be a non-emergency call to transfer a patient. But if one of the direct line, red phones on the wall rang, the klaxon horn would follow and we started a journey into the unknown.

The weekend had been exceptionally quiet. Just after midnight, the horn jarred us awake. Two of the red wall phones were flashing and ringing at the same time. This had never happened before. Roy and I jumped from our bunks to answer them. I could hear Milt pick up the

extensions next to his bed upstairs. He sat there holding
one phone to each ear.

"We just got a report there is a bad PI [Personal
Injury accident] on Hall Road." The duty guard from the
air base sounded like he had been running. "We heard
the crash, so it's not far from us." On the other line a desk
sergeant from the police department said loudly, "Bring
everything you've got. Reports are this is a bad one. Get
rolling!" Knowing Milt was listening, we waited for him
to speak, then dropped the phones and ran to get dressed.
Before we could get to the ambulances, he was coming
through the door pulling his jacket on and heading for
his wrecker. As was usual for me, during the first part of
a run, my heart was in my mouth and my thoughts raced
through a silent inventory of what we had in back. We had
taken the largest vehicle, throwing in extra stretchers in
case they were needed.

"Hang on!" Roy shouted, standing the ambulance
on its two right-side tires without braking. I tugged on
my seat belt to make sure it was tight and could hear
him grinding his teeth while he drove. It was his way of
handling stressful situations. Down the road we could see
lights, then parts and pieces of what had been two cars.
One was a 1957 T-Bird and the other a Nash Rambler
station wagon, at least that's what I thought it would be if
all the pieces could be put back together. We jumped out
and stood frozen in disbelief. The only sound was our siren
winding down. Everywhere around the perimeter dozens
of people stood motionless in the midnight air. Clad only
in pajamas and bathrobes, like statues, they stared at the

carnage in front of them. We were the first to arrive but in the distance we could hear the sirens of the police and our other two vehicles.

"Grab a stretcher!" Roy shouted, heading down the road to check for signs of life. I leapt to open the ambulance doors. The two men from the Thunderbird were dressed in Air Force uniforms and lay near their car. Both were dead. The road was filled with debris and bodies. Finally I reached a woman who was unconscious but breathing. We loaded her in the ambulance, then returned to search for more survivors. A woman in a bathrobe tugged at my sleeve and said in an almost whisper "Look over here." She gestured toward an area under a streetlight off the side of the road. The ditch was scattered with the body parts of four young children. Further down the road lay another motionless figure clutching a steering wheel in death that was no longer attached to a car.

My mind was racing. *What do I do first?* I screamed at myself silently, sliding on my ass down into the ditch and began gathering the pieces of the children, piling them on a stretcher. In a moment the scene was full of activity. The other ambulance loaded the two dead airmen and then helped us finish loading our victims. As we pulled away we could see our partners and the police continue to search for more people, but there were none.

Struggling to catch my breath, I sat beside the stretcher with the unconscious woman, while behind me on another stretcher lay her dead husband. Two other cots hung from hooks on the ceiling above my head loaded with their children. As I cleaned up blood, cleared her airway and held an oxygen mask on her face, I looked around and prayed to God not to let her wake up. "At least not yet," I said out loud as we sped toward the hospital. Moments later she stirred and moaned then stopped breathing. I think my prayer was heard and answered and I made no attempt to revive her.

Back at the garage we went mechanically through clean-up rituals to get the vehicles ready again. While we worked, the police from the scene pulled their squad car through the door and parked. Milt opened the bar and everyone sat silently drinking shots from water glasses. The air was almost too heavy to breathe. There had been no time for thought, only action. No emotions, only efficiency and speed to get the job done. We would think about what happened now, but only long enough to let our hearts stop pounding. Then we would package up all the events and shove them someplace very deep inside us. It was the only way our minds could allow us to go on. It was times like these, when the local police witnessed how our team worked together, that formed the bonds of camaraderie that led to Milt receiving all the police calls that needed an ambulance or a tow truck.

With the holidays fast approaching, making payroll was getting more and more difficult. Each Friday Milt paced the floor and checked with Lillian every hour to see if any more money had come in. This week the expression on her face told him what he didn't want to hear. As five o'clock approached, Lillian came out of the office and whispered in his ear, that once again, she had managed to pull it off at the last moment and was cutting checks for everyone - except him, of course. The sign of relief was visible as he leaned back on the sofa and closed his eyes.

One a Monday, about two weeks before Christmas, Lillian called in sick with a bad case of bronchitis. As sick as she had been in the past she had never missed day, but this time she ended up in the hospital. As Friday approached, Milt called Hazel down to see what she could do to put a payroll together. Hazel felt guilty invading Lillian's space, but jumped in to help. In the afternoon the intercom in the ready room came to life. "Milt, please come to the office immediately." Looking surprised by the formality and serious tone in his wife's voice, he put his paper down and left the room.

"Take a look at this," Hazel said sliding two thick file folders across the desk to him. "These are our accounts receivable."

Milt thumbed through the unpaid ambulance bills, some of which dated back three years. "So?"

"We need money, right? Well today I started calling some of these people. Guess what?" She leaned forward in her chair as if to almost whisper. "As far as I can tell, about 80 percent of those bills have already been paid."

"That's impossible." The gravity of what she had just said settled in, and her husband pulled up a chair and put on his reading glasses. "Then why are they in here?"

"Somebody has been getting this money, but it wasn't us," Hazel said picking up the telephone. "I'm calling an accountant and getting someone over here. We need to find out what the hell is going on." At last, the house of cards Lillian had built began to crumble.

The accountant confirmed that more than $180,000 was missing. Milt called his best friend at the precinct who agreed to accompany him on a visit to Lillian, who was home fresh out of the hospital. When they drove up to her house Milt couldn't believe his eyes. A beautiful sprawling ranch-style home with two new cars in the driveway greeted them. Knowing what she made working for him, and that her husband had been working at low-paying jobs for years, Milt shook his head. *It's impossible they could afford to live like this,* he thought to himself. Lillian tearfully confessed to everything. Although he could have put her in jail, Milt offered not to press charges if they signed everything over to him and his wife. Christmas came early. Hazel ensconced herself permanently in the office and there was never again a worry about paying the help on Fridays, making the building payment on time, or dealing with that pesky man from the gas company.

6

Merry Little Christmas

As Christmas week approached Milt stayed busy on the telephone calling everyone he could think of who might be available to help over the holidays. He managed to convince six people to forfeit their Christmas and New Year's parties to join us instead. They would be backup for the crew. Even the mothball fleet of old Cadillacs had been gassed, washed, waxed and stocked with supplies in case they were needed.

A joyous time for most families, Christmas also brought out the worst in some people. Heavy drinking coupled with family arguments and icy roads was a killer combination. Every year the holiday proved to be a never ending series of emergencies. On Christmas Eve the crew decorated the building and put up a tree in the ready room. As evening drew near, carols played on the radio competing with the chatter of DUI arrests on the police scanner. A steady stream of patrol cars entered through the rear of the garage. They were greeted by Milt with bottles of booze and thanks for everything they had done for him in the past year. One of the senior officers made a point to walk away from the group and over to me. "I wanted to say how great it's been working with you." He said with his hands in his pockets, looking me straight in the eyes. I was attracted to this rugged man but always feared getting close him because he was a cop and wore a wedding ring.

"Same goes for me, Clint," I said, extending my hand. "You've protected our asses quite a few times recently." He reached out to shake my hand and as he pulled away I swore I felt his little finger brush my palm and I broke out in a cold sweat.

"Let's try to find some time to get know each other better in the New Year," he said, adjusting himself in his pants while staring at me.

"Sure, that'd be great." I felt faint. When he was called back to his car, I looked around to see if anyone had noticed our conversation. He turned as he bent down to get in the car door and winked at me. "Oh, my god." I said under my breath.

It was almost nine o'clock. We played cards and dominos, occasionally glancing at the red phones on the wall. "It's too damn quiet," Milt said, dealing a new hand. Thick, wet snow fell outside and covered everything in a clean blanket of white, including the roads. No one said a word, but as the clock neared ten, nothing was happening. Without realizing it, we were all holding our breath. As a new hand was dealt, one of the phones on the table rang.

It was a line that was listed in the Yellow Pages and used for non-emergencies. Milt looked up from his cards and motioned for me to take it.

"Ambulance Service, how can I help you?"

"How fast can you get here?" a man's voice on the other end said nervously.

"What's the problem?" I asked. Everyone's attention was focused on me, so I hit the speaker button on the phone to let them listen.

"Someone's been stabbed. He's bleeding badly. You better hurry."

"What's the address?"

"14205 Shoener Road. It's a white two-story house that sits back off the road. The number is on the mailbox. There's a long driveway. I'll leave our outside lights on for you. Please hurry." I was waving my arm to get Roy's attention not realizing he was already on his way to the ambulance. Everyone stood up at the same time. I pulled the paper with the address off the pad and quickly wrote the phone number and address again for Milt, then grabbed my jacket and ran for the door. Milt picked up a direct line to the police. We listened to the police scanner repeat what Milt had just phoned in as we flew down the slippery snow-covered street.

The long driveway was hard to find under the snow. Not sure where it really was, we used the garage door as a guide and headed in that direction. A police car was directly behind us. As we unloaded the stretcher, we saw someone standing in a doorway and headed toward him but were stopped by huge pools and long streaks of blood in the snow. At first we saw footprints and blood, but as we approached the door we noticed someone had been crawling in the snow and bleeding profusely. Inside a man was laying on the living room floor in a pool of blood. It appeared he had been stabbed in the front and back with a large knife. We loaded him on the stretcher and headed back to the ambulance as the police began to question the caller. "We're going to St. Joseph's," I told the cop at the door.

"I have no idea who the guy is," the caller told the police officer. "He came from next door asking for help," he said, pointing to his neighbor's house.

I did my best to put compression dressings on the wounds, but there were so many I couldn't cover all of them. As I applied pressure to slow the bleeding, I rapped on the window and told Roy to step on it. He was on the radio to Milt telling him to send more police to the house next door. "Tell them to be careful," he said. "Whoever stabbed this guy might still be there."

"I shouted to Roy: "I can't do compressions the way he's bleeding. Go as fast as you can." I tightened the oxygen mask on the man's face, then leaned over and grabbed the stretcher, covering him with my body to keep him from sliding off as we rounded a sharp turn toward the emergency room. Milt called ahead and a trauma team was waiting. They met us with a gurney but seeing the amount of blood, shoved it out of the way and helped push ours into the emergency room. One of the doctors looked into the man's pupils, felt his carotid artery for a pulse, then looked up at the clock and wrote the time on the palm of his hand. He was DOA.

"You guys free?" The radio on my belt crackled as we wadded up the bloody sheets and headed out the door. "You guys free? Over." It was Milt's voice and he sounded rattled.

"We're at the hospital, just leaving now," I radioed back.

"I don't have anyone else to send. You need to get back over to the house next door to where you picked up your stabbing. There's another one," he said, taking a moment to answer another radio call.

"I don't have anything available. After you left, things got crazy. From what the cops told me, it's a woman and she's already dead, so don't kill yourselves on these roads to get there."

"Got it. We're on the way." I looking down at my white jacket, pants and sox, all saturated in blood. "No time to change now. They'll have to take me like I am."

We spotted a squad car with light flashing in the front yard and pulled in as close to the house as possible. A two-car garage had been converted into living space and was connected to the house with a narrow enclosed breezeway. No one was outside to guide us so we unloaded our stretcher and headed toward the only door we saw. A grandmotherly-looking woman in her late 70's held the door open for us. As we moved into the dark garage-living room, "Silent Night" played softly on a radio. The only source of light was from a big Christmas tree in the corner. The floor around the tree was strewn with Christmas packages in various stages of being opened. Three young children in their pajamas stood terrified clinging to one another with their backs against the wall. I felt bile rise in my throat and tears start to roll down my cheeks.

A policeman peered into the breezeway from the kitchen and caught Roy's attention. He motioned for him to come into the other part of the house, but said nothing. In a moment, Roy returned and whispered to me that the kids' mother was dead on the floor in the kitchen and that the cops had the ex-husband in there and were waiting for backup to arrive. The butcher knife he had used was still in the body.

We left the stretcher low on its wheels. Roy took the front and I followed behind. The breezeway was barely large enough for us to pass. Halfway to the kitchen we heard a struggle and shouting. Roy looked up to see that the handcuffed man had grabbed the butcher knife and was heading directly for the only exit, which happened to be on the other side of us. In a split second the officer shouted "DROP" and we both fell to the floor, making ourselves as flat as we could. A single gunshot rang out and the man dropped in front of us. Roy kicked the knife back toward the kitchen. The man was still breathing so the police re-handcuffed him to the stretcher and gave us the key. We loaded him and once again headed for the hospital.

His breathing was heavy and labored and there was a loud rattle when he inhaled. He shook his head hard enough to push off the oxygen mask, spit in my face and started violently kicking me. Roy pulled over and came back to help. He sat on the man's legs while I strapped them to the stretcher. He stared at me, daring me to touch him. As we pulled up in front of the emergency entrance he coughed up a huge amount of blood and stopped breathing. His eyes, now with dilated pupils, still attempted to hold the same hateful gaze in death.

Minutes later we loaded up and headed back to the same house, this time to pick up the dead woman who was still on the kitchen floor. What had started as a happy Christmas Eve with her new fiancé and her children opening Christmas presents, had turned into a nightmare when her uninvited, jealous ex-husband came to see his kids. Three young children - four, six, and eight - now sat side by side on a sofa with their hands in their laps watching in silent disbelief as we wheeled the body of their mother out of the house. The grandmother closed the door behind us. I sat in front with Roy. We both had knots in our stomachs. The thought of Christmas seemed foreign as we drove back to the hospital.

Vehicle after vehicle returned through the rear door and pulled back into line. Everyone pitched in to clean and resupply the equipment. The radio quieted down and when the garage lights finally went out, we all took a collective sigh of relief. It was well after four in the morning before people got tired enough to sleep. Like so many times before, Roy and I sat alone drinking as we shoved the events of the night deep into that quiet space we kept reserved inside us. *I wonder how much room is left in there,* I thought to myself before closing my eyes to sleep.

Christmas morning broke on one of the coldest

days in recorded history. Ice crystals painted intricate designs on the windows of the building and fog rose off the warm concrete floor and vehicles, giving the place a serene and peaceful feeling. Starting his morning routine later than usual because of the late night, Milt headed to the basement to light the boiler. As he had always done, he turned the wheel to open the large gas main and was about to strike a match when he heard a phone ringing. Not wanting to wake the men, he quickly closed the gas valve and headed back up the stairs. When he hung up, he returned to the basement, opened the heavy cast iron door to the boiler and turned on the gas. What he didn't realize was that he had not completely shut off the valve when he left twenty minutes earlier. As he struck the match he thought he smelled an unusual amount of gas.

The explosion blew the wood basement stairs up to the ceiling above and they rained back down onto him in pieces. The boiler door had blown off and was embedded in the concrete wall. Every window on one side of the garage blew out into the yard, and the windows along the opposite wall blew inward. Those of us who were sleeping were blown out of our bunks, suddenly finding ourselves standing on the floor in our underwear. We staggered into the garage that was filled with smoke and soot and over to the hole in the floor, fearing what we'd find. When the air cleared, we saw Milt standing in the bottom of the hole where the stairs had been a moment before. His eyes were the size of saucers and what little hair he had on his head jutted straight out.

"Ho, Ho, Ho, Merry Christmas," he said.

7

Burgers With a
Side of Sodomy

Esquire Magazine pretty much said it all in their May, 1997 issue: "*When two or more men spend any significant time together, one of two things inevitably will happen: violence or sodomy. Uniforms usually accelerate this process.*"

~

"It's Sergeant Campbell; he wants to talk to you," Milt said, handing me the phone with a surprised look.

"You busy?" the voice on the other end asked.

"No. What's up?"

"Have lunch with me. I've got something I want to show you."

Clint Campbell, dressed in plain clothes, pulled up outside in a patrol car. "Where would you like to go for lunch?" he asked.

"Just a burger is OK with me."

Clint was staring at me again and I felt uncomfortable. He was having a difficult time fitting behind the wheel of the car so I didn't think anything of it when his leg bumped my knee.

"I bought some old flats on Columbus Street and have been working like a dog getting them ready to rent. I'd like to know what you think. Do you mind if we go there first?"

"Sure, let's go see what you've done." I breathed a sigh of relief, starting to relax.

The old frame building had been painted dark maroon with white trim. Upstairs, he unlocked a door and stepped inside. "This is going to be my little space."

"Are you moving out of your house?"

"Nope, just feel like I need a place to get away from the wife and kids every now and then. Our place could drive you crazy on a good day," he laughed at his own joke. "Look at this." He stepped inside a bedroom painted flat black with a king-sized waterbed.

"Looks more like a playpen than an escape to me." I felt his belt touch my arm so I moved away slightly to see if I was imagining things. He moved closer again.

"Yea, I like to have a little place to bring my friends." I headed back to the sofa in the living room and sat down. Clint sat in a wooden chair, leaning back; he pushed his feet toward me on the coffee table. "Why don't we go in there and have some fun?"

What the hell is going on? Does he know I'm gay? Who told him? Is this some kind of set up? He's a cop. Thoughts raced through my mind. *I've heard stories about cops hitting on gay guys to get their kicks, but he couldn't....* "What are you talking about?" I said, fearing my voice would crack, struggling to keep calm. I saw a stack of mail on the cocktail table and began to open it, forgetting it didn't belong to me. I needed time to think.

"You know damn well what I'm talking about. You want it, don't you?" He rubbed his crotch that outlined an erection.

I started searching for the door, a window, any escape route. "What do you think I am?"

"Don't play dumb with me. I know you want to play." He groped himself again.

Shit, I've got to make a move. "I'm not interested in playing games with you, Clint. I don't know where the fuck you got your information, but you're wrong, dead wrong!" I stood up and began bravely walking toward the door.

"That could be a bad choice of words, Buddy." His voice shook a little as he pulled the front of his jacket open exposing his shoulder holstered gun. "You know, I could blow your fucking brains all over the room right now if I wanted to."

I couldn't believe my ears, and watched his hand carefully. Suddenly everything was in slow motion. Campbell's mouth continued to move but I couldn't hear what he was saying. My mind was going a thousand miles a second. I tried to gauge the distance to the front door and wondered if I could make it before getting shot in the back. *Does it hurt when a bullet hits you?* It seemed impossible I had so much time to think. Newspaper headlines flashed across my mind:

"*COP SHOOTS PERVERT*"

"Shit, Clint! What the hell are you trying to do? I shouted, hoping to shock him into rational thinking.

He pulled his coat closed. "Okay, you passed the test," he laughed nervously, sitting straight up in his chair.

What? What did you say?"

"I just wanted to be sure I knew who my friends are," he lied. "Someone told me you're queer. I had to find out."

I reached the door but it was locked so I stood there. "I'd better be going."

"There's no hurry. C'mon, let me show you the rest of the place." He rose, trying to conceal what remained of his erection.

On my way back into the garage I thought: *what a nightmare. I need some time to put the pieces of this one together. Shit, I didn't even get a hamburger.*

8

Friends & Lovers

I can remember my mother walking out into her
yard in the snow, brushing some of it aside to see if her
crocus had come to life. After months of grey and cold and
naked trees, anything green was a sign, a promise that soon
the robins would return and life would begin anew. The
spring of 1967 was no different.

My world consisted of living in a garage, sleeping
alone in a bunk bed and hiding my sexuality from
everyone. Like the men I worked with, I was horny all the
time but never showed it, and while they fawned over their
girlfriends as they paraded them through our workspace,
I kept my distance. On occasions they would try to set
me up with a blind date but I was always *busy*, which
no doubt made me the topic of rumors. I never let them
see any deeper into me. I was hiding. We shared enough
common interests: cars, football and our work that gave us
plenty to talk about, and that seemed enough.

~

It was my morning shift at the hospital when there was a knock on the pharmacy door. "Are you alone in there?" It was Dan, a nurse and one of the few who knew I was gay. "We've got to talk."

"Boy I'm glad to see you. You're not going to believe what happened to me."

"What in God's name did you do to Campbell?" he asked. "Clint was at my house last night. He was a wreck."

"What do you mean, he was at your house last night? What do you mean, what did I do to him? That son-of-a-bitch threatened to kill me!" I paused for a moment as the pieces of the puzzle fell into place. "Why you asshole!" Suddenly it was all crystal clear. "You told him!"

"I did no such thing. He must have put two and two together, that's all. We had dinner a few weeks ago and I mentioned that you and I are friends. I didn't tell him anything, honest. We've been getting together on the QT for months. I couldn't let on that I even knew him, that's why I never told you."

"When he threatened to blow my brains out, I practically pissed my pants."

"Well, he came by afterward and told me what happened. The poor guy was petrified that you were going to squeal on him. You did a good job convincing him that he'd made a mistake."

"Did you tell him?"

"Of course, I felt it was the only kind thing to do. He was pretty shook up. I told him I'd talk to you."

"I wish he'd thought more about *the kind thing to do* while he was threatening to kill me. You know, Dan, I think if I'd have said I was going to tell on him, he would have pulled the trigger."

"Don't be silly, him? He wouldn't hurt a flea."

"You forget I work with that guy in the real world. You've never seen him get violent like I have. He completely loses it sometime. I saw him bash a guy's head in with his flashlight one night at an accident scene. Anyway, you tell that asshole for me that he's on my shit list."

~

The road was clear so I pressed my luck and stepped on the gas. A short burst of a siren put my heart in my mouth as I checked the rear view mirror. The unmarked patrol car had its big blue light flashing in the window. Clint Campbell slowly slid from behind the wheel, so I began to walk back toward him. "We can't go on meeting like this," he smiled.

"That's the second time you've almost given me a heart attack!"

"I recognized the Corvette and sped up to see who was driving. When I was sure it was you, I had to apologize. I wanted to do it sooner but didn't know what to say." The tall cop looked down at the ground. "It was a real stupid thing to do. I would give anything if it never happened." He looked up sheepishly. "I don't know what else to say, except I'm sorry."

"Apology accepted. You need to know I would never say anything to anyone. Believe me, I know what it's like to keep your life under wraps. Sometimes I feel like telling everyone. I can't imagine the feeling of freedom that would come with that."

"Do you have time for a drink?"

"No, unfortunately, I'm already late. I need to run over to another hospital and pick up some supplies for my boss."

"I guess we'd better just leave it where it is for now then, eh?"

"Yeah, I think so. But do me a favor will ya, asshole? Stop scaring the shit out of me."

He grinned, "Okay, asshole." He got into his car and pulled up alongside me. "Hey, follow me, I'll give you an escort to the corner." He pulled ahead and drove off with his light flashing.

~

A week later I found myself standing next to a new pharmacist my boss had hired to work at East Side General Hospital in downtown Detroit. That hospital was owned by the same people as the one where I worked. Jack Van Blarcom was an intimidating man. At 6'-4" he had the frame of a defensive lineman. A heavy, permanent five o'clock shadow framed an outrageous but well-cared-for black moustache, and his deep voice, hairy arms and huge hands made my heart beat faster.

At the same hospital where the pharmacist was to work, I had been befriended by George, a very effeminate radiologist in his sixties. He spotted me the second we met and made it known that he knew my score. Without hesitation I admitted to being gay and we became close but careful confidants. Everyone in the building, including my boss, knew he was gay, and for whatever reason had decided to do whatever they could to protect me from him. I kept my distance during the day, but accepted several dinner invitations to his apartment to meet more gay people who worked in the hospital.

One morning the phone rang. "Lou?" the voice asked. "This is Jack, the new guy in the pharmacy," he said in his deep voice.

"Oh, hi, what can I do for you?" I was sure it was a business call.

"I think we have something in common." He hesitated. "We need to talk. Is there any chance we could have dinner tonight?"

As far as I knew we had nothing in common we needed to talk about. "Um, sure, what time?"

"How about eight at my place? I have an apartment in Indian Village Manor on the river. It's number 1240."

I hung up the phone but stood staring at it, then picked it up again and called the garage to have someone cover my shift. All the while I was trying to figure out what we had in common. It wasn't until he opened the door that night and I saw my friend George the radiologist sitting in his living room that I understood. My heart swelled as Jack smiled, gave me a huge bear hug and kissed me on the cheek. Over the next few months I reduced my shifts at the garage and we spent all of our spare time together. I loved to cuddle against him and feel the warmth of his breath against my neck as we slept.

9

The Motor City is Burning

Sunday, July 23, 1967 was just another hot
Michigan summer day. By eleven in the morning fans
couldn't keep up with the heat and the guys on duty at the
garage found shady cool spots to hang out. Trying not to
move anymore than necessary, everyone prayed the phone
wouldn't ring. Bored with doing nothing, I kept busy
waxing the two-year old Corvette I had bought by working
two jobs, buffing it out with a huge wheel that was used to
polish the ambulances.

Six-year old Mattie giggled as she sat on her father's
lap while he drove the family home from the beach.
The windows were open and the car was filled with
warm summer air. The sounds of The Jamie's 1958 hit,
"Summertime, Summertime" was on the radio and the
family sang along.

"We'll go swimming every day.
No time to work, just time to play
If your folks complain, just say
It's Summertime."

Imitating the family dog, Mattie loved to put her head outside the window to feel the breeze in her face. Without warning, a large truck swerved to miss a dog in the street and hit them head on.

The klaxon horn in the garage let go of a wail and everyone jumped to their feet. I turned off the buffer and ran back to the ready room. "It's a PI on Moravian," Milt said hanging up the phone. As he moved toward the door he turned back to us. "There are people trapped in the car." He ran for his wrecker and led the way out of the garage. It was 3:30 p.m..

As we got closer to the accident, Sunday traffic was backed up and standing still so we drove on the shoulder, and at times up driveways and onto the sidewalk, to keep moving forward. A siren did no good. There was no place for anyone to go. By the time we got there, people were standing outside their cars watching and the police were doing the best they could to clear a path for Milt so he could get his wrecker closer. We grabbed what we thought we'd need and ran toward the older Chevy coup. Inside the mother cried hysterically. Her and her husband's legs were pinned under the collapsed dashboard. The father sat semi-conscious in the driver's seat with his daughter still partially in his lap. Her head was outside with the triangular vent window firmly embedded in her skull; she was motionless and silent. I reached her neck and found a pulse. "She's alive," I said softly to Milt as he worked to carefully disconnect the vent from the window frame.

"Get another ambulance here," he snapped to no one in particular. "You and Roy need to get her out of here as soon as I get this loose." An officer heard him and radioed for a second ambulance.

I looked up and fifteen feet away my Dad was standing on the edge of the crowd. He and my mother were driving home in the other direction. He lifted the tape and came to me. "Is there anything I can do to help?"

"Thanks, Dad. Right now we're all waiting for Milt to get her free. Are you and Mom OK?"

"We're fine, son. How do you do this?" he said, shaking his head and looking down at the ground. "You be careful, you hear?" He went back to the car. They were part of a captive audience waiting and watching until the road could be cleared.

In a moment there was a loud snap of metal breaking loose from the window. Milt stepped back and I scooped up the child and ran toward the stretcher. The police were already clearing an exit for us. I sandbagged the sides of her head to immobilize it. The vent entered her skull just above her right eye but there was a surprisingly small amount of blood. I checked her airway and respiration, and then held her tiny hand as if to tell her we were there to help.

Milt turned his attention to the collapsed dashboard and the parents' legs. In a few more minutes he had them free and the backup ambulance with the parents followed.

The trauma doctor did a quick check of Matilda's vitals and a cursory exam of the skull problem, then picked up a phone. After explaining what he had in front of him, he sat listening to the neurosurgeon at Henry Ford Hospital in Detroit explain the options, none of which could be done at our location. "Then get a chopper here," he demanded.

Without offering any explanation, the doctor sitting in Detroit simply told him "They're all busy."

Knowing he had no time to waste, he said, "Looks like you two are it. No chopper can come. It's up to you to get her there. I'll do my best to stabilize her and then go over some things I need you to keep an eye on, but she's in your hands." He wrapped her head - with the window still in place - in sterile gauze and did a cut-down so he could start three different IVs while explaining what I needed to do during the trip. "I wish I could come with you or send another doctor, but we're stretched already. How long do you think it will take to get her there?"

"Who knows?" Roy answered. "If traffic is light, we could make it in forty-five minutes to an hour. If not, it's anyone's guess."

While listening, the doctor began shoving additional dressings, pre loaded syringes, extra vials of meds and replacement IVs in a large gym bag. "Take these. If you need help using them, radio us on channel 32. We monitor it. Anyway, let me know when you get there and how it went."

Traffic on I-94 was light, and when people heard the siren and saw the lights they thoughtfully moved to the side to let us pass. By six o'clock we were at the city's edge. A few minutes later we saw flashing lights ahead and watched as police routed all traffic onto an exit ramp. Seeing us coming, they quickly pulled one of their squad cars back and waved to let us pass and remain on the road. In what we thought was a stroke of good luck, we were on a completely abandoned expressway. "Great!" Roy shouted as he stepped on the gas. For a moment we both felt elated. Suddenly Roy began to swerve violently from side to side. He was dodging large chunks of concrete and bricks littering the roadway. People were standing on overpasses throwing them. "What the...," he shouted back to me. "I don't like this. You better hang on." Afraid to slow down and become an easier target, he did his best to keep his speed but still miss the junk in the road. Suddenly we heard a loud bang and felt something hit the roof of the ambulance, narrowly missing the windshield. At that same moment, two Detroit Police cars pulled up, one on each side and motioned for Roy to slow down. They pulled slightly ahead to run interference. The officer riding shotgun in each car rolled down his window and began to fire at the people on the bridges and they began to scatter.

"Where you headed?" a voice on the radio asked.

"Henry Ford. We have a brain injury," Roy answered.

"Follow us. We'll get you there."

Suddenly my little girl began convulsing and vomiting. I took a large blue bulb syringe and began aspirating the liquid from her mouth before it could get into her lungs. Without warning, she stopped breathing.

Grabbing a respirator bag, I checked her airway and started helping her breathe and at the same time began chest compressions on her tiny rib cage. With a violent jerk she came back and began breathing again. "How much longer?" I shouted at Roy through the window.

"I'm not sure." He swerved to miss a tire in the road.

It was time to swap out one of the IVs for a new one, and while I worked to get it started she stopped breathing again. Beginning chest compressions, I felt for a pulse, then put my head close to her mouth hoping to hear a sign of breathing but when none was detected, I pounded her hard once on the chest and switched to the respirator bag. She let out a sigh and started breathing. "It's getting dicey back here," I shouted. "Get us there, OK?"

We followed the squad cars up an exit ramp and suddenly were navigating a maze of city streets at a much slower pace. Everywhere you looked there were buildings on fire and large groups of angry people carrying whatever they could hold through broken store windows. "Christ, it's a war out there," Roy shouted. As he turned a sharp corner and accelerated, Matilda stopped breathing for a third time. She was aspirating a lot of fluids, and I didn't know what to do first - chest compressions, or use the bulb syringe. I tried doing both, and once I was sure there was no more fluid in her mouth, turned all attention to her chest. "Come on, baby, one more time," I begged, but she refused to oblige. Her color changed to ash gray, her skin began to look waxy; and it frightened me. I lifted her eye lids and the pupils looked like they were starting to dilate.

I worked frantically as the ambulance came to a stop and the back door flew open. A policeman reached inside to help unload. As I stepped onto the tile floor outside the emergency entrance, I slipped and almost fell. Looking down, I was standing in blood, lots of blood. The doors were smeared with it and long trails extended into the building. Inside it was complete chaos. People were shouting and running in every direction. A blood-drenched intern approached us as I continued chest compressions on my little girl. With just a cursory glance, he pointed at a dark area in the hall. "Leave her over there; she's dead."

"She's *NOT* dead!" I screamed. "I lost her twice on the way here and she came back. She's *NOT* dead." My head started to whirl and I felt like I was going to pass out. The cop helping me shoved the intern against a wall, grabbing him by his throat. I pushed the stretcher into the cop's leg to distract him and he let the terrified man go. My new partner yanked the stretcher with Mattie and me into the first trauma room, but it was already occupied with a team of doctors and nurses working on a black man with a bullet in his leg. "Can somebody help me? *PLEASE*," I begged, starting to sob. "She's *NOT* dead!" I cried, trying desperately to convince myself while keeping beat on the little girl's chest.

A nurse ran to us. Seeing I was exhausted, she pushed me aside with her hips and took over chest compressions as two other doctors joined her. "I've got a weak pulse," she shouted, as someone else arrived with a crash cart. The man with the gunshot was moved off to the side, while others continued to work on his leg and Mattie was pulled under the bright surgical lights. "Sit down before you fall down!" The nurse ordered as someone shoved a stool under me. No one needed to explain why we were there - the window sticking out of her skull told her story. Moments later the neurosurgeon who had consulted by phone entered the room and took over. I sat there sobbing from frustration, trying to watch through my tears as they moved the little girl onto a gurney and disappeared through the doors.

10

He's My Friend

Roy stood pinned against the ambulance by a small group of Detroit police officers. From a distance it looked like they were lecturing him, wagging pointed fingers close to his face. Some appeared to be shouting, and everyone, including Roy, looked pissed off. What started as a simple request to help, ended in an ugly confrontation during which the local police commandeered not only the ambulance, but us, too.

"We've got to get back," Roy insisted, holding his ground.

"You don't seem to understand. There is no getting back right now." The man in uniform gestured toward the city streets. "There is no safe way for you to get out of this city."

His uniform stripes and in-your-face attitude said he was in no mood to be challenged. "Even if there was, we need you here. You have no idea what we're up against. People are dying. Believe me, I have the power, and if you won't cooperate I can take your ambulance and throw your asses in jail."

This gave Roy pause as he looked up at the big dent in the roof of the ambulance while he thought.

"It's your choice. You want to cooperate or get locked up?" The unit commander folded his arms in defiance and waited for an answer.

"Whose gonna pay for …?" Roy started as he looked at the dent.

"Shit, son, that's the least of my worries right now. I've got bigger fish to fry."

The gates were just starting to open on five days of hell for the city of Detroit. What had started less than twelve hours earlier as a small raid on an after-hours club hosting a party for a couple of returning Vietnam vets, was escalating into what would end up being the most destructive riot in U.S. history. By the time the riots ended, 43 people would lay dead, and more than 467 would be injured, including police officers, fire fighters, National Guard, State Police and US Army soldiers. As I walked toward the ambulance, I could hear nothing but sirens. The smell of smoke was thick in the air. The city of my birth was on fire. "We'll help," I heard Roy say, and the group of men around him began to pat him on the back and do what they could to help us get the ambulance ready. They gave us a radio and told us where to stand by. Roy went inside to telephone his father and give him the bad news, and then had him call my folks.

Shortly before midnight on Monday, President Johnson authorized use of Federal troops, but when they arrived, many were white, and so the rioting escalated. We ate our meals in the hospital cafeteria and from vending machines. We slept in the ambulance when it felt safe; and when it didn't, we made do on the plastic chairs in the waiting room until someone led us into one of the nurses' lounges. On Monday afternoon we found and raided the doctors' lounge, helping ourselves to clean scrubs so we could abandon our filthy uniforms. The police left orders for an hourly radio check to keep tabs on us, but it was seldom needed as we were usually on the streets with them, hauling away the dead and wounded. The ambulance sported several new dents from bricks and bottles, along with a bullet hole in the rear window. When we needed gas, the police led us to where they fueled the patrol cars. All gas stations were closed to keep people from getting what they needed to start more fires. Everywhere you looked, entire neighborhoods were in flames. While some looted whatever they could carry, many black families wandered around, not sure where to go or what to do. A few shelters were opened for those burned out of their homes, but it was dangerous for families to get to them.

By Tuesday night the adrenalin we had been running on was gone. We needed to stop and recharge, but that wasn't possible. The only thing we took time to charge was the radio we had been given by the police, and we kept that alive by plugging it into any parked squad car we could find that had an adaptor. While charging our radio, we listened to theirs. It was frantic! Shouts for help were coming from both firemen and police who were overpowered and in trouble.

Thirty-year old Carl Smith was shot dead as he stood in an intersection shouting directions to his arriving equipment so they could attack multiple fires that had turned another neighborhood into an inferno. The police, trying to protect him, loaded his body into their cruiser and raced toward a downtown hospital. "Fireman down. En route to hospital. Ten-forty-five David," [Patient Deceased] they radioed. "We have a lot of guys fighting fires out here. Get another car and an ambulance to stand by near area Mack and St. Jean."

"10-4," the operator radioed back.

The radio on the front seat of the ambulance came to life with a call for R-One, the code assigned to us, and the call startled Roy. "Wake up, Lou, we've got a run."

Before we could maneuver out of the hospital parking lot, a cruiser pulled in front of us to lead the way. "Code 2 boys [no lights, no siren]. We're big enough targets as it is." As he finished speaking, a bullet ricocheted off his bumper in a trail of sparks, and the driver made a hard right turn onto a different street.

A fireman pulled a hose over to a hydrant on Mack Avenue. As he crouched to attach it, he removed his helmet so he could see what he was doing. In an instant a quart beer bottle hit him in the head and knocked him on his back. His scalp was cut to the skull and he bled profusely. Noticing what had happened, his buddy ran to help him sit up and put his hand on his friend's head, hoping to slow the bleeding. He spotted the police and ambulance approaching and waved his arm to get our attention.

"I know where I am," I said to Roy as we dressed the head wound and got the fireman on the stretcher. Sometimes I work at an old hospital near here. It's real close and they have an emergency room. We can take him there." I told the cops where we were going. As we pulled away, a dozen more bricks and bottles rained down on us.

East Side General was an old three-story brick hospital that had seen better days, but it was only blocks away. Roy left the window open between us, and I gave him turn-by-turn directions. As we approached Cadillac Boulevard, we heard gunfire and it spooked us.

"The entrance is on the left side," I shouted. "If you can back in, it would put us closer to the door." Roy parked and had just opened his door to get out when a burst of rifle fire hit the wall near him. He jumped back in and shouted for me to get down.

Inside, the hospital was busy with the local wounded. Everyone had been called back to work and most of them were as tired as we were. I could see familiar faces looking out through glass doors and I waved, but as I did three more shots were fired, and one of them came through the sheet metal behind me, narrowly missing my left arm, passing over the fireman's chest, and out the other side of the ambulance. I wasn't hit, and pulled the fireman onto the floor next to me. Everyone near the doors scattered.

The man's head dressing had gone from white to

red, and now there was a pool of blood on the floor. More shots hit the hospital brick wall; then a barrage of rocks and bottles hit all around us. Roy picked up the radio and called for help. For what seemed like an eternity, we waited amid intermittent attacks of bullets and debris. Finally there were blue and red lights and shots were fired into a house next to the hospital. Afraid to look up, I hadn't noticed the nurses and staff who came out to help. The doors opened and I saw their faces - among them the man I'd been spending all my time with, Jack. He looked as surprised as I was, grabbed my ankles and began pulling me toward the rear door. I turned and gave him a weary smile. With me out of the way, they were able to get the fireman into the emergency room. Inside, Jack put his arm around me while we walked and I introduced him to Roy.

The days that followed were a blur. We got permission to stay where we were and took whatever runs we were given. The small hospital staff treated us like family, and the doctors took time to pull off the dirty adhesive tape we had plastered on our own cuts so they could clean and suture them. We had real beds to sleep in and a hot shower for the first time in four days. By Friday the last major fire was under control and things had calmed down. The police we had come to know as friends, released us with appreciation so we could finally go home.

A month later, for unknown reasons, Jack was fired from the pharmacy; he moved back to Jackson, Michigan, near his family. I was heartbroken. Six months later a beautiful envelope arrived in the mail inviting me to a wedding between Jack and Maryann Davis, a woman I'd never heard of.

I sent a silver tray.

A month later a small, handwritten formal note card arrived saying only:

The wedding between
Miss Maryann Davis
And
Mr. Jack Van Blarcom
will not take place.

A few days later the silver tray showed up on my doorstep.

I never heard from him again. Later that year I ran into a mutual friend who told me Jack had gone out onto a golf course near his parents' home and shot himself in the head.

On a bright Saturday afternoon I watched as the front glass door into the garage waiting room opened, and a man with a little girl walked in, hand-in-hand. As they approached, my heart leapt into my mouth and I began to cry. Mattie's dad reached out for my hand to thank me, then turned to his perfect little daughter and said, "This is the man who saved your life."

Instead of looking up to see who I was, she wrapped her arms around my thigh and put her head against my leg. It was the most powerful moment of my life. I knew I wasn't the one who saved her, but that one single act I had been able to do - the dogged stubbornness not to let death win that day - had allowed me to complete what might have been the single purpose for which I had been placed on this earth.

Later in life, looking back on those times, I remembered feeling as if we were living in a two-tiered world. All the good, beautiful things and happy, peaceful people were on top, going about their business. But many of us existed on the bottom: the cops, firemen, ER interns, nurses and trauma docs. Our world consisted of dealing with the part of society that the others chose to ignore. Our world was filled with violence, destruction, death and heartbreak; yet something pulled us; maybe our souls were darker. Feeling inexplicably drawn to that world, we both hated and loved our lives at the same time. We thought and dreamed of a time we might experience a "*normal*" life, but the second we stepped out of our routine, we were drawn back by an overwhelming sense of duty, as though the fragile place in which we chose to dwell would fall apart if we weren't there. Although we thought of it as a duty, it was more than that. We developed instant, powerful friendships, knowing our lives depended on each other.

11

Alone Again Naturally

Chuck Dotson stood alone at the urinal. He was playing hooky from his job at Ford, where he chose the leather and upholstery fabrics that would go into next year's cars. He tried to smooth his windblown, semi-curly brown hair with one hand while unzipping his corduroy suit pants with the other. At five-feet-eight, his auburn moustache seemed too large for his face. The deep dimple in his chin drew attention to his mouth. I worked my way into the next stall and was deep in thought watching my stream swirl around the white deodorant cake and down into the drain. I was tired, and discouraged, and lonely. Since the end of the riots and return to a normal life of less - but still plenty of - blood, gore and death. I had begun to question where my life was going and I didn't like the answers. As I started to shake off the last drops before buttoning my fly, I looked up and found myself staring straight into his cute round Irish face. "Hi," he said. I shoved everything back inside my pants and felt a trickle of warm urine running down my leg. "Shit," I answered, trying to move toward the door while buttoning up.

"Wait," he shouted, trying to catch up with me as I ran down the hall and back into the mall. My heart was pounding; my mind was whirling a million miles an hour. Instead of running, I wanted to turn around grab him. In the parking lot, thinking I wasn't interested, he dropped back to put some distance between us. Afraid I'd lose him, I slowed down, then gathered enough courage to turn around and walk back to him.

"Sorry," I apologized.

"What the hell was all that about? I only said hi." He was staring at my wet pants.

"I can't believe I ran away from anyone as handsome as you. I'm Lou."

"Chuck," he offered his hand. "Can we go someplace and talk?" We turned and started walking toward our cars. With the Corvette, I had made a habit of finding a place on the fringe of big parking lots, away from other cars. I'd intentionally park diagonally across two spaces in hopes of avoiding chipped doors and cracked fiberglass.

"That's me," I said, pointing to my dark blue Corvette. "Where's yours?"

"Right there." He gestured to a silver XKE convertible parked only feet away. It, too, was sitting diagonally across two spaces. As we unlocked our doors, we looked at the way each other's cars were parked and broke out in laughter. "Great minds think alike. Follow me. I'll fix lunch for us at my place," he said, closing his door and starting the car.

Lunch never happened.

As soon as the door was closed behind us we tore into each other like love-starved animals. A trail of clothes covered the floor, and in seconds we were lost in each other's eyes, bodies and minds. Sex was awkward, brutally needful at times and lovingly tender at others. We abused and caressed each other to the point of leaving marks on our bodies. Afternoon turned into night, and by morning we still hadn't slept, and lay exhausted on sheets soaked in sweat, propped up on our elbows looking at each other. I turned to get out of bed; and he pulled me back and it started all over again. Neither of us went to work that day or the next.

Chuck's small one-bedroom apartment was close to both the garage and the hospital where I worked. It was suspiciously under-furnished and looked like he hadn't been living there long. He wasn't eager to share any details, and I didn't ask. Who we were and where we had come from wasn't important. It was enough that we could touch, hold and own one another completely.

When we were able to let go of one another, we tinkered with our cars and took short road trips. Neither of us cooked, so we ate out almost every night; he taught me to "almost" appreciate the sweet Southern Comfort Manhattans and Black Russians that were a part of every evening. Over dozens of long dinners in dark restaurants, we were as inseparable as we were in bed. For the first time in my life I felt loved and emotionally full to the point of exploding. It was like I had found the huge missing part of myself and when we were apart, I counted the minutes until we would be together again.

I loved being seen with him, proud of his confident masculinity. It made me feel safe enough to bring him to a family picnic, where my parents were welcoming and my three sisters competed for his attention - all but attacking him.

Over the weeks that followed I gradually moved more of my clothes into his closet, and our relationship grew deeper, faster than either of us expected. Then, without warning, I sensed that he began to distance himself, and it frightened me.

One afternoon I returned to see a strange car parked in the driveway. With an arm load of flowers and a bottle of wine, I unlocked the front door. When it opened, Chuck was sitting on the sofa waiting for me; at his side, his former lover of fifteen years, Jack.

My clothes were piled on a chair by the door.

Jack looked the other way while Chuck tried to explain, without making eye contact, that they were getting back together, to give it "one more try."

Just like that, it was over.

In disbelief I put the wine and flowers on the table in front of them, picked up my clothes and left. No matter how far or fast I ran, I couldn't beat the panic that filled me. I drove all night and found my way back by morning.

My eyes were still red from crying when I walked into the garage. Chuck stood next to Milt, waiting for me.

"I was worried sick," he started. I looked away, holding up my hand as if I could make them both disappear, and left the garage for the last time.

Convinced everything I had ever hoped for was slipping away from me, I headed to my parent's house. My father took one look at me and shoved me into their spare bedroom. "You OK?" he asked.

"No."

"Is there anything we can do, son?"

"There's nothing anybody can do," I said, sitting on the edge of the bed with my head in my hands crying. I wanted to tell him so badly but knew he would never understand.

"Try to get some sleep. Later, if you want to talk, I'm here." It was the most compassion I had ever experienced from my father. He closed the door gently behind him.

~

When I was very young, if I wanted to spend any time with my Dad, I knew it would involve two things: a coffee can full of bent nails, and a hammer. While he measured and cut and mortised and pounded, his five-year-old son sat in the sawdust on the floor at his feet, straightening bent nails. I thought this was how he kept me out of his way while he worked, but I was wrong. He was putting tools

in his boy's hands just as his own father had done to him.
Over the years, usually with more threates and demands
than love, he gradually taught me his trade. He taught
me to measure twice and cut once, to always buy twenty
percent more lumber than I knew I would need, then add
another five percent just in case. He demonstrated how
slow was better than fast, and that useful was as important
as beautiful. As I grew up he seldom praised me for what I
accomplished, usually finding fault and pointing out where
I could have done better.

At the most hopeless moment in my life, as I
prepared to run away to California in fear of disappointing
and embarrassing him and my mother, he came back to
me, sat on the edge of the bed and held me in his arms.
Time and health issues had mellowed him. Ulcers had
put an end to his drinking. The terrifying man of my
childhood was gone. Now facing his own mortality, and
not even knowing the details of who I was, he told me he
loved me and how proud he was of the man I had become.
I took those few, brief moments in his arms and the gift of
carpentry he gave me and treasure them still.

I would have settled happily for living with and
loving Chuck even if it meant I had to continuing living
my life in lies, but that wasn't going to happen. Now I
decided it was time for me to go someplace and "*be gay*".
I knew the further away from home would be best. The
problem was I didn't know what I was supposed to do
differently to get the "*be*" part of being gay down. If it
meant I was supposed to start feeling like I should wear a
dress or act like a girl, I didn't want anything to do with it.

The truth was I just wanted to be me and didn't want to hide anymore. I was completely comfortable living in the same old Levi 501s and T-shirts I'd been wearing all my life. The only shoes I felt good in were sneakers or work boots. I loved to watch football and the World Series. I lived to build things with my hands and drive fast cars. I didn't want to change any of that. It scared me to think I was going to start hanging around feminine gay men and sharing my life with them. They made my skin crawl. For the first time I gave enough thought to the fact that perhaps being "gay" could be many different things to different types of people. But for me the only way to be gay I had ever known was to be silent, invisible, insecure and scared to death.

The next morning I packed my clothes in brown paper grocery bags, filling the tiny space behind the seats of my Corvette, took the last thousand dollars out of my savings account, hugged my worried, confused parents goodbye and headed west.

Unfolding a map, I decided the road to "normal" might be route 40 to California. As I watched the pavement disappear behind me in the rearview mirror, I knew I was leaving one world that for me was too real and dangerous to stay in, and trading it for another that was completely unknown.

As it began to get dark, I realized I'd crossed the state of Michigan and was near the tiny town of Saugatuck, less than a hundred miles from Chicago. I pulled into a motel and got a room. Walking back to get my clothes from the car I saw Chuck standing alongside his XKE under a light in the parking lot. "What are you doing here? Why are you following me?" I pleaded, not believing how he could have been so close behind without me noticing. Exhausted and drained, I started to cry. "Leave me alone."

"I'm so sorry…" he began.

I held my hand up again to stop him. "Go home. Leave me alone. Can't you see I can't take anymore?" I begged.

"Where are you going?" he asked, still standing far away next to his car.

"West, someplace west. I don't know. It doesn't matter. The only thing that matters is getting the hell out of here."

"Can we eat something? I'm starved. You drove like a maniac; I almost ran out of gas trying to keep up with you."

"You eat. I'm going to bed," I said unlocking the door to my room and closing it behind me. A few moments later there was a gentle knock on the door.

"Please let me in. We need to talk."

"Go away. I got the message loud and clear."

"Please, I promise I won't stay."

I unlocked the door, went back to bed and lay on top of the bedspread curled up in a ball with my clothes still on. He climbed on the bed and wrapped his arms around me from behind and we both fell asleep crying. When I woke in the morning, he was sitting in a chair watching me sleep. Looking sadly into my eyes he said "Please come back. Everything is going to be OK."

"What do you mean OK? I said, getting out of bed, needing to go to the bathroom. "Can we be together?"

He hesitated. The look on his face said no. "Come back. Please come back. I never intended for anything like this to happen. I love you."

"I love you too but I guess that isn't enough. That's my problem now."

A moment later I opened the door for him and watched as he pulled out of the parking lot and disappeared down the road and out of my life forever.

12

California Here I Come

When the trip started more than two-thousand four hundred miles of road were waiting, but Chicago, Springfield, and St. Louis were already memories. The radio played "Everybody Plays the Fool" to me and I cried until there were no more tears. On the outskirts of Oklahoma City my car sputtered to a stop and was towed to a Chevy dealership. It was the alternator but they couldn't get the one I needed for a couple days so I got a room at the Holiday Inn and joined everyone around the pool. Giving in to exhaustion and frustration, I closed my eyes in the warm sun and emptied my mind, fighting every attempt by it to relive events of the last week. I found solace is Budweiser and sex, hooking up with anyone who gave me a second glance and soon I was able to breathe again and started looking forward to continuing the adventure I had begun.

"It's all set. You shouldn't have any more problems," the service tech said, putting my warranty book back in the glove compartment. "You have a flashlight in here?"

"I don't think so."

"If you're heading west on 40 and going to be doing any night driving you better get a good one. Be careful where you stop at night. The tarantulas are migrating this time of year."

"What? I asked laughing; sure he was pulling my leg. "I hate spiders!" After paying the bill I gassed up and bought the biggest, most expensive flashlight they had. The stretch of I-40 between Oklahoma City and Amarillo on the Texas panhandle is wide open and completely flat. I looked forward to being able to unleash the Corvette's 427 and see what it could do. It was a beautiful warm day so I put the top down, turned up the Beach Boys on the radio and pointed myself west again. As evening fell I was getting close to Amarillo and started to think about eating and finding a place to stay. Except for an occasional long-haul trucker, the road was deserted so I leaned on the gas, passing the last truck and claimed the empty road for myself.

The glow left in the sky after the sunset was fading, so I turned on the headlights. In the distance I could see what looked like a huge piece of rope lying across the pavement. As I got closer two black pools appeared, one on each side of the road. Suddenly I realized I wasn't looking at a piece of rope, it was thousands of big hairy spiders crawling on top of each other crossing the road. The pools on each side were where they waited before and after. My mind flashed on my topless car and I cringed at the thought of ending up with spiders inside with me. I punched the gas as hard as I could and watched as the needle on the speedometer approached 105 by the time I ran through the spider parade. When I was sure there were no more left, I let off on the gas, coasted to a reasonable 70, and took a deep breath.

By noon the next day I was driving through the outskirts of Albuquerque. A hand-lettered sign for Maria & José's Authentic Mexican Restaurant caught my attention. Having lived my entire life above the Mason Dixon line and leaving before Taco Bell invaded the northern states, I knew absolutely nothing about Mexican food. Convincing myself I needed more adventure in my life, I pulled in and parked.

Maria's teenage daughter brought a menu along with a little dish of chopped tomatoes with tiny pieces of green and red peppers. I pointed to the dish with a puzzled look. "It's salsa," she volunteered in a slow, monotone, completely bored voice. "It's picante."

What's picante? I thought to myself. "I'm hungry. What's the most popular thing?" I looked down the long column of choices. She pointed to the Super Mexican Combo Plate. "It has a little bit of everything."

"Good I'll do that."

"Do you want guacamole?" she said, staring at a fly on the ceiling.

"What's guacamole?"

"Never mind, I'll just bring it." She snapped her gum in defiant disapproval of the stupid gringo sitting in the booth in front of her, smiled weakly and took my ticket to the cook, who I assumed was José himself.

The questionably clean, huge oval Melamine platter sitting in front of me was overflowing with food. Except for the dark red sauce that covered most everything on it, the food peaking out was all suspiciously tan in color. It smelled wonderful and I couldn't wait to dig in. As I picked up my fork, Maria's daughter put a spoon into the salsa and asked if I'd like her to put some on.

"Sure, why not?"

Westbound miles were flying onto the odometer and a few hours later, as I reached the pine covered hills of northern Arizona, I thought I had to fart. But as your brain usually does when it knows that's not a good idea, my asshole slammed shut and I got the message. I needed to find a place to take a dump, and fast. Running across the parking lot trying to hold the cheeks of my ass together, I made it into a stall of the truck stop men's room just in time. My stomach rumbled loudly, and then what felt like liquid fire shot out of me. Convinced I had a terminal medical problem, I was afraid to move, fearing what I'd see if I looked in the bowl below me. Almost a full roll of toilet paper and eight or ten flushes later, I was confident enough to rejoin the living and considered trying to find a doctor as I walked back to the car. Sliding into the driver's seat, I elevated my burning ass so it didn't touch the leather. Leaning far to one side, I maneuvered back onto route 40 and once again headed west.

By the time signs for Barstow were outside the window, I had added two and two together and figured it out. I had never eaten food as spicy or hot as my Super Mexican Combo Plate at Maria & José's.

"Milk. Drink plenty of cold milk," the gas station attendant told me after I whispered my problem in his ear. While he laughed and gassed up the car I went inside and came out with a half-gallon, glad to know my rectum wasn't permanently damaged.

The huge peaks of the Sierra Nevadas formed what looked like an impenetrable wall of stone ahead of me. As the sun began to set, a long line of taillights appeared climbing the pass through the San Bernardino Mountains that separated the desert from California's Inland Empire. Cresting the high point, the valley floor below was filled with city lights as far as I could see. I was certain Santa Monica must be just around the corner. As traffic raced down the steep decline, an overhead sign read: "Los Angeles 103 miles." Disappointed, I pulled off the road and stopped for the night. I didn't know exactly where I was but I did know Mexican food wasn't going to be on the menu a second time that day.

13

Rapture of the Beach

Michael and Anita weren't really my cousins, although I told everyone they were. Actually they were friends of Auntie K's, one of my bosses at the hospital where I worked. Kay was a woman I dubbed my second mother, and I was able to tell her anything, knowing nothing I said would shock her or be repeated. So when I told her I was running away to California she called Michael and Nini and made arrangements for me to stay with them until I could get settled.

Michael, a tall, handsome man in his mid 30's, managed a drug store for The Guild in Northridge. Anita, his wife and in her second marriage, was in her mid-forties and bemoaning the loss of her childbearing abilities. Nini had many phobias, including an extreme fear of elevators. To aggravate the problem, she also despised climbing stairs. It wasn't a great combination when you live on an upper floor in Barrington Plaza near Santa Monica. To my surprise they greeted me like family and in a matter of moments I began to feel at home in their apartment.

Santa Monica is the true definition of a picture postcard. Its pier extends into the bay and every night, as it has for over a hundred years, the rides and Carney midway glow in bright colors. Even in the late 60's it was considered the place to live if you couldn't afford Brentwood or Beverly Hills. The cool ocean breeze always managed to dissolve the choking smog that looked like a bowl of orange soup hanging over the rest of Los Angeles. Ocean Avenue, the main waterfront street sits on a cliff high above the beaches and Highway One. It was here Lawrence Welk and his big band played to as many as seven thousand people a night inside the Aragon Ballroom for ten years in the 1950's. Leveled by fire in 1970, today high rise apartment buildings fill the area. At the end of Ocean Avenue, West Channel Road leads you on a downhill drive through Santa Monica Canyon to Will Roger's Beach. A stone's throw down Highway One once stood a magnificent mansion William Randolph Hearst built for his movie star lover Marion Davies. At the corner of West Channel and Highway One, a pair of notorious beach rest rooms played host to thousands of gay encounters. Los Angeles Police Chief, Darrell Gates, wasn't shy about busting queers and his vice cops stayed busy, occasionally snaring embarrassed Grammy musicians and movie stars with the usual group of beach queens looking for a blow job.

Across the road, just off the corner, Bill Crocker,

also known as Betty by his friends, headed for the door of his bar, the S.S. Friendship. He carried a huge, bronze porthole under each arm he had bought at a salvage auction. Bill had an irresistible affinity for anything nautical. His rapture of the deep was on full display in the huge wooden bow of a ship that penetrated the front wall of his bar and extended onto the sidewalk. "Where's my jigsaw?" He shouted at the boy behind the bar as he headed for the office. When he returned the saw was sitting on the bar next to a water glass full of Vodka. A short, hard drinking man in his fifties who looked seventy-five, Bill Crocker knew he had a goldmine and loved being the center of attention. Just as everyone in the area knew the last parking space in Santa Monica Canyon would disappear before the morning fog burned off, they also knew the entire beach crowd would pack themselves into Bill's Friendship Bar by three-thirty every weekend afternoon.

In its seventy years, the Friendship laid claim to a lot history and some mythology as well. Many of Hollywood's most famous drank inside its beer spattered walls. The National Enquirer supposedly even ran a story claiming Marilyn Monroe gave birth to an illegitimate baby girl in the back of the bar when it was called Doc Law's Friendship Cafe.

Gay men started coming to it in the 1940's, and it wasn't long before Will Roger's Beach became known as Ginger Roger's beach. Gay writer, Christopher Isherwood describes the Friendship bar fictitiously when he called it the "Starboard Side" in his novel, "A Single Man":

> "The Starboard Side has been here since the earliest days of the colony. Its bar, formerly a lunch counter, served the neighbors with their first post-Prohibition beers, and the mirror behind it was sometimes honored by the reflection of Tom Mix. But its finest hours came later. That summer of 1945! The war was as good as over. The blackout no more than an excuse for keeping the lights out at a gangbang. A sign over the bar said, 'In case of a direct hit, we close immediately.' Which was meant to be funny, of course. And yet, out across the bay, in deep water under the cliffs of Palos Verdes; lay a real Japanese submarine full of real dead Japanese, depth-bombed after they had sunk two or three ships in sight of the California coast."

Over the years there have been different owners, but one thing never changed. Above the bar, a piece of a ship's keel salvaged from a wreck in the 1930's bears the scrawled names of patrons. Once written in red, many of them were painted white in the 1980's in memory of their owners who died from AIDS.

Two doors up the street I finished a steak sandwich at the bar in The Golden Bull. Nini and Michael mentioned it would be a good place to start looking for a job and gave me a heads up about how gay the neighborhood was. "I'm sorry, kid. We don't need anyone right now," the bartender said, putting the check next to my glass. "Try the Friendship next door. You might find something there."

Bill Crocker was busy standing on a pair of beer cases with his jig saw cutting two new round holes in the front of his bar. I stopped and watched until he noticed me and turned off his saw. "I'm putting in a couple new glory holes," he said with a grin. "What can I do for you?"

"I need a job. I'll do anything."

"Just get in town?"

"Yes, from Michigan."

"You gonna stay? Most guys don't. There are too many flakes in this city." He was checking me out and seemed to like what he saw. Without waiting for an answer he said: "Come back this Sunday. I'll try to find something for you." He started to go back to his portholes but turned and said, "Wear what you're wearing now." I looked down at my Levis, white T-shirt and work boots and felt lucky. Sunday, worried he wouldn't remember me, I arrived before the beach crowd. "That's one for you," he said noticing me at the bar.

"One what?"

"Your first point. You showed up. That's more than

most do. See that pile of beer cases over there? Put them over here." He tossed a Friendship T-shirt in my direction and said "Put this on. It's minimum wage. You won't get rich, but everyone splits the tips, so you'll get your share."

As I finished moving the last box the beach crowd exploded into the bar, swamping all three bartenders. In moments the bar was shoulder to shoulder with the most beautiful assortment of men I had ever seen. The Pointer Sisters blared on huge Klipschorn speakers and the floor, covered in the beach sand that arrived with crowd, was alive with dancing. Gym-perfect, tanned bodies, most with sun-bleached blond hair partied hard. I tried to resist the temptation to stop and watch when a horrible feeling of inadequacy swept over me. All I could see was how many incredibly handsome men surrounded me and never thought for a moment I was one of them. Perhaps the gods give this blindness as a gift to prevent young men from being egotistical, but it is a gift not everyone gets. The men before me were only the latest crop of hardened wannabes, looking for their break into show business, willing to do anything to get it.

A six-foot-six body builder stood alone in a dark corner towering about the crowd on the dance floor. His face showed lines that come with age. His hair was thinning but his tan was what people noticed. His head was planted on a Tarzan torso with muscles that had been developed to the point of not looking possible. Standing motionless, posing, he occasionally reached into his tank top to pull out a pair of scratched glasses that were missing their ear pieces and held them off his face so he could scan the bar. Just as quickly he would shove them back into his shirt, hoping no one had noticed, and posed again. An attractive older man was talking to Bill at the end of the bar. As I passed them carrying bags of ice, Bill grabbed me and introduced me to his friend. His name was Richard and I got a very good feeling from him. Across the room, several of the boys from the beach stopped talking and began watching us. It made me uneasy. "Will you have dinner with me?" Richard asked.

"That'd be nice, but I don't know what time I'll be done. It's my first day." Bill raised his fingers to let me know eight so I finalized my first date. When Richard left many eyes followed him to the door. Bill Crocker turned to me and said: "He likes you. Richard works for Paramount. You just met your first movie mogul." Instead of casting couch visions all I could think was that he probably needed someone to clean his house.

14

Suicide is Painless

"Through early morning fog I see
visions of the things to be
the pains that are withheld for me
I realize and I can see ...
that suicide is painless
it brings on many changes
and I can take or leave it if I
please."

- by Johnny Mandel
Theme song from Mash

By 3:30 in the morning, most of the bottle of Jamaican rum I brought with me from the bar was gone. What remained was sticking out of the sand between my knees. The beach was deserted and the water smelled like dead fish. The surf broke in a fluorescent electric blue glow that only comes with a red tide.

There wasn't much money left, a car payment was overdue and I was spending too much time thinking about my dead pharmacist friend, Jack and replaying the movie of Chuck's car driving away from the motel in Saugatuck. My Hollywood director friend lived in a circle of people way outside my league and while they were very nice to me, I was a curiosity to them and nothing more. I was tired of watching the plastic Hollywood freaks that hung out in the bar and longed to be around normal, masculine people who could talk about something other than themselves.

At the edge of the water I expected to see dead fish, not knowing the smell was from rotting plankton, a microscopic animal that lives in the sea. I bent over, picked up a hand full of wet sand and threw it into the air. It glowed like fireworks. Finishing off the last of the rum, I found myself walking out into the surf. When the water was deep enough to hit my crotch I hesitated. Feeling overwhelmed and far from home with no place to turn I kept walking until suddenly I began to float and lose my balance, falling head first into water over my head. Instead of panic, there was plenty of time to think. *All I have to do is take a couple deep breaths and let my lungs fill with water.* I surfaced and saw the moon's reflection on the water and began swimming back toward shore. Crying, I dialed the operator from a pay phone and placed a collect call to my youngest sister. When I heard her sleepy voice accepting the charges I wanted to hang up, but instead thanked her for answering and being there. She could tell I was drunk and wanted to know if I was OK and all I could do was thank her again for answering and tell her I loved her. I had decided to give things another try.

No one knows how the universe chooses the people it puts together in a bar on any given night, but many agree when the moon is full, the group will be strange. On this particular night as I worked, I had managed to become the focus of attention of an attractive bearded man. He made no attempt to hide his interest and the bulge in his shiny dark brown leather pants gave a hint at what he was thinking. Intrigued and horny, I wandered by him and he reached out and stopped me by putting his hand on my belt buckle. "You cut or uncut?" he quizzed.

"Huh?"

"It's a question. You have a foreskin?" he said, pointing down at my crotch.

"No. Why? Is that important?" I asked defensively.

"That's a shame."

"I didn't have any say in it."

"I like men with skin. Let me take a look at it. Maybe there's something we can do." He pulled me closer to him by my buckle and reached for the buttons on my 501's before breaking into a big smile and with a deep belly laugh, introduced himself. "Hi, I'm Hans." And in that moment, without realizing it, I met a man who would become a big part of my life, even saving it once, and we became instant brothers.

When Hans told me his last name was Von Braun, I of course questioned a connection to Werner, the German scientist who defected and helped build rockets

for the United States. "He's my uncle," he told me. Before
I could stop long enough to consider it, I had left Nini
and Michael's and moved into his dark, one bedroom
apartment on Fourth Street. A passionate, protective,
very intense relationship formed that demanded we spend
every second together, most of them in bed. We wore one
another out until we collapsed. For several weeks we lusted
after one another then just as quickly as it had begun,
Hans decided to continue his quest for the perfect foreskin
and was back in cruise mode. I loved him deeply, yet for
some reason I wasn't devastated, in fact I was relieved. I
didn't want to lose him but asked if he wanted me to move
out and he said of course not, so for the next six months
we shared his apartment and continued to get even closer
as friends.

What he did for a living remained an ever changing
mystery. Each day he would dress in street leathers, jump
on his motorcycle and head south on the freeway. In the
evening he returned home dressed in a variety of costumes
ranging from medical scrubs to paramilitary uniforms. It
got to the point where I couldn't figure out which Hans
I was going to meet in the morning; the Psychiatrist, the
MD, the biker, cowboy or beach bum. He was a male
Auntie Mame on steroids, always trying to consume as
much of life's banquet as fast as he could. I was confused,
but content to lovingly be a part of the daily secretive
parade of colorful characters he chose to inhabit. My only
concern was that one day I might answer a knock on the
door and find the police standing there.

It was after nine and although he always told

me not to, I had fixed dinner and was waiting for him.
Finally giving up, I stashed what was on the stove in the
refrigerator and scrawled a note for him to heat it up if he
was hungry. With car keys in hand I headed for the door
but stopped in front of the ringing phone. A distressed
woman caller was looking for Doctor Von Braun. Deciding
not to answer, I listened while she left a message on the
machine. I was bored with the gay bars I'd been going
to and needed something different so I headed up Santa
Monica Boulevard toward West Hollywood. At a light I
was cruised by a guy in a Mercedes. He motioned for me
to pull over but I kept going instead. A few blocks away
an interesting mix of people stood outside a bar I had
never been to so I parked and thought I'd give it a try. I
was surprised that the crowd inside included women, so
I sat at the bar with a beer watching. A few minutes later
two young kids who looked like hustlers came over and
introduced themselves, wanting to know if I was interested
in partying with them. I declined and headed for the
bathroom hoping they would be gone when I got back.
They were nowhere in sight when I sat down at the bar
again.

Bored and wanting to leave, I chugged most of my
beer but gave up finishing it because it tasted bitter. As I
got behind the wheel I began to feel strange and nauseated
so decided to head for home. My head was spinning. It
was difficult to keep the car in a single lane so I pulled
over and parked. Feeling worse, I knew I'd better get home
and off the road before the police stopped me. By the
time I reached the apartment all I could do was pull the

car in front of the gates to the garage and leave it there. I
stumbled up the stairs and as I tried unsuccessfully to get
my key into the door, it suddenly opened. Hans took one
look at me, threw me over his shoulder and headed down
the stairs, tossed me into the passenger seat of my car, then
drove like a maniac toward St. John's Hospital. I woke
up on a gurney in the hallway. Hans looked concerned.
"There were enough barbiturates in your stomach to kill
you. Where the hell were you?"

"Some bar on Santa Monica Boulevard. I think
some guys put shit in my beer."

"Don't you know to never leave a drink on the bar?
Always take it with you. You're lucky I was home. They
probably saw your car and figured you'd be an easy hit."
The next day I drove to a car lot and sold my Corvette for
enough to pay off the loan and buy a used Chevy pickup.
To celebrate Hans suggested we pack up the truck and
head up Highway One above Malibu and camp out. We
found a place on a deserted stretch of beach behind a rock
outcropping and threw our sleeping bags on the sand.
"I was worried I was going to lose you," he said softly,
drawing circles in the sand with his big toe and watching
the water make them disappear.

"Thank you for saving me."

"Don't do that again." We zipped the sleeping
bags together and cuddled. He reached over and grabbed
me. "Damn, still cut." He smiled and kissed me.

I awoke to the sound of something eating.
Squinting through the morning haze, I saw a huge, three
hundred pound sea lion ten feet away. He was oblivious to

me, busy finishing up what was going to be our breakfast. He had also consumed half of the canvas bag that held it. I nudged Hans and we both lay silently watching until he was full and headed back to the water. "Have you ever been to San Francisco?" he asked out of nowhere.

"Yeah, I wasn't impressed." I rolled over and began rubbing his back.

"You've never been there with me."

PART TWO

**I'm going home
to my city by the bay**

15

Transition

The Castro district during the 1970's was just another San Francisco ethnic enclave, the entrance to Eureka Valley, a group of residential neighborhoods near the top of Market Street. Tucked against the bottom of Twin Peaks, the city's two highest hills, it enjoys some of the best weather, always more sun than fog.

The gay community didn't invent the Castro district. San Francisco's Irish and Swedish populations did quite an excellent job of that. Its ethnic roots were evident in the imposing

architecture of the Most Holy Redeemer Catholic Church and convent that sat at the neighborhood's heart. A disproportionate number of taverns, more than ten, were dotted around Castro Street's short two-block retail strip. Rather heavy, balding men with pock-marked red noses inhabited the tiny bars at any given time during the day or night. Since the turn of the century faithful, middle class Catholic families had lived, shopped and raised their young here.

Castro in the late 1960's and early 70's was a confusing neighborhood in transition. When you stepped into a store you were never quite sure how you would be greeted. Many older business owners embraced us and looked forward to our business, while other merchants were disillusioned, angry holdouts who not only resented our presence, they despised who we were. But money has a way of changing attitudes and eventually even the most disagreeable characters took the cash and moved to the suburbs.

Walking from Market Street through the Castro in 2013 is an entirely different experience. The grand Castro Theater still sits proudly as the centerpiece, but for those of us who lived there during the seventies, besides the theater, little remains of what we knew and loved. The buildings are all still there, but the businesses, people and the magic "can-do" energy are gone. For a period of time, the AIDS epidemic almost made the Castro disappear. Some of our favorite watering holes faded away, their barstools left empty by thousands who vanished so quickly. Now only Peggy and Charlotte's Twin Peaks Tavern, Louie's barber shop, Ernie's legendary Cliff's Variety, Izzy and Bob's Sausage Factory survive in their original locations. The Castro has once again changed to meet the needs of a less gay, wealthier young family demographic, but now some of the families have two Dads or two Moms. People still walk down the street carrying cameras trying to capture the place where so much history, optimism, magic and violence took place in a short time span but there is little of the old left to photograph.

The first gay bars in the Castro area began to spring up in the late 1960's. The Men's Room on 18th Street and The Missouri Mule on Market near Castro were famous for Sunday brunches and Bloody Marys. These bars were a favorite hangout for older men. In the early 1970's, The Nothing Special on Castro enticed the morning alcoholics. "Mother" was always behind the bar with a cigarette dangling from his lip, and a heavy hand on the pour. David Ford's Midnight Sun opened in a tiny, marble floored former bank building on Castro just above 18th Street. Looking more like it belonged on Haight Street, it was decorated in an ever-changing array of themes. My favorite was the circus trip that covered the ceiling in bright orange and white parachutes draped to look like tents. Jesus Christ Satan, a strange little man who fried his brain on multiple doses of questionable quality, inexpensive acid was the unofficial mascot of the bar and could usually be found sitting cross-legged on top of the jukebox, dressed in layers of robes and outrageous jewelry. The cockroaches loved the circus theme too, and the day the tented ceiling came down to make way for a new look, they claimed the entire building briefly as customers, like roaches, fled into the street in panic.

Michael Frowley, a middle aged gay Irishman and his handsome, straight business partner, Rod, opened The Pendulum, the Castro's first bar catering to black men and their admirers. No one knows where Peter King came from, but the tall, skinny, effeminate Chinese man was hired to feed the patrons on Wednesday, the slowest night of the week. Free food and fifty-cent beer kept the bar packed but after awhile Peggy King's spaghetti gave way to a dubious KFC fried chicken knock-off and the crowds moved on to other taverns offering free food the same night.

The last straight neighborhood bars to give in were Gallagher's in the middle of the first block of Castro and The Eureka Bar on the corner of 18th and Collingwood. The short bald headed bartender at Gallagher's taped a sign on the bar mirror; "*Free Drinks If You Hate The Fags*", which produced a short lived but dramatic increase business. Some of the more adventurous, straight-looking gay men got a kick out of sitting on barstools, bashing their queer brothers for a few minutes while downing a free shot and beer. But soon that door too was locked and the sign changed. The Eureka Bar was the last straight drinking establishment to close. It briefly morphed into the Castro's first lesbian bar, Francine's.

By the seventies rents were on the rise. Judy's tiny Chankly Boar bookstore disappeared when her new Chinese landlord raised the rent 500%. It became The All American Boy, a clothing store. Some Castro gay bars were already busy reincarnating themselves into their second and third versions like the real corner grocery store on 18th Street that suddenly became The Corner Grocery Bar, then was reborn again into the Opera Cafe' which segued directly into Moby Dicks. It seemed drinking establishments were morphing everywhere. Frank & Jean sold their Cocktail Lounge and Watergate West was born, only too quickly to become The Badlands. Bob opened his Castro Café next to Toad Hall and it became home to many neighborhood characters, including a young black singer named Sylvester who constantly told everyone how famous he would be someday as he washed dishes behind the counter. Scott Smith and Harvey Milk opened their camera store and Star Pharmacy on the corner of 18th and Castro, hired Jackie, the neighborhood's first self-proclaimed fag-hag. Embracing the gay community, she quickly became a local celebrity one-woman powerhouse to raise money for neighborhood charities.

A woman affectionately known as Crazy Girt stood on the curb waiting for the light to turn green so she could cross 18th Street. Her inability to complete each crossing was a sadly comical ballet of stepping off and on the curb over and over again in circles long before people understood the meaning of obsessive compulsive disorders. If she wasn't on the curb you'd find her exhausted and frustrated, sitting alone talking to herself on the bench by the pay phone.

Everyone in the neighborhood looked out for Girt and protected her from harm. No one knew where she went at night, but each morning she was back at her post looking clean and cared for. One Thanksgiving she appeared looking disheveled for the first time. A bartender took her to the Castro Café and ordered a turkey dinner. When he tried to pay for it, Bob, the owner, told him he received a check every month in the mail to pay for her meals. One day Girt didn't return to her corner on Castro and 18th Street. Mr. Anderson retired, and overnight his historic treasure of a pharmacy on that same corner, with shelves filled with ancient, glass apothecary jars vanished and became the Elephant Walk. Adopted as a new home by the wealthier Castro queens, it would earn its place in history in 1979 after the White Night Riot.

16

Keep Your Hat On

My first visit to San Francisco had been a few years earlier as a generic tourist, the kind you see fresh off the plane, walking around holding half open maps while craning their necks to get better looks at Coit Tower and the Trans-America pyramid. The more affluent tourists had their half open maps splayed across the steering wheels of rental cars. Their eyes were the size of saucers as they flew down steep hills going the wrong way. I fell prey to all the typical tourist things like riding cable cars, going to Fisherman's Wharf and hanging out in an overpriced hotel room in the Tenderloin because I was freezing to death in my shorts and T-shirt. This time was different. I was with Hans and it seemed like he knew everything and everyone who lived in the city. We each packed a gym bag of warm clothes and he led me far from the crowds and deep into the beating heart of the real city.

The cabbie stepped on the gas and shot up the steepest part of Castro Street, pinning us against the back seat. "Where the hell are we going?"

"To Jack and Gordon's house, they're expecting us," he said, tapping the cab driver on the shoulder, pointing where to turn. "They're throwing a party for us and some of my friends, you're going to like them." We made a turn and headed up another hill. Beautiful Edwardian and Victorian homes stood in a colorful array along both sides of Elizabeth Street as it ran across the top of hills that formed a ridge between the Castro District and Noe Valley. "We're here," Hans said, jumping out of the cab pulling me after him. Three Harleys were parked on the small front lawn and the street was littered with pickup trucks. A large group of very big men surrounded us, and before we could say hello we were holding beers and hugging. I thought I'd died and gone to heaven. Introductions were quick and I tried to burn the image of each hairy face deep into my brain, knowing I'd not want to forget a single name.

Jack grabbed our bags and the group moved inside, then out into the backyard where huge pots of water were already boiling. "It's that time of year. I hope you like Dungeness crab," Gordon said as he started throwing them into the pots.

Across the yard, Hans talked to several people while they looked in my direction. "They wanted to know if we are partners," he said later. "I told them you're available. Better watch out, you're fresh meat for this group."

I wish, I thought. "Who's the bearded guy by the tree?"

"Dave Peterson. That's his partner, Ron over there.

They're both merchant seamen. They're not in town very much, but when they're here we have a lot of fun." Hans no sooner spoke when Dave began walking toward us and it felt like I'd been set up.

"How long are you going to be here?" he asked staring directly into my eyes and putting his hand on my shoulder.

"Just the weekend. Hans set the trip up."

"Think you'll have time for a drink and maybe dinner?"

"I hope so. Is Ron OK with that?"

"Oh hell yes, we're just good buddies now. We've been together a long time." He looked to see where Ron was in the crowd.

The pot of crabs and a pot of artichokes were dumped onto newspaper and bowls of different dipping sauces were uncovered. Moments later a feeding frenzy began and the group would not be satisfied until the last crab and artichoke had been left in a pile of rubble on the table. As soon as my beer was empty someone would put another in my hands. I had never eaten so much rich food or drank so much beer in such a short time, and soon all I could think about was finding a place to lie down. "You look green," Hans said realizing I wasn't going to be joining him and the others at the bars. "Come on, I'll find our room and you can get some rest."

"I don't want to wreck your night."

"Don't be stupid, we've got plenty of time. Besides, you're a star and you don't even know it. They've been lining up to find out more about you, asking me to put a good word in for them." Dave and Ron found the room and came to say good night as did several others in the group. Outside motorcycles and pickups were leaving. By morning I could add Dungeness crab and artichokes to gin on my short list of things I had overindulged in to the point of vomiting them through my nose. For the rest of my life I wouldn't be able to bear the smell of them cooking, let alone eat them.

By four in the afternoon I felt semi-human and was able to keep soft food down. Hans called and changed our return flight to add another two days to our trip. "Get your butt out of bed. You've had enough rest. I've got a city to show you that you're going to love." He threw a bag on the bed with a black leather vest in it. "Here, I got you a present. Put this on." For the next two days and nights he led the way through what seemed like endless numbers of bars, discos and bath houses. We ate in intimate, family restaurants tucked deep into neighborhoods far from the Grayline tour busses. Each passing hour I felt more at home and deeper in love with San Francisco.

On our last night, Hans took me to Febe's, a leather bar on Folsom Street. "You need a hat to go with that vest." Upstairs, Nicodemus, a slightly insane, dirty old man resembling Santa Clause, ran *A Taste of Leather*. His emporium included everything from motorcycle jackets, vests and sex toys, to a special homemade brew of amyl nitrate popular with the leather crowd. And of course, leather motorcycle hats. Hans insisted I try them all on until I found one that pleased him. "I feel like a fool, I said trying to take it off.

"You look great." He paid for it and led the way to our next stop. I walked behind him through the bar looking down at the floor, hoping no one would notice how silly I looked in my new hat.

The Gentlemen's Quarters on 18th near Dolores was a small neighborhood bar. Painted entirely black inside, it took your eyes a few moments to adjust before you noticed the ceiling was completely covered in men's underwear of all sizes and shapes. An extremely good looking, half-dressed bartender seemed to know Hans and waited to take our order. "Do you know everyone in San Francisco?"

"Only the best ones," he winked at me.

Our drinks came and with them, the bartender brought two leather cups with dice. "Wanna shake for the drinks?" he asked, putting a cup in front of Hans who immediately pushed it in front of me. "Oh, forgot to tell you, we're playing strip dice." I looked down the bar at three other people sitting in various stages of nakedness. One was down to his shorts.

The jukebox was playing the Bee Gee's "*How Do You Mend a Broken Heart,*" and for a moment I disappeared in thoughts about Jack and Chuck in Michigan. "What the hell," I said, picking up the cup and shaking the dice. Of course I lost, and the first thing to go was my leather vest.

"I'll give ya a handicap," the bartender said pulling his T-shirt over his head with a broad smile and throwing it on the back bar. Several rounds of drinks later he stood there in only a jockstrap and a pair of boots. I was down to my Levis and new hat. "It's your turn." I shook and lost again, this time offering him my hat. "Nope, you need to keep your hat on; you look too good in it. I'll take the Levis."

"You can't take them. I'm not wearing any underwear."

"So?" My Levis were added to the pile of clothes on the back bar and my bare ass began to stick to the barstool.

"Your dice are loaded."

"Of course not," he said with a grin. "Tell you what. You can have your clothes back, but first you have to dance on the bar. And, you can't take off the hat." I looked at Hans who grinned and shrugged his shoulders acknowledging he had set me up again. The bartender poured shots for the three of us and after a couple rounds the music changed to "Staying Alive" and I gave my solo performance to appreciative applause from the other almost naked men in the bar.

That night we flew back to L.A. and the following week Hans rode back to San Francisco with me in my truck. Jack and Gordon insisted I stay with them as long as I wanted. "Well, I guess this is it," I said, hugging him in the airport. "Do you think you'll ever move up here?"

"You never know." he said with a bear hug and kiss on my forehead. "I'm not great at goodbyes." He turned and disappeared into the crowd without looking back. I stood there feeling empty, alone and afraid. Like Dorothy in the Wizard of Oz, people had been coming and going entirely too fast.

I never wore the hat again.

17

Scared Shitless

For most of us arriving from cities and small towns across the country, the Castro and gay life in San Francisco became our universe. We didn't pay attention to what was going on in the rest of the world. We were consumed by this new place we called home. Our days and nights were spent with each other, and for many of us, there was no interaction with the straight community. It was an entirely new feeling having lived in fear of our families finding out. Getting far enough away from home allowed us to not care for the first time. We were "*out*" to each other, and that was enough for the moment. The panacea of being openly gay in gay San Francisco allowed many to feel self-worth for the first time and the feeling was intoxicating. But too soon the euphoria of our freedom wore off, and we found ourselves with life and death choices to make. Did we want to spend the rest of our lives sitting on barstools and struggling to survive? Or were we willing to step out of gay play time long enough to allow our talents to surface and lead us back into productive lives in our new home?

There was a social pecking order and I arrived near the bottom of it. I had a truck, driver's license and a trade and these were the things that would allow me to pull myself up. Without those and the people who befriended me, I would have had the same fate as the men who stood in line every morning in the fog waiting for the first bar to open. I spent too much time wallowing in self-pity that I wasn't as handsome or wealthy as many of the men around me, but deep inside I knew I was probably smarter than most.

The morning finally arrived when I turned the key in the ignition only to watch the arrow on the gas gauge stay on empty. I had a five dollar bill in my wallet, some loose change in my pocket, and that was it. What now? I asked myself, leaving the truck parked in Gordon & Jack's driveway and starting a walk down the hill to the Castro. I felt hopeless, on the verge of tears and panic. "Pass me the salt," an elbow nudged me while I waited for my eggs at the counter in the Castro Café. "It's not the end of the world, you know."

"Is it that noticeable?"

"Where are you from? I haven't seen you around here before." He turned his head toward me and a pair of piercing blue eyes on a kind face greeted me.

"I just moved up from LA, but I'm from Michigan. I'm afraid I'm not having a very good week," I apologized. "I can't find a job anywhere. You probably hear these stories all the time."

"This city can be tough on newcomers. A lot of guys arrive who don't want to work, just party. What do you do?"

"I'm pretty good at scraping people up off the street. At home I worked on ambulances; lots of guts and gore. Don't want to get back into that again."

"Can't help you there, but I've heard they're short a good waiter at the Country Club down on 17th and Florida. The bar downstairs is called The Speakeasy. The restaurant is upstairs. You might try there. I hear the owner is a pretty nice guy."

"I've never waited tables before."

"Oh hell, just lie. Anyone can do that stuff. Who knows, it might be something that could put a smile back on that cute face of yours." For the next half hour we sat talking, and after he was gone I realized neither of us had introduced ourselves. I wanted to thank him.

I paid the check with my five dollar bill and left with only a quarter in my pocket, jumped on the Market streetcar and watched my last coin bounce down the chute inside the fare box. The sound was so final; it became a recording I could play back in my head for the rest of my life. By three o'clock the bar on the first floor was open. "Someone told me you're looking for a waiter."

The bartender pointed to a small office in the back. "Ask for Ray, he's the owner". The door was open but I knocked anyway. "Are you looking for a waiter?" The man sitting behind the desk looked up from his work. It was my blue-eyed breakfast partner. "You have any experience?" he asked with a big smile on his face.

"Sure, I'm your man."

"References?"

"I think I know the owner." We both laughed and I followed him upstairs to the restaurant. He handed me a white apron, corkscrew, pen and an order pad.

"Good luck. Tips are good here. Ask for Chuck in back and he'll walk you through what you need to do. The cook's name is Carlos. Tell him I said to feed you before it gets busy." And with that I landed my first job in San Francisco.

By eight o'clock I had about twenty dollars in tips in my pocket. Things were going smoothly and everyone was welcoming except Carlos in the kitchen. His huge body was soaked in sweat running off his face. Every time a waiter clipped an order above the window he screamed at them. He made it clear I was to tell him when the salads were served so he would know when to fire the entrée.

An older gay couple reached the top of the stairs and the host seated them in my station. You could tell by their body language they weren't getting along and had been sitting at the bar downstairs too long. "What can I get for you gents tonight?" I asked handing them menus.

"We'll I'd like some wine, if I had a wine list." the one who looked and sounded like a whiney Truman Capote snapped.

"Cut him some slack," his partner said looking up from his menu.

"Go fuck yourself." I pretended not to hear, struggling to get the cork out of the wine. Without thinking I put the bottle between my knees and pulled harder. "For Christ sake, who taught you how to open wine?" He reached between my legs, grabbed the bottle and began to pour. One of the other waiters watching busted out in laughter. They both ordered medium steaks, and when salads were in front of them I told the chef. By the time they finished them, their argument had almost become a fist fight. "Cancel our steaks," I was told as I cleared the salad plates. "We're leaving."

When I relayed the news to Carlos, he swore at me. "I'm sorry; the chef already has your steaks on the fire."

"We don't want them. We'll pay for the wine. Bring us the check."

I ran back to the kitchen and this time Carlos waved his huge butcher knife at me. "I'm afraid the chef said you'll have to pay for them. You can eat them here or take them home with you." Things were going from bad to worse. The quiet one shoved the loud one back into his chair when he stood up to leave and almost knocked him over. I was told to bring their food and they would eat it, but now they had decided to fight with me instead of each other.

"These steaks are too rare. Tell the chef we said MEDIUM." I took them back to the kitchen and while giving me a threatening look, Carlos threw them on the fire.

"They're still too raw. I don't want to see any blood in this meat." When Carlos saw me coming through the door with the steaks a second time he threw a pot across the kitchen. This time he checked for blood before sending me back out with the meat, making it clear the next blood I saw would be my own. To emphasize the point he slammed his knife into the counter and left it standing in the wood.

"Now they're burnt. This is garbage." He threw his fork on the floor. As I reached for his plate he stabbed at my hand with his steak knife. It passed between two of my fingers nicking the thin flesh connecting them and stuck into the table top. I stood in disbelief for a moment. Everyone stopped eating and watched in silence. There was no way I was going to take the meat through those swinging kitchen doors a third time. The longer I thought, the angrier I got. I needed this damn job and these two idiots were wrecking it for me.

"Listen you bitchy old queen," I said, pulling his steak knife out from between my fingers and pointing it in his face. "You can either eat these fucking steaks or wear them." I picked up his plate and slammed it down on the table again. "One thing I can tell you; you're going to pay for them." I wiped the blood off my hand onto their table cloth and stormed away, handing my apron, corkscrew, pen and pad to the host as I passed. By the time I reached the bottom of the stairs, my new ex-boss, Ray Ruehl was waiting for me. "Don't let em get to you, Lou. They've been thrown out of here before. Not everyone is like them." I couldn't believe my ears. Rather than being angry, he was trying to console me. For awhile we sat at the bar drinking in silence. "Clearly, waiting tables isn't your thing." He leaned over and gently bumped my shoulder with his head so no one would hear. "What else can you do?"

"I'm a pretty decent carpenter, but I don't have any tools," I said almost in tears.

He pulled out his walled and put two fifty dollar bills on the bar in front of me. "Go buy yourself what you need. I'll meet you tomorrow at noon at my other place, The Covered Wagon on the corner of 12th and Folsom. I need a few benches built that people can sit on and I can store beer cases under. If I like what I see I can probably find a few more things to keep you busy."

"Ray, I don't know how to thank you."

"Don't worry. I'll figure something out." He smiled and ordered two more beers for us. In the weeks that followed, he kept me doing small carpentry jobs. Pay was never discussed, but every Friday the envelope always had more in it than I hoped for. I never did tell him the story about how I spent my last quarter. Something told me he had a story like that of his own.

18

Motorcycle Matinee

In 1964, Life Magazine ran a fourteen page spread called "Homosexuality in America." The article called "Life inside the gay community...a sad and often sordid world," sensationalizing and judging homosexuality as a mental illness, dirty little secret, and illegal. Photos showed police arresting gay men while upstanding heterosexual citizens looked on with disgust. But no matter how hard they tried, it was already too late to shove the gay community back into their closets.

In the 1950's, most masculine gay men, and those into leather, hung out in waterfront bars along the Embarcadero with the merchant seamen. In 1962, the city's first dedicated leather bar, The Why Not, opened briefly in the Tenderloin and later that year, The Tool Box on 4th and Harrison, and Febe's on Folsom and 11th opened a day apart. Chuck Arnett, a local artist who worked in The Tool Box, painted a huge black and white mural of leathermen on the bar wall that became an icon in the community. When Life magazine did their article,

a photo of it was stretched across the two opening pages. Arnett created hundreds of posters and ads for the bars over his lifetime and was revered by the San Francisco gay community for his artwork.

By the early 1970's, the South of Market area had been nicknamed the Miracle Mile for the sheer number and variety of leather bars and baths. The Stud, No Name, Barracks, The Slot, Ambush, Lone Star, The Eagle, and

on Market Street, The Balcony, catered to not only the
men who rode motorcycles and serious S&M players, but
also to the subset of curious, weekend leather wannabes,
who did their best to look masculine and fearful while
exchanging recipes and decorating tips. Untold numbers of
cows gave their lives to clothe them.

～

The Ramrod, at 1225 Folsom, was partially owned
by Hollywood film editor, George Wilbur and San
Francisco drag personality, Luscious Lorelei (Paul Bentley).
Its name implied a country western theme, and while it
attracted a few cowboy types, it was quickly adopted by
the San Francisco leather community. The costumes later
worn by the hyper-male, cartoonesque Village People were
surely inspired by what they saw on Folsom Street.

Every Sunday afternoon, movies played to a
standing room only audience that filled the dark back
room. There were scores of men in leather and Levis
packed so closely together it was difficult to breathe, but
they managed to do that and lots of other things. Thanks
to George and his connections, the film could be a first run
pirated version of "Star Wars," or a classic like "Gone with
the Wind." Whatever the choice, it was always fun. One
of the crowd's favorites was a reel of nothing but dozens of
Loretta Young's swishing entrances through a sequence of
more and more elaborate doors lifted from pieces of her
1950's television series.

I felt the back of my shoulders touch his chest,
then his breath on the top of my head. As I bent my
head back so I could look up, I stared into the face of an

exceptionally tall version of Bluto. His dark eyes and full black beard looked familiar. Dave Peterson broke into a smile, wrapped his hairy arms around my chest and held me for the next forty-five minutes while we watched the movie. As it ended he bent down and whispered in my ear; "Hi Lou." He kissed me on the neck. "Remember me? Dave. I met you at Jack and Gordon's house."

"Sure. I owe you a dinner. There wasn't enough time before we flew back to L.A." We found a place along the wall to get away from the crush of people and spent the next hour talking and laughing.

"What are you doing tonight?" he asked.

"I was going to have a few more beers and head back to Jack and Gordon's. I'm worried I'm wearing out my welcome. They've been so good letting me stay there.

"Why don't you come over to Sausalito tonight and stay with me? Ron is at sea and it's a big empty place." I felt light headed when I nodded yes. "Are you driving?" he asked as we walked out the door.

"My pickup's over there." I pointed noticing something wasn't right. Dave saw my concern and followed me. The back window was smashed and everything inside was gone. "Fuck! I just lost all my tools. They took everything," I said on the verge of tears, knowing what they took wasn't much, but it was all I had.

"I'll drive," he said wrapping his arm around my shoulder to console me and pointing to his own truck. We'll come back tomorrow and get it fixed." He drove toward the Golden Gate bridge and headed north across the span to the first exit.

19

38 Caledonia Street

There were two ways to get to Sausalito; the way we came the night before or by boat. Before the Golden Gate Bridge was completed, Sausalito was a place where the car ferries landed and people could connect to trains heading north. When World War II began, shipyards sprung up around the area and Sausalito was inundated with workers. By the 1970's, it had returned to being a quiet town on the edge of the bay. The ferries that once carried cars now arrived loaded with vacationers from all over the world. Disney couldn't have designed a more

Take a Ferry to Sausalito

&

Take A Fairy Home

THE SAUSALITO INN

picturesque place.

The Sausalito Inn was only steps from where the
ferry unloaded passengers and was a favorite place for the
gay and straight locals to mingle with tourists. The bar
always had a bowl of souvenir match books that said "Take
a Ferry to Sausalito and Take a Fairy Home". The spelling
of the last Fairy is debatable but the message was the
same and always produced bursts of laughter. Something
fun and interesting was always happening in town. Carol
Burnett and Walter Matthau sat at a table in the window
of the Sausalito Inn being filmed for the movie Pete and
Tilley. The Kingston Trio entertained diners at their
Trident Restaurant and a walk down Bridgeway took
you past the No Name bar, a popular straight haunt.
Occasionally I stopped and watched sexy Shel Silverstein
sitting near the open front window as he drew cartoons for
Playboy. He looked up and winked at me once and made
love to me with his eyes.

The buildings closest to the ferry were a mixture of
bars, restaurants and souvenir shops, but the further away
from the ferry you got, the more normal life began to
get. The streets were always clogged with tourists so daily
chores like going to the bank or Laundromat were almost
impossible to do on weekends making life difficult for
people who lived there.

Dave and his partner Ron worked for Pacific Far
East Lines and sailed on the Mariposa and the Monterey,
a pair of wartime cargo ships that had been converted
into small, 600 passenger cruise ships that routinely ran
between San Francisco, Hawaii and Los Angeles. I stayed

with Dave and his mostly absent merchant seaman partner in their flat above Poor Richard's Beauty Shop at 38 Caledonia Street. When they were at sea together, it was just me, and the cat and the incredible view overlooking a marina full of sailboats toward the million-dollar homes on the Belvedere Peninsula.

Life at Dave and Ron's was unpredictable. Late one night I awoke to the sound of the screen door opening, then slamming shut. Moments later someone pulled the covers back and climbed into bed with me. Reaching for the light, I was surprised to find a very attractive naked woman. "Where's David?" she asked with breath smelling like Scotch.

"At sea," I answered, looking at the alarm clock.

"Who are you?" she wanted to know, lifting up the sheet to see the rest of me.

"Lou, and who are you?" I asked pulling the sheet back down.

"Patti." And with that she reached over, turned out the light and cuddled up next to my back in the spoon position. A few hours later her lover Betty came crashing through the same screen door. After lots of shouting and negotiating they left together, but not before Patti ran back and kissed me on the forehead. "You're a good cuddler." The next morning she called to apologize and invited me to lunch. Her office on the 18th floor in the financial district had fantastic bay views, and her receptionist was expecting me. "You can go right in."

"There's no one in here," I said sticking my head back out the door.

"Don't be silly, she's in there. I think she had a rough night." Walking back behind the big walnut executive desk, the receptionist put her finger in front of her lips and waved for me to come. Patti, nicely dressed in her two piece black Armani suit and frilly white blouse, was sound asleep, curled up in a ball in the knee hole. "Should I wake her?" she whispered.

"No, I think she needs the nap more than food."

That Sunday Patti, Betty and I went to Casa Madrona for brunch. One of the jewels of Sausalito, the hotel looked more like a series of bright blue connected cottages cascading down the side of the mountain facing San Francisco bay. We all agreed that sitting on the Casa Madrona terrace having brunch on a warm, sunny day was where we wanted to be when the big quake hit.

20

The Seaman's Semen Bar

It makes me smile to think how fearful some gay men were to go to the leather bars South of Market. They were nothing compared to risking your life to hang out in the Tenderloin.

When I first arrived in San Francisco in the late 1960's, the Castro wasn't the world famous gay Mecca it became. The hippies, love-children and a few gay people were living and playing in the Haight Ashbury, but downtown the Tenderloin and Polk Gulch areas of San Francisco were the favorite haunts for most gay men. Sweet Lips, [Dick Walters] was still walking the planks behind the Cockpit bar on Turk Street where Truman Capote could occasionally be found on a barstool, holding court.

The Tenderloin was a dangerous place with the highest crime rate in the city and the police treated it as a holding area where they could confine the darkest aspects of city life. Poverty was everywhere, as was sex, drugs and alcohol. If you were homeless or mentally ill, you could get by living on the streets or in doorways. It wasn't an easy life and it certainly wasn't pretty.

The Tenderloin before the turn of the century was known as St. Ann's Valley and was considered far enough away from the water's edge to be on solid ground and safe during an earthquake. The scientists felt they proved this when they dug up remains of a woman dating back five-thousand years. Over time the district became known as the Uptown Tenderloin and was second only to its neighbor, The Barbary Coast, for easy women, cheap booze, police payoffs and crime. It was here in the late 1800's that Alice B. Toklas was born, and while living with her friend Gertrude Stein at 922 O'Farrell perfected her pot brownie recipe.

The western edge of the Tenderloin was a wealthy Jewish area that separated the down-and-outers from the rest of town. City Hall sits in the southwestern corner of the neighborhood, the Hilton Hotel is on its eastern edge and the upper slope of the Tenderloin meets lower, prestigious Nob Hill along Geary Street. One block away on Post Street, in an area with a Nob Hill zip code, is a no-man's-land that is sometimes called Tendernob. This is where seedy meets society.

What the 1906 earthquake didn't knock down, the fire department did while setting backfires and explosions in hopes of saving the rest of the city. The aftermath was an area where nothing remained but ashes and a few piles of bricks.

Writer, Robert Louis Stevenson and then-newspaper reporter Mark Twain walked the rebuilt Tenderloin streets and lived in the post earthquake brick apartment buildings. Later, Charlie "Bird" Parker, Benny Goodman and his big band, and Billie Holiday entertained and hung out here. Dashiell Hammett lived on Post Street and wrote his Sam Spade detective novels and The Maltese Falcon using the Tenderloin as the backdrop.

The real slide into crime happened as a result of the Second World War. During wartime, the port of San Francisco expanded and contracted to fit the needs of the Navy, but when the war ended, hundreds of dock workers and merchant seamen were left out of work and stranded in their hotel rooms. Poverty was everywhere and the neighborhood quickly took on a horrible new and dangerous identity.

Perhaps John Waters, the gay film maker who gave the world Hairspray and Devine eating dog shit, best describes the Tenderloin and one particular bar I became intimately familiar with, The Trap:

> "*The Tenderloin was scarier than you can imagine. It was really scary. There was the scariest bar I ever went into in my life there called The Trap, and it was a trap. You went in and you didn't come out. It was not a gay bar; I don't know what it was. It was psychopaths and criminals basically.*"

Dawn light had barely hit the window when the

phone began to ring. "I thought I'd let you sleep in," the voice on the other end said. "Can you come get me?"

"Where are you?" I asked trying to open my eyes and find a pencil in case I needed it.

"I'm in San Francisco. I got in early this morning. Come have a beer with me. I'm at The Trap."

"I'm on my way," I said rotating my feet out of bed and tucking the phone against my shoulder while trying to pull on my Levis. "Watch your back," I added knowing that he had just been paid and had a lot of money on him. The drive into the city was easy and I was in the Tenderloin before I knew it, but spent fifteen minutes in the maze of one-way streets trying to find a parking place.

The Trap was a full frontal assault on all your senses. Even the door was encrusted in filth and the second you opened it, your lungs filled with the smell of stale beer, piss and body odor. There were no dark corners. What light couldn't filter through the dirty, partially painted windows was supplemented by a ceiling filled with strips of glaring, bare fluorescent bulbs. The patrons were always an unusual group, but this morning the mix was heavy with merchant seamen, most of who clung close to the bar. The tables were filled with drag queens, transvestites and down and out hookers of both sexes. It was not by coincidence they were all there. They knew when the ships came in, memorizing the schedules in the newspaper. They also knew that every horny seaman who disembarked carried his sea papers, union card, and his off-duty pay in a black zippered leather pouch, making them easy targets to spot.

Dave greeted me by opening his legs and making

room for me to stand between them. "I'll get you a beer., he said, handing me his. "I missed you," he whispered, squeezing me between his legs.

"How long have you been here?"

"Since it opened." he said in a voice I knew meant he had more than a few beers already. The Trap opened at six a.m. The hour was important to the locals, they needed someplace to hang out. Life was tough and rough, and survival was on everyone's mind. The street people all knew their next stop could easily be San Francisco General or the city morgue if they weren't paying attention.

"I need to take a leak," I said, half asking where it was. Dave pointed to a dark opening without a door. A small red bulb hung from the ceiling barely lighting the room. A very drunk seaman stood at the trough with his hand against the wall to steady himself. His bulging wallet was part way out of his rear pocket. I took my place on the other side of him, half tempted to push his wallet deeper in his pants but decided that wasn't a good idea. A skinny transvestite wearing bright green platform heels with laces that went up to her knees came in with a full Budweiser and without warning, slammed it into the sailor's head, making a move for his money. The bottle burst and a mixture of glass, beer, blood and scalp flew in all directions. The sailor fell against the wall, and when he did, I kicked the wallet he dropped behind me, swung around and shoved my foot as hard as I could into his attacker's crotch. The drag queen fell out the door into the bar on her ass.

"Shit," the bartender said seeing the mess he had to

clean up. He took the dirty bar rag hanging from his rear pocket and plastered it onto the man's head and led him back to the bar. I picked up his wallet, followed and made sure he got it back.

"Are you ready to go?" I asked Dave, wiping the blood off my shirt and out of my hair with a rag the bartender shoved across the bar for me.

"Let's have another beer," he said to both me and the bartender. So we sat there, but instead of facing the mirrored wall behind the bar, we turned around on our stools, leaned back and watched the show in the center of the room feeling safer seeing what might be coming rather than being surprised by it.

"Go down Mission Street," Dave said, pointing where I should turn. "I need to pick up a few things." A moment later we pulled into Sear's parking lot. First he carried a Craftsman worm-gear circular saw to the counter, and then kept making trips, adding armloads of tools to the pile. "If you're gonna work you've gotta have tools," he explained, answering the questioned look on my face.

"Whoa. Wait! I can't pay for this stuff."

"So who's asking you to? You've gotta have good tools if you're going to keep me in the style I'm accustomed to," he laughed while unzipping his pay pouch, pulling out a stack of fifty dollar bills.

I couldn't believe anyone could be this generous. "I'll pay you back as soon as I can get on my feet."

"Actually I'd prefer you to stay on your back for a while longer," he said punching me on the arm and loading me up with boxes.

21

I'll Rip Your Balls Off

Juanita Musson was never a beautiful woman, nor was she articulate or polite. Like mythology's Minerva who sprang from her mother's head dressed in full fighting armor, Juanita just suddenly appeared on the scene, but instead of armor she wore a muumuu that had already been worn too long and an assortment of large Spanish mantilla combs which she sometimes substituted with a tacky tiara. At almost three hundred pounds she was definitely a force to be

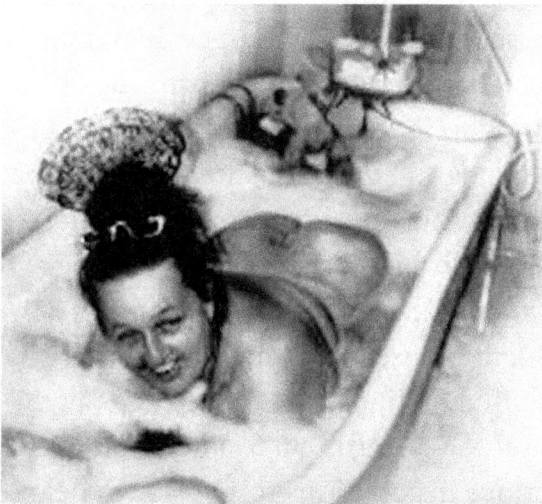

reckoned with and never shied away from a good fight.

Juanita was a restaurateur like none you've ever known. I suppose she could be compared a bit to the Soup Nazi character on Seinfeld, but in truth was far more savvy. During the 1960's and 70's she became a cult hero to a huge and very diverse group of Bay Area people. Love her or hate her, you could not ignore her. You'd frequently find her latest antics described in Herb Caen's daily column in the San Francisco Chronicle. I first became aware of Juanita while I lived in Sausalito. She inhabited what was left of a rotting, but historical old, wood car ferry that, after its final trip across San Francisco bay, had been left to die in the tideland mud of Sausalito's inner bay. Juanita's Galley, as all the future reincarnations of her restaurant would also be called, wasn't much. But with Juanita on board, it quickly became infamous, then just as quickly managed to burn down.

Juanita's arch enemy competitor in Sausalito, at least in Juanita's mind, was Sally Stanford, and her beautiful waterfront Valhalla restaurant. Another larger than life, beloved San Francisco character, Sally was born Mabel Busby, an Oregon girl who in her teens was an experienced bootlegger. She came to San Francisco in 1924 and by the forties was running one of the most successful bordellos on the edge of Nob Hill. In June of 1945 the planning meeting to establish the United Nations was held in the San Francisco Opera House. Years later Herb Caen would write: "The United Nations was founded at Sally Stanford's whorehouse". Sally's girls entertained many of the delegates, and serious negotiations took place in her bordello's living room at 1144 Pine Street.

In 1949, California governor Pat Brown had police raid her place and shortly afterward, Sally closed it down, took the money and left town. In 1950 Sally used that money to open Valhalla in Sausalito. Inside its heavily flocked wallpapered walls and among windows facing San Francisco bay adorned with heavy red velvet draperies, she held court over the rich and famous of the world. Always at the front door when people arrived, she greeted

them dressed to the nines with a beautiful Macaw parrot on her arm. To imitate and humiliate her, Juanita began to greet guests arriving at her decaying, rented ferry boat in her usual muumuu but added a one-eyed rooster to her shoulder and named him Chicken Shit Smith.

Legend has it that when Juanita's ferry caught fire and burned, Sally felt so sorry for her that she invited Juanita to be a guest hostess at her Valhalla until she could find a new place. No one knows for sure if what happened that first night was pre-planned by the two of them for publicity or spontaneous, but Juanita, feeling no pain, apparently decided to lay her three hundred pounds on the floor against the door, refusing to let anyone enter or leave until Sally had the police come and forcefully remove her.

Sally married many times, always taking her husband's last name, but in 1971 she registered her final name change. Sally Stanford had named herself after her favorite football team. She went on to become the mayor of Sausalito in 1976 at the age of seventy-two.

Juanita always had a knack for finding down and out places with cheap rents, so it was no surprise the next place she would turn up would be an old hotel and mineral spa at Fetter's Hot Springs in Sonoma County's Valley of the Moon. Like the Sausalito ferry boat, the buildings were in a similar state of decline and chaos. But Fetters was home and soon became a familiar destination for her loyal following of diners and experience seekers.

~

On a sunny Sunday morning while a group of us were drinking Tequila Sunrises on the deck in Sausalito, the topic of whatever happened to Juanita came up. It was decided we should all go to her new place at Fetters for Brunch. Gordon and Jack had come over from the city on their Harleys so the rest of us piled in Dave's bright orange pickup with the huge cab-over camper and headed north toward the wine country.

At just under six feet, I was the smallest in the group. The rest resembled a mixture of Hell's Angels, football quarterbacks and salty bearded sailors. There wasn't a feminine bone on display as we got out of the truck and off the bikes, so everyone was surprised by Juanita's greeting of: "Hello girls, nice to see ya again!" Just as affectionately, she shot us her middle finger, smiled and walked back inside the kitchen door.

Juanita's style of decorating depended on the principle that if some was good, more was better. Cleaning was never high on her list, so a layered, heavily cluttered, mishmash of dusty broken things once again set the theme for her new place. The group inside the dining room was an assortment from a Fellini movie. Tables of well coiffed, white gloved little old ladies fresh out of church mixed with bikers in full leather and suburban families with an occasional Hollywood celebrity or local politician mixed in. Waiters and waitresses scurried like their lives depended on it, looking like they had just been picked off the streets of the Haight Ashbury in their second-hand paisley cowboy shirts and granny dresses with flowers in their hair. They had names like Bay Laurel and Redwood and reeked of patchouli oil. Beauregard, Juanita's large monkey, roamed the dining room freely, stealing drinks and things off people's plates with complete impunity.

With a full house, Juanita knew it was show time. She went into the kitchen and gave members of her crew last minute instructions on the parts they were about to play that would earn them the pity of the diners and more than double the amount of tips they'd normally receive on a Sunday. The planning complete, she was about start the performance. No two weekends were ever the same, and while the theme was always familiar, every week an attempt was made to take the dialogue to new heights of profanity and absurdity.

Half the dining room had meals in front of them when suddenly the kitchen door swung open and Juanita stumbled through it, a dusting of flour on her face, her hair and muumuu disheveled as she started patrolling the tables of her diners. In the center of the room she stopped, looked up at the ceiling and shouted: "Every one of these fucking plates is supposed to have a fucking biscuit on them, and I'm going to find out why the fuck they don't." Some of the church ladies paled from hearing the word fuck being used, let alone three times in the same sentence. Juanita turned and marched herself back to the kitchen, nearly knocking a woman off a chair with one of her huge breasts. Suddenly the door swung open again and a terrified, scrawny waiter with a plate of biscuits almost as tall as he was stumbled into the dining room. "You've got five seconds to get those fucking biscuits on those plates or I'll rip your balls off!" Juanita screamed, throwing herself through the open door, disappearing like the wicked witch of the west. With fresh, hot biscuits on the plates, people turned their attention to their meals, content having had their promised dose of Juanita's crude theater.

"Are all you girls' seamen?" she asked standing at our table with her pet pig, Erica tucked under her arm. "No I'm a carpenter," I volunteered.

"Hey, I like you, you're cute." She turned her breasts toward me. Wary of the size of them, I pulled my chair in. "I'll tell ya what. I need some work done around here. I have some bathrooms that need fixing. I can't pay ya much, but I'll feed ya well." We exchanged phone numbers. Later that week, I came back with my tools and began sorting through piles of old toilets and sinks stacked behind a shed, trying to find enough to get three more bathrooms working again. "I'm having a wedding here next weekend," she said, "so I'll need those bathrooms."

"I'll be done by then."

"You should stick around. The wedding is going to be a hoot. Real unique couple if you know what I mean," she said winking at me.

Saturday morning a large group of people began to arrive in BMWs and Mercedes. They looked like Marin socialites and the bride and groom were cute. I had spent all week trying to figure out what Juanita meant by unique and seeing the group gave me no clue. I was more comfortable being alone than among strangers, so I found myself a place on the porch roof just outside a window where I could watch without being in the way. Juanita surprised me at the window with a galvanized pail full of beers and ice. She put it down on the sill, uncapped one and handed it to me. With her cold fingers she reached over and pinched my tit. It was her way of thanking me for what I did.

During the ceremony the best man spotted me sitting on the roof with my bucket of beers and kept staring in my direction. Finding him and his heavy, permanent five o'clock shadow attractive, I lifted my bottle in a silent toast. He became distracted and turned away from the groom's side to get a better look. Moments later the bridal couple was forgotten while most of the guests looked back and forth from the best man to my perch on the roof. The ceremony ended with a kiss and a woman singing something horribly off key. Soon the sun began to fade and the serious partying started. Another bucket

of beers appeared at the window, but this time they were
delivered by the best man who climbed onto the roof in
his tux and sat down beside me. Not knowing what to
say except "thanks," I popped one open and handed it to
him. I thought about pinching his tit, but didn't. We sat
there for almost an hour watching the festivities without
speaking another word. At one point, Juanita walked
by below us. Looking up at me she said; "You're bad!"
Breaking into a big grin, she continued on her way.

Around three in the morning I woke to loud
shouting and a woman wailing in the distance. The groom
had apparently decided he'd rather spend his honeymoon
night in the sack with his best man instead of his bride.
There were lots of car doors slamming. A few minutes
later, a gentle knock on my door revealed my drinking
buddy had been left behind without a ride and he wanted
to cuddle.

~

In 1975 the old Fetters Hot Springs Hotel burned
down. Unfortunately, Christine Hill, a waitress who
worked for Juanita, died in the fire. Juanita sent me
the same Christmas card with her bare ass in a bubble
bath several times during the years after my brief stint
working for her. Years later I ran into her one more time in
downtown Vallejo as she was sweeping out a tiny Victorian
house, proclaiming it was going to be her next location.
I never checked back to see if it happened. She lived out
her final years in a group home in Sonoma and died in
February, 2011 at the age of eighty-seven. A woman who
took care of her near the end called her a "nurturer" and

indeed she was. She always served a delicious plate of food and after experiencing what came with it, everyone left with stories to tell for generations and high regards for her.

Her ashes were scattered in Sausalito Bay and there is comfort knowing her spirit is still there.

22

Angel on Collingwood Street

As it turned out, living in Sausalito wasn't easy or practical. Tourists crowding the town made it impossible to get even simple things done and all the best opportunities for work were in the city. I pulled a note card off the wall inside Star Pharmacy and dialed the number. "*Room for Rent in the Castro – Call Don*".

"It's on Collingwood at the top of the 21st Street hill. Do you have a job?" the voice on the phone asked.

"I'm a carpenter."

"Good. I'm gay. Is that a problem?"

"So am I."

"The rent is a hundred and fifty a month. If you want, you can come by later today. I get home from work around six."

Don's flat was amazing. There were views from every window. It was clean, minimally furnished but beautifully decorated. It just didn't feel like home. He obviously had a good job, but I couldn't help thinking he might be looking for a roommate for friendship because he was lonely. He welcomed me, and although we led completely different lives, we became close immediately. I moved in with my bed, some cement blocks and boards for a bookcase and an old steamer trunk I bought for ten dollars that was filled with my clothes and tools. The hill leading up to the apartment was amazing, too. You had to stay in first gear all the way and could never back into the driveway because, when parked, the truck sat on a forty-five degree angle. If you opened the door without holding onto the steering wheel, you'd fall out and could roll all the way down the hill. *Note to self; don't try this after drinking.*

San Francisco gay men easily adopted the old mantra that man is by nature a hunter. Sex was everywhere, not just in the bars, parks, public toilets and the baths. It was at breakfast, lunch and dinner, walking down the street, driving in a car, at the Laundromat, the super-market, in the theater, waiting for a bus, riding in a taxi - even while waiting your turn to get checked out at the city clinic on Sixth Street. Everyone gave in to their animal instincts. It was impossible to connect sex with love and monogamous relationships because of the sheer volume of it that was going on. Fidelity and trust were words associated with banks and lending institutions but seldom in regard to personal relationships. If you expected or demanded that your partner would be faithful in San Francisco, you were in for a huge disappointment. In this regard, I concocted my own unique way to preserve my sanity. For me, life became an absurd ballet, a tightrope walk, of never loving while lusting and never lusting when serious friendship or work was involved. It was loosely based on a line my father taught me; "Never shit where you eat." Living this philosophy confused everyone who came into contact with me. Trying to justify that way of thinking now makes my head hurt, but it made sense and seemed to work at the time. Later I learned that by adopting this way of thinking I was pushing myself deep into a life of loneliness and regret.

Moving back into the city put me closer to carpentry work, but the temptation to hang out in the bars was strong, and soon I fell into the habit of drinking and not working. I spent my afternoons in the bars or playing in the Jaguar Bookstore. At night I'd get too drunk to drive up the hill, so I'd check into the Castro Rock Steam Baths and continue a drunken orgy until I passed out. When they weren't at sea, Dave and Ron would track me down, scold me and drag me out of the bars and back into the daylight. "Look, Lou, I can help you get the Union papers you'd need so you can go to sea with us." Ron promised. "But I won't until you get your shit together. I'm pretty sure I could get you a job in the Slop Chest. That's the crew's store."

"I'm going to Palm Springs this weekend to do an art show for a friend of mine. Why don't you come?" Dave asked. "I'll split the commissions with you." By the second day I had no appetite and couldn't keep anything down. When we got back to San Francisco, someone gave me the name of a doctor and I went to see him.

"You've got the flu. Go home and rest." But after a week nothing was better. One morning I looked in the toilet, my urine was brown and the face that stared at me in the mirror had dark yellow eyes. "You've got Hepatitis A," was the diagnosis the second time after blood tests. "There's no quick cure. Get yourself a big bottle of One-A-Day multiple vitamins with minerals and take four of them a day. Eat as many bananas as you can stand. Get plenty of rest. Drink plenty of fluids, but no alcohol of any kind. In fact, you can't drink for a year."

For more than a month Don came home at lunch time to make sure I was OK and that I ate something. He made a bed for me on the living room floor and put a dishpan there so I could vomit without having to get up and go to the bathroom. Every inch of my body down to the follicles of my hair hurt. After a month I asked God to kill me if I was going to keep feeling that way. My drinking days were ended and, although I would try, I wasn't able to do anything physical, including work, for two months. A letter arrived from Pacific Far East Lines accepting me, and I was scheduled to leave on my first trip but was unable to go because I was sick.

Don appeared in my life as if through divine intervention, like someone had put him there just to take care of me. Almost immediately after I was better and able to work, he was transferred to Atlanta. Once again I was looking for a place to live.

23

The Master
of Goldmine Drive

Dean Kwetcher sat alone sipping a gin and tonic
at a table up against the plate glass windows of Twin
Peaks Tavern. It was five-thirty and he was on his way
home from a liquor distributor, where he worked as a
bookkeeper. Dean was a cute little man, almost delicate,
with facial hair that simply didn't look it belonged on him.
He shared a two-bedroom apartment in Diamond Heights
with someone named Rod that he had found the same way
I found Don; a card on a bulletin board advertising for
a roommate. Although the views of the city and bridges
from Diamond Heights were second to none, the houses
sat covered in fog most of the time, and the neighborhood
was on the edge of being too far from the Castro. Still
unable to drink, I sat at the bar with an Irish coffee that
had a huge head of whipped cream almost making up for

the fact that it was missing the whiskey. It was a perfect choice for the cold, grey afternoon. Wanting to get closer to the windows to watch the action on the street, I saw an empty chair at his table and asked if I could join him.

"Sure, I've noticed you around the neighborhood for awhile now," he said extending his hand. We made introductions and sat for the next hour exchanging life stories and joking about how different our versions of San Francisco were. When he tried to buy me a real Irish coffee I confided the details of my recent health drama, confessing I was looking for a new place to live.

"I'm sharing an apartment with a roommate on Diamond Street. He's about to buy a big new house a block away. It has three bedrooms and he told me last week he'll need another roommate. Maybe you should come and meet him."

"Are you two lovers?"

"Heavens, no. I hardly see him. We just share the expenses. It's worked out pretty good so far."

Dean wanted a lover so bad he would do anything. When he met someone he immediately began showering them with gifts and making plans for a future together. So smothering was his affection that people literally ran away from him. He lived on a constant roller coaster of desperation, euphoria of certain love, always followed by loss and a period of deep depression. Although Dean could certainly have afforded to live alone, he needed someone near him, and was smart enough to recognize this.

I sat across the table from Rod Phillips sizing him up while he did the same to me. The expensive suit he wore said he had a good job, and by his measured words and vocabulary I could tell he was intelligent. He looked like the kid at school everyone picked on; short, overweight and pudgy to the point of resembling the Pillsbury dough boy. His skin was shiny, like it was stretched too tight. He wore a smile well and appeared friendly, albeit condescending, even before he opened his mouth to speak. After exchanging greetings, his first words to me were "Where do you hang out?"

"Since I work there, I'm usually around the Castro area during the day."

"How about at night?"

"Either the Castro or down on Folsom."

"I'm a South of Market man myself. I like the people who inhabit those places. I find hunting is really good there." While he spoke his eyes filled with a look that unsettled me, but I concluded he was a harmless leather queen and let it go. The conversation changed to the mundane, and gradually I became more at ease. As soon as we had agreed on the rent, what was included, and when he expected to move into his new house, he ended the interview abruptly and excused himself. Dean, who had sat silently, looked at me and shrugged as if to say go figure, then smiled and reached across the table to shake my hand. "Welcome to the fold," he said refilling his wine glass.

As I helped them move, I was surprised that most of the furniture, at least all of the beautiful pieces in the apartment, belonged to Dean. Rod of course took the largest bedroom, but the other two were nice and everyone had their own bathroom. Dean and I became friends but Rod was seldom there longer than the time it took to change from his work suit into street clothes.

There are some men who look good in leather. The ones I've seen who did it with complete credibility were unusually big men with questionable hygiene mounted on motorcycles. The first time Rod stepped out of his bedroom in full leather drag I had to bite the inside of my cheek to keep from laughing. Nothing fit, including the image. There were shiny bulges from trying to squeeze too much into pants and shirts two sizes too small, but there were no bulges where they were needed. *He looks like a kid whose mother bundled him up to go outside and play in the snow,* I thought, making it even more difficult to keep a straight face.

For several months, life on Goldmine Drive was normal and we fell into a routine that seemed to work for all of us. Dean got home from work first, would pick up the house, and start cooking something to eat. He'd spend the rest of the night reading before going to bed. I'd usually arrive second, shower, change my clothes and watch a round of evening news before going out for the night. Rod was always the last to arrive, but left on his motorcycle in full leather only minutes later. At different times during the night he and I would return alone or with someone and disappear into our rooms.

On a foggy Sunday night I awoke to cries for help. I lay on the bed half awake, not sure I had heard anything, when the cry came again, only louder.

"Someone please help me!"

Dean knocked on my bedroom door, and when I opened it, he looked scared. There were sounds like a struggle coming from Rod's room, then a loud scream and more sounds like things were being thrown around. "Help" rang out again as I pounded on the door.

"Rod, open the door."

"Leave us alone, everything is OK." But behind him I heard more cries.

"Open the damn door!" I shouted while Dean asked if he should call the police. "Not yet," I told him.

"For God's sake, help me. Get me out of here," a voice begged from behind the locked door.

"Open this fucking door right now or I'll break it down," I shouted; then in a voice loud enough for Rod to hear, I told Dean to call the police. Moments later the door opened and Rod stood looking wild and crazed. Behind him, a naked young blond kid in his twenties held a bundle of his clothes in front of himself. A pair of wrist restraints dangled from his arms. As soon as he saw me he rushed out the door, shoving his poorly chosen master aside and stood shaking behind me.

"Get the fuck out of here," Rod screamed. "All of you. Get out of my house." He slammed his bedroom door, splitting the jamb at the hinges and continued shouting at no one and throwing things around. The blond boy was dressed and on his way out the front door before I could turn around.

Dean, on the verge of hysteria, paced up and down the hallway rubbing his forehead. I poured him a glass of scotch and we sat at the kitchen table in silence. "Where will we go?" he finally asked in tears.

"Let's not worry about that tonight. Don't cry. I'll find us a place in the morning." I let him spend the rest of the night with me in my room behind a locked door. He curled up under the covers, and I lay on top, wondering if there were any guns in the house.

24

Kindness of Strangers

On that cool April morning in 1906 when the ground stopped shaking, the fires started. Many people spent the day searching for loved ones in the rubble while others gathered whatever they had left and began walking away from the ruins of San Francisco to search for a place they could feel safe. Golden Gate Park and the hills of

Twin Peaks became destinations for refugees.

On Corbett Street, just above the corner of Clayton, eight-year old Alberta was being helped into one of her best dresses by her mother who had just completed the same task for her other daughter. The woman knew what needed to be done, and worked with her girls to set up a stand in front of their house so they could help people less fortunate than themselves. From a leaky old wooden barrel, like angels of mercy, the girls spent their day ladling out water to people in passing wagons and on foot as they wound their way up the Corbett Street hill to safety.

Almost seventy years later, after spending her career working in San Francisco's building inspection department, Alberta Dolan, now alone after the death of her sister, had acquired an extensive portfolio of "distressed" houses and apartment buildings. She didn't know it, but she was about to become my own personal angel of mercy.

~

"My, you're out and about early," Michelle said, unlocking the door of his beauty shop two doors up from Harvey and Scott's Castro Camera. "I don't have anything for you to do right now, but I do need a good plumber."

"Call Alex, you know the guy with the huge frizzy Afro?"

"I've called that crazy Russian three times, but he's still a no-show."

"That's not why I'm here. I've got an emergency and I need your help." He pulled me inside the door, removed my baseball cap and walked around me in a circle looking at my head. "It's not your hair, so what's the emergency?"

"My roommate and I are being thrown out by the leather queen who owns the house. It's a long story, but we're going to be sleeping on the street unless we can find a place."

"Funny you should ask - I've just moved out of the cutest little house up on Clayton Street. I lived there for a long time. Take a look at it, the number is 1449, and I think it's still for rent. Look at this mess." He opened the door to a private stash of liquor bottles under his shampoo sink. Water flooded the floor and left him standing in a puddle as he began peeling a wet label off a bottle.

Michelle was pushing sixty and fighting every inch of the way. His post-acne complexion, large nose and deep wrinkled face were something only a mother could love. The gay community cherished him for his brazen, comical drag shows, and he was a tireless fundraiser for any worthy cause. His singing voice resembled Carol Channing's, although some compared it to Lee Marvin's. "Want a cocktail?" He pointed the bottle with the missing label at me.

"It's eight in the morning, I'll take a coffee." I got on

my knees and looked for the problem. In twenty minutes
the rusted leaking trap was off the sink and a new one
from Cliff's hardware was on.

"You're a life saver." Michelle finished the note he
was writing. "Alberta is the woman who owns the house.
Give her this and hopefully it's still available. Her address
is on the back. She's a bit eccentric, but who in this city
isn't? You'll love her."

Alberta finished reading the note, shoving her
glasses back onto her face no fewer than three times while
doing it. She had a kind, round face like my mother's,
blue eyes that twinkled through her wire rims, and I fell
hopelessly in love with her. She tried to tuck the note into
her dress pocket, but noticed the pocket wasn't where
it was supposed to be, and her dress was on backwards.
Embarrassed, with a slight nervous cough, and cute
innocent smile, she disappeared, returning seconds later
with the pockets and neckline where they belonged, and
the zipper on the back, instead of the front.

"Tell me all about you, Lou. I think we're going
to be friends," she said, beginning a conversation that
would last for the rest of the afternoon. She made a pot
of tea, but we were interrupted many times by the phone
and the doorbell; nonetheless, each time she returned
more interested than ever, asking direct but never prying
questions and encouraging me to do all the talking. While
I spoke, she listened and thought, and when she was about
to speak, she always began by clearing her throat. I decided
this was her way of buying time to think about what she
was going to say, like people who use the words "and" and

"uh" over and over. "You bite your nails," she scolded me affectionately, touching my fingers.

"It's probably something left over from being traumatized when I was a kid." I confessed to her. I went on to describe Dean and how we met at the Twin Peaks bar, what each of us did for a living, about the violence that had happened at Rod's house, and why we needed to move quickly. Before I knew it, I had dumped my entire life in her lap. During all this she said nothing, but I felt a constant stream of love and understanding coming from her.

"Do you have nice furniture?" she asked.

"Dean does."

"Can we go see it?"

"Sure." I put her in my truck and we drove to Rod's house. Thankfully no one was there, and she was impressed with the way we lived.

"Let's go look at Michelle's little house," she said finally inviting me to see the inside of the place I hoped Dean and I could call home. The house on Clayton Street was nothing more than a tiny rectangular shoebox covered in white shingles with a flat roof. My eye went to the two single garage doors and I began to dream about a small shop for myself. "Does the garage come with it?"

"Yes. I have things stored on one side, but you can have the other half." The house was tiny, but everything we needed was there; two bedrooms, a nice eat-in kitchen, a small bath that needed remodeling and a living room with a corner fireplace and picture window with views of the Bay Bridge. It hadn't been cleaned since Michelle moved out, but it felt like home. "Can we afford it?"

"If you're willing to clean it up and take care of a few things that need to be fixed, you can have it for $350 a month."

"Great. Do you mind if I remodel the bathroom?"

"Of course not, I'll pay for the materials. Don't you want Dean to see it first?"

"He's going to love it." I wrote a check for the deposit and she gave me the keys.

By the time Dean reached the Castro and Twin Peaks Tavern that afternoon, I had already taken everything we needed to the house so we could start cleaning and painting. Dean stood inside the front door and started to cry, and he kept crying as he walked through each room. When he reached the bathroom he began to wail. "I've already asked her if I can remodel it. I'll start as soon as we get moved in." His disappointment hurt and I began to feel bad for making the decision without him. "We needed a place. We were lucky to get something like this." He nodded in agreement through his tears, picked up a broom and began to sweep.

By springtime the little house on Clayton Street could have been a spread in Architectural Digest. It was so packed with Dean's furniture, we worried the varnish on the legs of the wing chair next to the fireplace would melt. As promised, I remodeled the bathroom and was forgiven for moving him into a place he felt was below him. Alberta popped in and out with suggestions and projects, thanking me for what I did and how I did it. My little shop in the garage was cramped and always busy. No matter how I begged, her side remained full and unavailable.

I knew the balance in my checkbook wasn't even close to what I had in the bank. The statement seemed artificially high, and never having balanced the account, I asked Dean for help. "None of your checks to Alberta have cleared. All the rent you've paid her, including the first deposit, is still in your account."

I rang Alberta's doorbell to see if she could tell me what happened to my checks and was led into the kitchen. Confused, she began pulling draws open that should have had silverware, but were overflowing with checks instead. "How about making us a pot of tea?" I asked, and for the rest of the evening we sat sorting thousands of dollars in checks, some dating back more than a year. I found the ones I had written, and watched while she made deposit slips out for everything. The next day, I took her to the bank.

~

Dean loved Gladys Knight, Fanny Flagg, Ramos Fizzes, and cleaning house. Although I had never seen him in drag, he kept a pair of dark blue, stiletto high heels in his closet. While working in my shop in the garage, if I heard Gladys Knight singing "The Midnight Train to Georgia," the sound of the vacuum, and clacking on the wood floors, I knew he was wearing his heels and cleaning house.

We were never more than just friends. In fact, we led completely different lives, frequently just passing one another on our way in or out of Alberta's little house. He respected my work and tolerated cleaning up the sawdust I

would drag upstairs when I had to use the bathroom, and I respected his privacy and was courteous to his friends, making myself scarce when he entertained at home.
Our living arrangement gave us both what we needed; a sense of security, the economy of sharing expenses and friendship. We kept a watchful eye out for one another for several years.

We heard master Rod sold his house on Gold Mine Drive and bought an old Victorian on Castro Street.
One evening when he returned home from work in his expensive suit, he found his boyfriend from the night before dead in his bed with a noose around his neck tied to the headboard. The medical examiner determined it was accidental suicide by autoerotic asphyxiation.

When Dean finally met Mister Right, he turned out to be a tall, lanky cowboy from Texas with a new Jeep who lived for line dancing and country music. I reminded Dean not to hold on so tight, coached him on how to build his relationship, and told him that he didn't need to give his boyfriend anything but his friendship. When they had spats while dating, I'd quote his favorite person to him. "You know what Fanny Flagg said about Mister Right, don't you? When you finally meet him, shoot him."

We both laughed.

25

An Experience in Living

Wisps of long gray hairs on the ancient Chinaman's bald head were all that was left of his once handsome, three foot long queue. He grimaced, pulling up the collar on his heavy wool coat to protect his ears from the windblown fog as he searched for the right key. The brown paper bag under his arm filled with the day's receipts threatened to fall to the ground. It was eleven o'clock, and as he had done for fifty-three years, Peter was locking his South China Café on 18th Street for the night. Light from an old neon sign inside flickered strange shades of red on the tall wood booths. Worn tables and chairs filled the open spaces. It was here, during the day, where three generations of women sat and made won-tons, and the rest of the family briefly came out of the kitchen to eat their meals together. A young man passing on the street noticed the old man struggling and came to shield him from the wind.

He lit a cigarette then lowered his lighter to the keyhole. The old man briefly handed him his package while he locked the door, and when he was finished, politely bowed from the waist and without a word, retrieved his bundle, turned and walked into the night up the street toward home.

During the day, Peter senior always dressed in a dark suit and tie, sat on a small wooden chair shoved tight against the wall near the front windows and directly behind the cash register. There was barely enough room for his equally ancient wife or his handsome gay son, Peter junior, to take money from customers. The old man's attention never left the cash register. His dark brown eyes were cloudy now. Only when his son or wife was present would he allow those cloudy eyes to focus more into open space or on the old metal ceiling as he sat quietly, playing back movies of his youth in his mind. Young Peter ran the restaurant now. The most popular thing on the menu was still the huge bowl of combination won-ton soup for one dollar that kept many of the neighborhood's Irish Catholic families, and now the younger gay men, alive. If you didn't have enough money, all you had to do was promise to return and pay later, and people always did. Frank Capra could have picked the businesses and people for his movie "It's a Wonderful Life" straight off the streets here.

It was the early 1970's, and for a moment we were allowed a brief glimpse into a few of the oldest businesses in the neighborhood and their pre-turn-of-the-century trappings. The aroma of freshly oiled wood floors flooded your senses when crossing the threshold into the old hardware store on Market Street near Castro. Every wall was filled floor to ceiling with wooden cabinets so high you had to use the Putnam rolling ladder to reach them. Here you'd find any piece or part you might need to repair things in your Victorian home: valves for gas chandeliers, porcelain knobs for your toilet flush, hinges, door stops. On the balcony, at her desk just behind the wood railing, the owner's wife took the money sent up to her on a small trolley that rode on a wire. She'd record the sale, and then send change and the receipt back down to the sales clerk who still wore a green visor. When you left, you walked away sad and grateful at the same time, knowing what you just had the privilege to experience would soon disappear and fade into history.

Fred and Rolland ran a small butcher shop and knew each of their customers by name. The cases were always filled with the freshest, most wonderful things, and they were happy to fix a crown rib roast, a fresh ham, or to bake a Christmas goose encrusted in rye dough for your holiday. The long line of white porcelain and chrome chairs in Louie's Barber Shop were staffed by men in their seventies who had worked there most of their lives. Down the street, a plump, jolly old man who had worn the same oil stained leather apron every day of his adult life, repaired shoes in a shop filled with noisy, turn of the century machines that could bring any pair back to life for the third or fourth time for only a couple of dollars. And Rose, her husband Meyer, and their son Bruce stood behind the counter of Mueller's Delicatessen, always offering a spoonful or more of Rose's fresh chopped chicken livers made that morning or whatever wurst was the newest and best.

In spite of the hills, San Francisco has always been a walking city. Little old ladies in hats and white gloves dressed to go shopping in their sensible, thick heeled-shoes, trudged along with a bag of groceries in each arm as they climbed the steep hills on their way home.

~

Sunday walks were always the highlight of my week. They were all day events, great exercise and gave one time to reflect on the history of the city and neighborhood you lived in. They always started early in the morning with breakfast at Norse Cove Café on Castro near Market. Nora, a slender, rather severe looking French woman always stood at the register. The menu was on large chalk boards behind her, and you told her what you wanted to eat and then took a seat. Nothing was written down, but a few minutes later whatever you ordered appeared on the arm of her skinny, bald husband who ran the kitchen. While you ate, if you needed anything else, you raised your hand and it would be brought to you. When it was time to leave you simply went to the register to be asked by Nora, "What did you have?" It was the honor system, more or less. Nora had eyes in the back of her head, and even if every table was full, she knew exactly what you and everyone else had eaten. She was one of those women who could give you *the look* and make you feel guilty even though you had done nothing wrong.

The path seldom changed. After breakfast I'd start at the Bank of America building on the corner of Castro and

go down Market Street, pass Polk Street and City Hall, the
Orpheum Theater, the bums hanging around Sixth and
Market, the cable car turn-around at Market and Powell,
then head for a fascinating old bar in the Ferry Building at
the Embarcadero. There you could run into any number of
old-timers with red whiskey noses, occasionally including
the city's favorite columnist, Herb Caen. Sitting on a
barstool you could learn more San Francisco history from
the mouths of the people who lived it than by any amount
of reading.

Out of the bar, a right turn, and you found
yourself walking by the odd-numbered piers along the
Embarcadero and any number of cargo and passenger ships
that were at call in the city. Sundays were quiet times. The
piers were usually deserted, but you could start hearing
the crowds of tourists long before you reached Pier 39 and
Fisherman's Wharf. People packed into cable cars were
disembarking, and long lines waited at the turntable for
the car to be turned around by the brakeman and head
back up Powell Street for the return trip. While people
waited, street entertainers - an assortment of jugglers, fire
eaters and solo violinists - entertained them. In a small
patch of grass nearby sat a beat-up weathered cardboard
refrigerator box with a poorly handwritten sign reading
"The Human Jukebox". A slot, outlined in fading yellow
paint, marked where you could deposit twenty-five cents
enticed the curious, and occasionally someone would
break from the line and drop in a quarter. Like magic, a
dog-eared trap door with cardboard hinges would drop
down on a frayed hemp line and a very unkempt man in

his sixties wearing a tattered top hat would shove his head and trumpet out of the opening and enthusiastically play a heart-rendered, albeit slightly off key, version of "San Francisco". When he was finished, he would duck back inside, and yank the door shut until another quarter fell.

A cold Anchor Steam Beer was always a good companion as you walked down the Wharf. Past the fishing boats and barkers selling walk-away shrimp cocktails, the 1930's Art Deco architecture of the Maritime Museum at the waterfront foot of Polk Street waited for you. The famous C.A. Thayer cargo schooner and an old San Francisco car ferry called tourists aboard, and occasionally I would join them.

The walk on Polk Street toward the Civic Center was up-hill as you left the waterfront. Passing the beautiful old Alhambra Theater, eventually Swan's Oyster Depot would call, and you'd stop for a plate of fresh oysters. More than a score of gay bars on Polk Street would manage to keep you engaged until late in the afternoon. Passing City Hall, you were only a block from Market Street where you'd turn right and head back toward the Castro, but not without warming a barstool at The Mint first. At this point you could cheat if you wanted, and jump onto one of the classic old streetcars the city had restored, but what was the point? There were at least another half dozen bars along the last few blocks and Mister Right could be waiting in any one of them for you.

26

Fire

VIEW OF SAN FRANCISCO, FORMERLY YERBA BUENA, IN 1846-7

At six o'clock in the morning on Christmas Eve, during the Gold Rush in 1849, San Franciscans experienced their first major fire. The town was nothing more than an unorganized mess of a few brick buildings that formed the core, surrounded by hastily built wooden houses, tents, and even old hulls of ships that could no longer float. The thousands of people arriving to search for gold, and those who supplied them, lived in anything they could find for protection from the elements. During the first three years, six major fires, one after the other, leveled the city despite the best efforts of people to protect it. Even today, in defiance of all our modern technology, if you hang around San Francisco for any length of time you are bound to become familiar with fire. Rows of tinder dry, multistory redwood buildings, many sharing common walls, still allow city residents to occasionally experience, and become victims of, a perfect storm.

~

In San Francisco's exploding gay community, the profit potential of gay bars made for strange bedfellows. The lure of easy money found straight people with big checkbooks teamed up with gay men and women full of ideas and talents to make things happen. In 1971, Ron Estes and David Monroe of the popular Lion Pub on Divisadero Street had an idea. They were joined by Tom Sanford, Sam Hall, and Sam's close friend, Marjorie De Remer, a wealthy retiree from down the peninsula.

Marjorie was a no-nonsense, well-coiffed straight lady with a kind heart. She had hands horribly disfigured by arthritis, and a penchant for driving new Corvettes. Because of their partnership, on May 28, 1971, Memorial Day weekend, Toad Hall was opened at 482 Castro Street.

The friendly bartenders under Stan Walker's management made the bar a favorite neighborhood hangout. Night after night people waited in line to get in. But, like much of San Francisco's history, Toad Hall's brief eight-year run would be punctuated with fire.

The first fire happened because bartenders love candles. Someone began having fun with one in a wine bottle that dripped down its sides. More were added as they burned, and soon the bottle disappeared under candle wax. By the spring of 1972 the mountain of wax had grown about three feet high and caught the bar on fire when someone forgot to blow out the candle before closing. The wall behind the candle burned, but the damage was minor, and the bar opened the next morning. Stan hired his friend David Swain to make the repairs and was so impressed with the work, he had him continue to improve the bar over the next year.

The second fire also started during the night. On Saturday, June 15, 1974, two weeks before the gay Freedom Day Parade, Toad Hall burned again. This time it was completely gutted. By the time the fire department dragged their hoses out the door, all that was left was charred wood and mountains of beer bottles. Many in the neighborhood came to help, myself included. Trucks delivered debris boxes every hour and we kept them full.

The local dealers kept everyone's pockets filled with black beauties and pot and we worked around the clock. It was a time of rebuilding, and with the Freedom Parade and the thousands of people who would flood the city less than two weeks away, there was no time to waste. David needed help, so Stan Walker hired me.

The third fire started when scaffolding that David and I were moving late one night bumped a temporary wire strung across the bar for lights. It started a fire inside the wall. No one thought about fire extinguishers since the place had already burned, so we used beer to put it out. Shaken, we sat down, smoked a joint, and then went back to work.

Sunday, June 30th, 1974, was the day of the Parade and Toad Hall was ready to open. It was only a sheetrock box painted flat black, and the paint was still damp. We propped up the singed pieces of what was left of David's beautiful new bar top and supported them with plastic garbage cans. We had been working - on speed - around the clock to get it finished, so I wasn't there to celebrate the reopening.

By eight in the evening the bar was packed when someone told the manager he thought there was a fire in the back. When Stan opened the steel door into the office, a wall of flames shot out and nearly burned him - the fourth fire. He tried using a garden hose from behind the Castro Café, but the fire department arrived and put it out quickly. Although the office and bathrooms were trashed, someone dragged an extension cord into the bar for lights and the local beat cop gave the go-ahead to reopen. The next morning they found that the cause of the fire was a hot water heater.

～

My roommate told me later that I slept for three days, sleepwalking to the bathroom occasionally. When I finally awoke, it was to the sound of the phone ringing. It was my friend, Scott. "Are you alive?"

"I think so. What day is it?"

"Thursday, the 4th of July."

"I need to eat something."

"Can you come over tomorrow? Harvey wants to get that cabinet built."

"Shit, sorry. I'll run down to the bar after breakfast and get my tools."

"It's almost dinner time, Lou."

I grunted and hung up. I still had eggs and bacon at the Castro Café even though it was almost dark. David Swain was sitting at the counter. "You missed the fire."

"What fire?"

"The one that burned up the bathrooms, and the office, .. and your tools."

～

During the next five years fire would gut or damage The Pendulum bar, Cliff's Variety hardware store, apartments above the grocery store on the corner of 18th and Castro and the Elephant Walk across the street.

For a couple months after the fire, I continued to work at night inside Toad Hall. I knew when the morning bartender arrived that I had thirty minutes to clean up my mess.

Michael Schoch was one of those rare human beings who could quiet a noisy room by simply walking into it. His hair was a mass of tight, dark curls that looked like he had just stepped out of a shower, and his face always had a smile. He wore a neatly pressed flannel shirt and Levis that emphasized his large upper torso. The smells coming from the coffee and flowers he carried created an invisible aura around him as he moved through the dark bar. "Good morning, Lou," he said, hitting me on the ass with the bouquet.

"Morning, Michael. God, how do you pull it together like this at six in the morning?

"Pills!" he replied jokingly, holding up the coffeepot. "Come and sit for a few minutes." I pulled up a barstool and watched him methodically begin his morning set-up. In a matter of moments Orff's "Carmina Burana" was playing, flowers were arranged in a gallon olive jar and placed by the cash register, lighting levels set, candles lit, and his fresh coffee beans put on to brew. Instantly, the dreary, smelly place was transformed into a warm, friendly home. "So tell me, what do you do with yourself when you're not working? Where are you from? How'd you get here? God, Lou, I've been trying to get to know you for weeks now. It's obvious you're not going to volunteer anything." He pushed his face close to me across the bar so he could look into my eyes. "Let me in there!"

"There's nothing special to know. When I'm not here I'm down on Folsom. I drink too much. I fuck around too much. I guess it's not a real exciting life compared to yours. I came to California a few months ago, running away I guess, like a lot of other people. One day I just shoved my clothes in the car and ended up in Santa Monica. This is the first real job I've found since I came up here." I envied this man. He was so beautiful, and so popular. I couldn't imagine why he would be interested in me. *Why is life so easy for him and so shitty for me?* I thought.

Michael reached across the bar and grabbed me by the arm. "I've been trying to get you home for weeks now. I've told Gary all about this mysterious carpenter I spend my mornings with. He's a terrific cook and wants to make dinner for you. Damn it, I'm going to be your friend, so you might as well get use to it." We exchanged phone numbers, then he leaned across the bar and kissed me on the forehead. "Now unlock that door and get the hell out of here so the breakfast club can come in."

⁓

On Sunday morning my phone rang. "I'm home alone; Gary is working, and I'm hungry. Wanna go to Jackson's and have brunch with me?"

"It's my walking day, but sure, why not? I should be at Market and Church in about forty-five minutes. Meet me there and we'll walk together."

I could see Michael standing on the sidewalk talking

to someone. All around them the contents of the burned out "Naked Grape" bar cluttered the sidewalk. As I got closer I recognized Hans. "When did you get to town?"

"I live here now; in fact, until last night I lived upstairs." Hans pointed to broken windows above the bar.

"Thanks for calling and letting me know."

"I've been trying, but you're never home."

"How long have you been here?"

"About two months. I bought this bar. It's been doing OK until this morning around three." I felt like staying to help him clean up, but invited him to join us instead. "Thanks, but I have to be here. I've got help coming to take care of this mess and an insurance agent to deal with."

"You need a place to stay?"

"No. But thanks for asking. I'll move in with my boyfriend for awhile."

As we walked away I whispered to Michael: "I bet the new boyfriend has a foreskin," and I began to tell him my long story about Hans.

~

Jackson's was packed as usual for Sunday brunch. Michael leaned across the crowded bar and kissed his partner Gary Mac Donald good morning. "What are you boys having?" Gary asked, leaning across the bar to kiss me too. "You must be my boyfriend's new boyfriend," he whispered and laughed. "It's nice to finally meet you, Lou."

"Ramos Fizzes, of course," Michael grinned.

"Not for me. I learned a long time ago that gin

and I don't get along. I'll have a Bloody Mary with lots of horseradish." Every table was full and waiters scurried past us carrying plates of eggs Benedict and omelets.

"Do you want to eat here at the bar, or do you want a table?" Gary asked, handing us menus.

We looked at the line of people standing outside. "The bar works for us."

"Good, that way I'll have more time to spend with you."

We expected a long wait, but our food was in front of us before we knew it. In the distance we heard sirens getting closer and closer. Everyone looked out the windows to watch the fire truck go by, but instead it came to a stop in front of the building. A lone fireman jumped off and began dragging a hose through the restaurant. When he opened the door to the kitchen, smoke billowed out into the dining room. Everyone put down their forks and sat watching and trying to decide what to do. The smoke quickly turned to steam, and moments later the fireman returned from the kitchen, dragging the hose behind him. "Nothing to worry about folks, go ahead and finish your meals. Everything's under control," he said, closing the door behind him.

Gary banged a cocktail shaker against the bar. "Can I have your attention please? The kitchen is temporarily closed."

27

Sawdust

Word travels fast when you're the cheapest decent carpenter in town. I was getting to the point where I could pick and choose which jobs to take. I was tired of working in bars late at night and looked forward to finishing up the ceiling at The Round Up on Folsom and 6th Street. "Daylight work after this," I said out loud to confirm my decision.

From my perch high above, I watched as the morning bartender completed stocking the coolers. "I have to take a dump," he said, looking up at me on his way to the bathroom.

"Thanks for sharing."

"Don't mention it. I thought you might want to watch."

"You're a sick fuck. Let me know how it comes out." I went to work nailing the last of the old redwood boards to the soffit above my head. *Nailing upside down is punishment,* I thought.

The sound of timbers groaning and cracking stopped my mental complaining. Suddenly a loud crash shook the building. *Earthquake!* I thought. Clouds of dust filled the air so thick I could barely see and I looked for the shortest path to the door in case the shaking started again. "Are you OK?" I shouted for the bartender. There was no response, so I climbed down from the scaffolding. Where the bathrooms were was now a hole into the basement. "Are you OK?" I shouted down into the dark.

"I think my leg is broken."

"Don't move. I'll find a flashlight and be right back." With the light I could see him. He was still sitting on the toilet with his pants around his ankles, but he and the commode were on their side in the basement along with the rest of the rotten bathroom floor. *They should have had me working in here instead of on the ceiling,* I thought as I dialed 911 for an ambulance.

~

Tommy Zelinski gave me a job building a large greenhouse behind his plant store next to the Castro Baths. A few weeks after I finished, my phone rang, and it was Bill Graham. "Your friend Tommy rented a booth in my plant show at The Cow Palace. He tells me you're a carpenter. Do you want to work for me? I need good, dependable people."

Michael Maletta, a barber who staged big gay disco parties, called a few weeks later. "I understand you work for Bill Graham. I need some carpenters for an event I'm doing at the Embarcadero." The job he offered involved building a wood scaffolding four feet high and thirty feet long with stairs on each end in the middle of the dance floor. Along each side we needed to install long troughs. With hundreds of people drinking beer non-stop and dancing, urinals had to handle scores of people at the same time. All night long, lines of men waited their turn to climb the stairs and take a leak while they watched everyone dancing below. Word had spread around town that "special secret performers" would be there at midnight. At one-thirty in the morning, the lights went black and when they came back up, the Pointer Sisters were on stage and the crowd went wild. The next morning Herb Caen wrote in his column that rumor had it the Pointer Sisters did a gig at a big gay disco bash last night on the Embarcadero. When he called their New York hotel in the morning, he was told they were there and getting ready for their show at Madison Square Garden.

For months no one except the eight hundred stoned, sweaty gay men at the party could confirm the rumor until someone produced a Valium prescription bottle with Bonnie Pointer's name on it that they found on the floor under the stage.

Ray Herth began recommending me to people who bought homes from him, and I started remodeling kitchens and bathrooms. I bought a new table saw and shaper, and my little shop in Alberta's garage was busy all the time. Through Ray I met Jim Reid, and got my first chance to show off the cabinet making skills my dad taught me by spending more than two months in his

home on upper Market Street building a custom library.

I was happiest when working alone at my own pace and on my own terms. The biggest thrill was being treated as an equal by the business people who hired me. I kept my prices reasonable, but raised them enough to be proud of what I earned. My self-esteem had never been higher.

28

The House
That "T" Built

My truck was filled with expensive custom moldings for Jim's library from D'Christina Millwork south of Market. But I was at The Ambush in the middle of the day. If I said I went there just for the music, it would be a lie. But here I was, sitting on a bench with a beer in my hand, listening to another one of Mel Ford's reel-to-reel tapes. Where else could you find a mix that had "Staying Alive" by the Bee Gee's, followed by Pavarotti singing "Nessun Dorma," melting into "Sweet Virginia" with the Stones singing "..*got to scrape the shit right off your shoes,*" segueing into Vikki Carr crying, "It must be him"?

Mel was a shy, nerdy black guy who made music tapes. He knew each bar's clientele so well he could make them do whatever he wanted, compelling his listeners to stay and see where his music would take them next. His talent for doing this translated into more beer and liquor sales, making him a valuable asset to bar owners. He made his creations in the back of an old Dodge van that many suspected was also his home. The carpeted space had two large Teac tape decks, a turntable and stacks of record albums.

Kerry, one of The Ambush's owners, walked from behind the bar and handed me another beer. "It's compliments of the three guys sitting by the front door." I looked up and raised my bottle to say thanks, but didn't recognize anyone.

"We like your boots," Ken Williams said as he climbed onto the bench next to me. "Is that real sawdust?"

"Is there any other kind?" I brushed it off my pants from my knees to the boots he was admiring. "I'm supposed to be working, but decided to play hooky. Where are you guys from?"

"New York City. We're staying with a friend who happens to need a carpenter. If you'll have dinner with us, I'll introduce you." And that's how Ken Williams, a supremely well-endowed, very outspoken, and completely crazy Texan came into my life. But he didn't come alone. His partner, Chas Collins, a quiet, intelligent, handsome man, and their friend, Michael Donovan came with him. Michael's claim to fame was his face and blue eyes on thousands of "I Like The Box" billboards for Marlboro cigarettes. By accepting that beer, I had opened a door that would lead me on a wild ride as a part of their lives and into a friendship as deep as brotherhood. We exchanged phone numbers and agreed to meet that night for dinner in the Castro. "After dinner, I want you to show us the baths."

I saw a familiar face sitting at the bar and excused myself. "I think we're married," I whispered in his ear while hugging him from behind.

He turned to see who it was. "I still have that sign. I couldn't throw it away, hoping we'd cross paths again," he laughed. We met at a gay pride parade a year earlier. David was on his motorcycle alone, and I was standing with friends. When I saw him I couldn't resist the urge to climb on the back of his bike and wrap my arms around him. A few minutes later someone ran up behind us and put a "Just Married" sign on the taillight. As we passed, people began to shout and applaud. By the time we reached City Hall, we finally figured out why. "You busy?"

"Not really."

"I think it's time I took you home to show you my etchings." We finished our drinks and he followed me to help unload my truck. His apartment on 20th Street was filled with daylight and huge, colorful canvases. He was a talented painter.

"My etchings," he said, handing me a beer, pointing to his work.

"Incredible. I want one."

"You can't afford me… But then again, maybe you can," he smiled. "I've got some dynamite acid. If you don't have any plans for the rest of the day…."

The window shade in his bedroom had several large brown water stains that kept changing into profound words in different fonts that demanded my full attention. The word **Listen** appeared first, so I did, then **QUIET**, so I was. But when the word *SEX* appeared, I rolled over. David was lying on his back, staring at the ceiling and counting something. *This isn't going like we planned*, I thought to myself. "I'm going to the bathroom," I told him. "Where is it?" He started counting again at one, so I found it myself.

A dark blue and yellow shag throw rug in front of the toilet had faces and heads of people I knew popping out of it at my feet. One at a time, they would appear then disappear. "Are you all right?" he asked through the door. "You've been in there more than an hour."

Without discussing it, we gave up on the idea of sex. "I'll make us some tea," he told me disappearing into the kitchen, leaving me sitting in the living room alone. I thumbed through a tall stack of magazines and newspapers on the floor, but didn't look at or read anything in them. I was finishing up arranging them in alphabetical order when I realized he had been gone a long time.

David filled the kettle, putting it on a 1940's Garland gas stove with a beautiful nickel top. He began wiping up a few drops of water he spilled and noticed how much better the nickel shined as he rubbed it. By the time I entered the kitchen, the stove was in a million pieces. Parts of it were all over the room and he was busy trying to get the knobs off. "How's it going?" I asked. He looked up sheepishly, realizing he'd forgotten about the tea and had decided to do a deep cleaning instead.

"I have an idea," he said, returning to the living

room with a joint. "Why don't we smoke some grass to
mellow out? We'll just take one little hit on this and put
it out. It's really strong." I sat next to him on the couch
while he lit it and passed it to me. I passed it back to him
and before we realized it, there was nothing left. I leaned
forward to say something, when I somersaulted out of
my body and floated up to the ceiling. *Great*, I thought,
looking down at the two of us sitting on the couch. *Am I
dead? If I can't get back in there I'll be dead.* "Maybe we
should go outside," David said, jarring me back into my
body. "If we go outside and people don't laugh at us, we'll
know we're OK."

I started laughing.

"No laughing!"

I stopped laughing and we walked down his stairs
and into the street. An old lady was pulling her two wheel
grocery cart up the hill, and we broke out in hysterics,
turned, and ran back inside the apartment.

In those days, street drugs were lids of grass;'the
amount that would fit on the top of a coffee can until it
started to fall off, and cost fifteen bucks. Your friendly
neighborhood dealer always had psychedelics and they
were pure, plentiful and cheap. Four or five types of
acid, chocolate mescaline and MDA were fifty-cents
each. Cocaine and heavier drugs were available, but there
weren't many buyers in the semi-employed burgeoning gay
community of the time.

By the late 1970's acid started getting strange
and people began to have bad trips. Locals blamed it
on the mob, thinking they had become involved in the

production and were cutting it with strychnine. But the real culprit was the CIA, who had been monitoring the tripping hippies in the Haight Asbury. They decided to secretly test new combinations of chemicals on them to see what happened, hoping they might find a military application to use in war and to control civil disobedience.

~

"OK, I've been to the baths. Now take me to the place they call The Glory Hole." Kenny was reading from his list of must see places in San Francisco. "It's on Sixth Street."

"I know where it is."

"What is it?

"It's a big, dark building with lots of tiny rooms with big holes in the walls. It's completely anonymous sex and always busy."

"Just drop me off. You guys can go have a drink on Folsom Street and I'll catch up to you in a little while."

Two hours later Kenny walked into The Ramrod. "That place is fantastic. I've never had so much fun." We sat around drinking beer and laughing, but they were flying back to New York in the morning and soon we were hugging and promising to keep in touch, and then they were gone.

A few months later my phone rang late one night. It was Ken. "How soon can you come to New York?"

"I don't know, maybe a couple weeks, why?"

"I need you to build something for me."

"What?"

"A Glory Hole."

When Ken and Chas bought their three-story brownstone in New York's Chelsea district, it wasn't a fashionable place to live. The neighborhood was filled with peep-shows and whores, and there was a steady stream of hookers and pimps near the corner of 8th Avenue and 21st Street.

Their house was like Grand Central Station; people were constantly coming and going at all hours of the day and night. No one went out until after midnight, and since they didn't have an extra bedroom, they made a special room for me in the basement. It was the old coal bin with no windows. I could sleep all day and go out with them and play all night.

We went to see the building they had rented. It was in the Village, across the street from The Eagle leather bar. "Wow, what a perfect location," I approved.

"We only rented the main floor, but there's a second floor and basement if this thing takes off like we think it will," Ken said unlocking the door.

We measured it, then I began to make a list of materials. "I'll need about 200 sheets of ¾" plywood for the walls and doors. Pick up sixty pairs of hinges, sixty door handles, five-hundred eight foot 2x4's and a shit-load of flat black paint, rollers and brushes. You'll need to buy a Skillsaw, big drill and a hole-saw. Oh yes, sandpaper, that's important. Don't want any slivers," I shuddered at the thought. "We'll use screws instead of nails, that way you can take it apart and move it if you need to."

The tiny office I built next to the front door with a glass window is where they would sell memberships and collect entry fees. When I saw the sign go up with prices, I couldn't believe my eyes. "Are you serious? Do you think someone's going to pay eighty-dollars for a membership and twenty-bucks every time they want to come in?"

"No problem. Those boys in San Francisco are giving it away at fifteen-bucks and three-dollars a visit. New York queens would never come if it was that cheap. In this city it has to be expensive to be good."

He was right, on opening night they were lined up around the block to buy memberships.

~

As I packed my bag at their house for the flight back to San Francisco, I had one question. "Tell me, why are all the stacks of record albums around here called "Disco Hits"? Are you guys in the record business?"

"Sort of." Kenny pulled the cellophane off one album and pulled out two large sheets of blotter paper. Each sheet was scored with tiny perforations and divided into five-hundred small rectangles, each one with a tiny record printed on it. "Each square has a drop of pure THC, the chemical that's in grass that gets you stoned. Each album has a thousand hits." Suddenly all the traffic coming and going made sense and I began to get nervous. "This is the house that "T" built, bought and paid for," he said, shoving an album into my bag.

"My theme song has always been "Stayin Alive." Thanks, but I don't think I should take this on the plane."

"I'll mail it to you then, like I do all the others."

~

In the San Francisco airport, at the luggage carousel, I found myself standing next to Hans. "What's up?"

"I just got back from a meeting," he said, pulling his bag off the belt.

"What are you doing? I haven't seen you since the morning after the fire in your bar."

"I'm the head of security for Hewlett Packard." He had once again climbed out of a cocoon and morphed into something wonderful and new.

29

Elephants & Empresses

The headline in the San Francisco Chronicle on the morning of January 9th, 1880 read: "*Le Roi est Mort*" ("The King is dead"). In the article that followed they reported: "On the reeking pavement, in the darkness of a moon-less night under the dripping rain, Norton I, by the grace of God, Emperor of the United States and Protector of Mexico, departed this life."

In 1849, after receiving a forty-thousand dollar bequest from his

father's estate in England, Joshua Norton first appeared in San Francisco. He got involved in several successful real estate ventures, but when he bought into Peruvian rice at exactly the wrong moment, he lost everything he had made and his father had given him. Distraught, he vanished, surfacing in the city a few years later, but this time severely mentally unbalanced, anointing himself as the Emperor of the United States. Accepting San Franciscans quickly adopted him and his long list of eccentricities, following his antics daily in the newspapers. To survive, Norton issued currency in his own name, and oddly enough it was honored in many local businesses, including the finest restaurants and stores. For almost thirty-years he spent his days roaming the streets, examining the conditions of the city's cable cars and sidewalks while wearing an elaborate array of military costumes. He seldom relinquished his tattered top hat.

On January the 8th, 1880, at the corner of California and Dupont (now Grant Ave.), he collapsed and died on the street. Instead of a pauper's funeral, members of San Francisco's Pacific Club made sure he received a proper burial. That Sunday as many as thirty thousand San Franciscans lined two miles of city streets as his funeral passed. He was buried in the Masonic Cemetery in a grave that had been bought and paid for by the citizens of San Francisco.

In 1934, when the city needed space to grow, the voters made the decision to move all the graves in San Francisco to Colma, just outside the city limits. Locals insist that today, Colma has more residents underground than above it. The remains of Emperor Norton were moved and now rest peacefully in Colma's Woodlawn Cemetery. The grave is marked by a stone inscribed "Norton I, Emperor of the United States and Protector of Mexico".

Joshua Norton had become a lost footnote in San Francisco history. In the 1940's, José Sarria came along, heard his story and decided to adopt him.

After being discharged from the Army, José decided to stay in San Francisco. He began waiting tables at The Black Cat, becoming known for his campy performances of arias from the opera Carmen while he worked. He soon earned an affectionate reputation as "The Nightingale of Montgomery Street". Near the end of every evening he stood up and encouraged people in the bar to be open and honest about their lives. "There's nothing wrong with being gay; the crime is getting caught". He would tell them. When the bar was ready to close, patrons would join him in a chorus of "God Save Us Nelly Queens" sung to the tune of the British national anthem. Occasionally he'd push the crowd outside for the last verse, serenading men in their jail cells across the street that had been picked up earlier in vice raids.

José Sarria wasn't just a drag queen with a pretty face. He had been the target of vice arrests in both bars and public places, and it was his suggestion to gay men to start demanding jury trials in self defense. Soon the courts were overloaded, and judges began demanding that prosecutors have actual evidence against people before allowing the cases to go to trial.

Every Halloween, after midnight when the festivities of the day were officially over, police arrested drag queens under an old city ordinance making it illegal for men to dress in women's clothing with "intent to deceive". Fed up, José went to attorney Melvin Belli, and the two of them found a way around the law by giving out handmade labels to the drag queens in the shape of a black cat's head. They read "I am a boy". After that, when stopped, men in dresses would show the label, proving they were not attempting to deceive. This put an end to police raids on Halloween.

Working with others, José Sarria helped start the League for Civil Education (LCE) in the early 1960's. The organization gave educational programs on homosexuality and offered help to men who were being persecuted for being gay after being snared in police raids. He ran unsuccessfully for the San Francisco Board of Supervisors in 1961 for the same seat that Harvey Milk won sixteen years later. His résumé of work on behalf of the gay community in San Francisco is astounding. He was instrumental in starting many organizations to benefit gay people, including SIR, the Society for Individual Rights, and The Tavern Guild which initially was a group of bar owners who hired attorneys to post bail for their patrons when they were arrested in bar raids. He was also instrumental in establishing the Imperial Court of San Francisco, a system that today has chapters in cities across the United States, Canada and Mexico, raising millions of dollars for charity.

I watched the people I had naívely held in distain

before coming to California and grew to respect them. It was the drag queens who proved to be the bravest, most fearless fighters for gay rights. While masculine gay men wearing business suits cowered in their closets, the boys in dresses and wigs were out in force, defending our rights. They adopted their alter egos and campy names not only because they were fun; they did it to give themselves a tiny measure of anonymity to protect their livelihoods.

Three years before the Stonewall Riots in New York City, it was a group of San Francisco drag queens who, late one night in August of 1966, had finally had enough of being harassed by the police. They fought back in Compton's Cafeteria on Taylor and Turk in the Tenderloin. They decided it was time to start fighting, not just for gay rights, but for the most basic of human rights and dignity that we were promised under the Constitution but were being denied. Along with their Stonewall counterparts in New York, they began the long walk down a road that eventually led to the White House in 2012, and convinced Barack Obama to be the first president in history to demand and obtain

human rights for all LGBT people in America.

José Sarria was the first in a long line of characters, both men and women, in The Imperial Court of San Francisco. In his nineties, José purchased the plot next to Emperor Norton in Colma's Woodlawn Cemetery. He will reign in perpetuity as "Her Royal Majesty, Empress of San Francisco, José I, The Widow Norton". No doubt future generations of gay San Franciscans will continue their annual pilgrimages to the graves and remember both him and the Emperor Norton.

Gene Bache had somehow been endowed with every talent God hands out to gay men that makes every straight woman envious. He had impeccable taste, could create a fantastic home from what he found at a thrift shop, put together beautiful floral

arrangements, build absolutely believable theatrical sets, and could do it all in a matter of minutes. He was revered in the community as Empress II, Bella. So when he came to me, asking that I build him a flower shop on Castro Street, I was flattered because he could have just done it himself.

"OK Bella, where's this magical new shop going to happen?" I looked at the buildings surrounding us on Castro Street, but they were all occupied.

"You're standing in front of it," he said, taking me by the shoulders, turning me around to face the front of Mueller's Delicatessen. All I could see was a window filled with sausages and hams. "I rented this window from Meyer and Rose." They stood inside smiling and waving at us. "I know exactly what I want. We'll take out these big plate glass windows and get some smaller wood-framed ones…" And for the next hour, while waving his arms to indicate what went where, he described his vision down to the smallest details. "Make a list of what you need and I'll have it here tomorrow morning. Oh, I forgot to mention, I can't pay you right now for your time, but it'll be good exposure for you, if you know what I mean," he said with a wink looking at a cute man walking by. For the next few days my sawhorses and power tools shared the sidewalk with pedestrians. The big windows disappeared and a small counter that he could work on appeared. The new windows were stored in the walkway to the apartment in the back during the day and his flowers filled that space at night when he closed. Everyone stopped to ask what I was building, thinking it was a crazy idea. But by the end of the week, Bella, with a little help from me, worked his magic once again and a sidewalk flower shop was born. It was an immediate success and the neighborhood adopted it as its own. As I was packing up my tools he said: "You know the Freedom Parade is only a couple weeks away, and it's a real big deal for the Empresses." Bella shoved a flower into my shirt pocket. "I have another little project for you and Michael. Doris needs an elephant."

"What?" I asked, exasperated.

"I told her it would be a good idea for her to ride an elephant in this year's parade."

"And that has something to do with me because?"

"Well, I found one, and it'll cost six-hundred dollars, but I need to pay for it right away if we want to get it here in time. I need you and Michael to find the money. Sell ads on it or something." He busied himself with flowers so he wouldn't have to look at me.

My mind was busy thinking of more practical problems. "Who's going to pick up the poop?"

"Let the queens behind it deal with that. We've got bigger things to worry about. Michael said you would help."

I turned and walked two doors down the street and into Toad Hall to confront him. "I know, she wants an elephant," Michael shouted from behind the bar as I came through the door.

"How'd you get me into this?"

"She asked me first. I told her I couldn't do it by myself. She suggested you." For the next two hours, between serving drinks and being the most charming person in the world, Michael tried to concoct a scheme to raise the six hundred dollars. "It's too late for a fund raiser, but I have an idea. Meet me at the P.S. on Polk Street tonight at eight."

When I came in, Michael had already spotted Hank Trent seated at the end of his bar and sent him a drink. Hank raised his glass to us, smiled, and downed the double Early Times that Michael knew was his favorite. Every time it looked like he was about to get up and leave, Michael would send another drink. "This should soften him up," he said, asking the bartender to put it on his tab. After six doubles in the span of forty-five minutes, Michael thought he was ready. "I'll give you a sign when I want you to come over." He walked down the bar, stood next to Hank and put his arm around him.

"What do you want now? I never see you unless you want a donation for something. What is it this time?" Michael whispered in his ear. He turned and looked at him in disbelief. "You're out of your fucking mind. I'm not buying any elephant for that queen."

"Wait, wait. It'll be a good investment, Hank. It's going to be the *only* animal in the parade, and *everyone* will be talking about it. We'll put a huge sign on each side of it for the P.S. Restaurant."

He was just drunk enough. "How much is this honor going to cost me?" Michael whispered in his ear again as he signaled for me to join them.

"You know Lou." Michael said, directing his attention to me.

"No, I don't."

"Yes, you do. He's the carpenter who's working for everyone. Lou's going to be personally responsible for all the signs." I gasped and took a swig out of Michael's drink to punish him. Hank put one arm around each of us more for support than in agreement. He called the bar manager over, and in a few minutes there was a stack of cash in front of us.

"Do you want a receipt?" Michael asked.

"Get the hell out of here, and those signs better be on that elephant or I'll come looking for you two." Michael kissed him on the cheek, took the money and we left before he could change his mind.

The big day came, and so did the huge van carrying Doris's elephant. Two handlers unloaded the young female and told Doris she needed to become friends with it before trying to climb on its back. As she patted its forehead, the elephant shoved its trunk up her dress, almost lifting her off the ground. Bella arrived with the signs for Hank's P.S.

Bar & Restaurant, but we were told by the handlers that absolutely nothing except Doris could be attached to the beast.

"I'll be back." Bella said, running into the crowd in a panic. She returned with four handsome, half-naked men who walked along side carrying the signs.

After much cajoling and some serious threatening, Doris climbed on and the parade began.

Hank Trent would tell stories about how much business that elephant brought to his bar for years, and Bella would remind everyone it was all his idea.

30

Lions & Tigers & Bears

The Kabuki Theater in San Francisco's Japanese
Culture Center was definitely haunted. When you opened
the doors into the pitch black, abandoned, but almost
new auditorium, you knew there was something sinister
about the place. Bella closed the flower shop early to
meet us. At her predecessor's urging, Empress Doris had

decided the Kabuki would be the perfect venue to stage her first fund raiser for Operation Concern, a gay charity in San Francisco. It was dusty and dirty, but it seemed like a magical place befitting a live version of "The Wizard of Oz".

"I've got a lot of fundraising to do," Doris addressed the group of supporters who had come to help. By the time she finished speaking, the wheels began to turn on what many called an overly ambitious project by inexperienced people. There was literally no budget, so to do her first fundraiser, we had to have another fundraiser first.

Chuck Zinn began casting his show, but there was a problem: "We can't afford dwarfs. What are we going to do?" Bella took off his shoes, threw them on the floor and knelt down on top of them. "See, I'm a dwarf now. We can stitch shoes to the knees on their costumes and do it like this. We just need to make sure everyone wears a cape to hide their legs when they walk."

Chuck turned to his partner Tony. "You're going to be the mayor of Munchkin City. Now go find the other twenty Munchkins I need." He let it be known it wasn't going to be a drag show. "I want an open casting call to go out, not just to the gay community, but to anyone who wants to audition. We need money from the entire city to make this thing profitable. If we have a big cast, they'll sell tickets to their families and friends."

And so the line that formed around the block the next week was filled with cute little grade school girls in gingham dresses with their mothers standing next to drag queens wearing ruby slippers, all of whom wanted to be Dorothy. Michelle, at almost six feet four, took a break from his beauty shop and stood towering over the rest. He had his Yorkie tucked under his arm. Chuck Zinn walked the line, coming to a stop next to him and looked up at his face. Michelle shrugged his shoulders and in his deep baritone voice said, "Thought I'd give it a shot." Chuck smiled and walked on.

Noticing some little girls carrying sheet music for "Somewhere over the Rainbow", he shouted, "This isn't going to be a musical. There's no singing. It's a play adapted from the book." You could see the disappointment on all the little girls' faces.

"Dorothys, you stand over there. Wicked Witches, over here, Tin-Men, Lions and Scarecrows, take a seat behind me. Glendas, all wait out in the hall until there's room for you. For the next three days, Chuck Zinn casted his show, astounded by the talents that walked through the door willing to perform with no pay. Dorothy ended up being a little girl from Lafayette. Later, Herb Caen would write in his morning column that a credible and entertaining performance was staged by the gay community with an eleven-year old real Dorothy and a terrifying Wicked Witch of the West played by a leather queen named Bob.

~

"We've got a problem," Bella told Michael over a cocktail at Toad Hall with the breakfast club. "We need money."

"I'll bring one of the owners of the bar. Maybe she

can help." Michael invited Marjorie DeRemer to watch a rehearsal. Sensing why she was there, and excited about what she saw, she opened her heart and her checkbook. "I'll be happy to help make this happen, but I might have a favor for you to do for me later."

"Of course, you name it," Michael agreed.

And so:

*Imperial Productions of Empress Doris X
in association with
the San Francisco Tavern Guild Foundation
presents a benefit for
Operation Concern
Frank L. Baum's fantasy,
The Wizard of Oz.*

~

We arrived with keys and flashlights. "What have you gotten me into this time?" I asked Michael. "Remember I've got to make a living too. I can't give this thing all of my time."

"The hard part will be over when the sets are built; Bella will help with that. Then we just stand in the wings, give lighting cues and push scenery around."

We were standing in the middle of the Kabuki's eighty-foot wide, multimillion-dollar stage. Above our heads was a forty-foot tall fly filled with scenery, scrims and curtains. Below us was a forty-foot round turntable with a twenty-foot elevator in the center. It could lift performers and sets up from the basement and raise them fifteen feet in the air above the stage while it turned. On the far left and right were two, small, rapid drop elevators. "This would be perfect for making the wicked witch disappear," I said, pointing my light to show Michael one of them.

"Why isn't this theater being used? What do you think happened for them to leave a place like this sit empty?" A loud banging noise from below stopped him, and was followed by moaning. "Shit. What was that?"

"It came from the basement. I don't see any stairs, but there's a freight elevator. Let's go down and check it out. We need to see what's down there anyway."

"You sure you want to go down there?"

The moaning began again. It was a man's voice, and it sounded like he was hurt.

"We better check." Michael found the switch for the elevator and we slowly descended into the dark.

"Here it is." I flipped a switch and the basement lit up with bright fluorescent lights. Under the center of the stage, there was an enclosure around the elevator in the turntable and you could see where someone had tried to pry the doors open with a crowbar. "Look here." A ragged hole had been cut through the masonry wall into a shaft big enough for a person to fit through. Michael shined his flashlight inside but saw nothing. We split up and went searching for the source of the sounds we had heard upstairs. A few minutes later we met in the center of the basement. "I can't imagine where the moaning was coming from."

Michael noticed stacks of wood and canvas scenery flats leaning against the walls. "We won't have to build much. Do you think we could use these?" He pointed to a pair of massive curved stairways on casters.

"Maybe for the Emerald City. They're already painted green. Let's get out of here. This place gives me the creeps."

A few nights later, Bella brought two cast members and we began to build the sets. "There are stacks of things we can use in the basement. You should come down."

He looked up at me. "I'm not going down there."

"There's an elevator. It's not hard. You need to show me what you want so I can bring it up."

"There is no way you're going to see me in that basement," he insisted.

With a five-gallon bucket of white paint, the pagodas and Japanese gardens painted on the flats disappeared and Bella had the blank canvases he needed to create Munchkin Land. Like Salvador Dali, he sketched the outlines of every flower, tree, and building at lightning speed. In two evenings he had drawn the complete one-hundred foot long and twenty-foot high outline of the Munchkin Land set. Two nights later, he returned with more help to start painting them. "So tell me why you won't go into the basement," I asked as he finished a huge yellow daisy.

"Everyone knows this place is haunted. There's a story that when it was built in 1968, they wanted to use it for traveling Kabuki shows. They were planning this big Cherry Festival to kick off the opening, and since San Francisco had a sister city thing going with Osaka, they sent a troupe of famous Kabuki performers from Japan to do shows to get it started. People say that on opening night the star performer died when an elevator collapsed while he was standing on it and trapped him in the shaft below. Supposedly his ghost haunts the place. The owners won't talk about it when you ask."

"And you believe that really happened?"

"Who knows. People say they've heard and seen strange things in here." The lights on the stage suddenly dimmed to a faint glow, and as if on cue, the groaning sounds from the basement began again. "I don't think were in Kansas anymore," Bella said throwing his paint brushes into his tool-box. "Come on girls, we're getting out of here. We'll come back tomorrow when it's light. No more nights in this place for me."

It was getting close to dress rehearsal time, and we thought we had everything under control with construction when Bella looked up from a copy of the script he was reading to make his list of props. "Look here guys, it says that in the enchanted forest Dorothy and her friends get turned around on some kind of magical bridge that rotates when they try to cross it.

"There was no magical bridge in the movie."

"There weren't any Jitterbugs in the movie either, but it's in here and it needs to turn really fast, so we can't use the turntable."

"OK, what do we do?" I asked.

"I have an idea. I know you and Michael said you don't want to be in the show, but I think you're going to make your stage debut as bushes."

"Huh?"

"We'll get you both some green tights and dye some long-sleeved shirt greens and paint some sneakers the same color. I'll cover them with big green leaves. We can use ski masks with leaves sewn on them to hide your heads. You can stand at opposite corners of the bridge and turn it around. Aren't I wonderful?"

When no one from the theater office was around, I drilled a one inch hole in the stage. We built the covered bridge on casters with a steel pin we could drop into the hole in the floor. Bella painted and covered it in ivy to match our costumes.

"Well, I guess we're the Bush Sisters now," Michael said during a dry run as he tried to shove the pin into the hole in the dark. We decided to coat the hole with glow-in-the-dark paint. It worked, and we were stars. Naturally, as if we didn't have anything else to do, we stopped working on the sets and built the Wizard of OZ float for the 1975 Freedom Parade and spent time to make sure Doris and her elephant got the credit for her first fundraiser.

As planned, the show ran for three nights of sold-out performances. After the first show everyone left excited, and by morning Oz was the talk of the town.

After the first performance, Marjorie came backstage to congratulate us. "It's truly magical. I can't believe what you did with so little money. Now about that favor you promised me. I have a friend who runs a school for developmentally disabled children down the peninsula. I know her kids would love something like this. Do you think you could add one more performance? We'll invite her and the other schools in the area with kids like hers. I'll pay whatever it costs to do a special matinee just for them."

~

School bus after school bus arrived, and almost three-hundred special needs children of all ages marched into the Kabuki lobby where, thanks to Marjorie, ice-cream and cookies were waiting. You could see the concern on the teachers' faces. They were worried about the outing and huddled each of their classes into small groups making them easier to supervise.

"We've got a noisy house full of kids out there," Chuck Zinn said peeking through the curtain. "Everyone speak up and slow down. Make sure they can hear and understand everything you say. Remember, make big gestures and exaggerate."

The curtain rose, and the moment they saw Bella's Munchkin Land set they started to scream and applaud. When the Munchkins appeared, they screamed louder. Two children, with eyes the size of saucers, ran up to the edge of the stage. When their teacher rushed to bring them back, she stopped and stood there with them in awe. When the Wicked Witch of the West disappeared down the elevator shaft in a puff of red smoke, we had to bring up the houselights and stop the show so teachers could calm their children down, and convince them everything was OK, and that it was just a story.

But they weren't buying it.

When Glenda the good witch appeared, they ooooed and aaahed. Too excited to stay in their seats, some ran around and danced in the aisles, even though there was no music.

When the curtain finally came down, the cast gathered on stage. When it rose again, instead of taking a bow, they stood there crying as the children rushed from their seats and climbed the stairs to join them. Everyone wanted to touch Glenda and her magic wand. The Tin-Man gave away his tinfoil-covered cardboard axe, the Scarecrow his hat, and the Cowardly Lion hugged as many as he could before he sat on the edge of the stage with a little boy in his lap and broke down in tears.

More than thirty-five years later, I still treasure the little medals Michael and I were given for our part in making it happen.

If the Kabuki Theater in San Francisco's Japanese Cultural Center did indeed have a curse or a ghost, the unbridled love from the cast and the thrilled children who filled seats that day made it go away.

31

Sunrise in
"The City"

The day after Halloween in 1972 was a Wednesday, and the sun came up over the Oakland hills in San Francisco at exactly 6:35 a.m.. I know this because I smelled Folgers coffee being roasted, and I could read a distant clock tower in the headlights of cars coming off the Bay Bridge. I could see and smell all of this from high on my perch in the crotch of a tree in Dolores Park. Getting comfortable was difficult because the synthetic fabric of my white nurse's uniform was stuck in the crack of my ass, and when the J Church streetcar occasionally passed directly below me, it would shake my tree and blow cold air up my dress. A large, white nurse's hat sat cockeyed in my black Tammy Wynette wig, which managed to get hooked into bark on the tree. Every time I moved, it threatened to come off. My legs were incredibly heavy, and looking down, I noticed two of the front wheels on my left roller-skate were completely worn to the bearings. Both of my knees were bloody and long streaks of blood caked in pools at the top of my white soxs. Some of the glitter from my moustache and beard had fallen on the sticky mess which made it oddly more festive than gory. On closer inspection, I noticed a line of ants had begun to climb up my legs. *Not a good sign*, I thought.

All I could think was, *this is all JR's fault*. Short, extremely hairy and way too macho for his age, JR simply didn't give a shit. He came to San Francisco to live and have fun. One of many stars behind Toad Hall's bar at night, his dancing eyes enticed scores of men into leaving large tips, and his face lit up whenever anyone challenged or dared him to do anything crazy. It was all JR's idea.

~

"What are we going to do for Halloween?" he asked one evening as I sat on a barstool.

"Hell, I don't know. I'll probably go down to Folsom and hang out with the boys."

"*BORING!*" he shouted, pouring me a double Dewer's adding a splash of water. "I've got a better idea. How about nurses on roller-skates?"

"I'm not getting dressed up in drag. Don't even go there."

"I think I can get ten or twelve other guys to do it too. I'll take care of everything," he said. "I love going down to Mission Street and fighting those huge Mexican women in the thrift stores for the larger sizes. I'll make the hats myself."

"Not interested." I said, doing the best I could to protect my masculinity while taking a gulp from my drink. "Besides, are you insane, roller-skating on these hills?"

"There's safety in numbers," he snapped back shoving his open palm in my face. "Just give me thirty damn dollars. I'll take care of everything. Don't worry, we're going to have fun." As I reached for my wallet I felt my hand stop as if to warn me this wasn't a good idea.

Not much was said for a couple weeks after that and I began to think it had been forgotten when the phone rang. It was JR. "Five-thirty tomorrow at my house. I've got everything ready."

"Really? I don't think...."

"You better come. There's going to be fifteen of us. Don't worry, we're going to have fun!" He hung up and left me holding the receiver.

Some of us decided to meet at the bar, and by three-thirty the next afternoon, eleven of the fifteen, myself included, were looking into our drinks, trying to figure how to get out of this mess. Five-thirty was coming too fast and none of us were ready. You could feel panic in the air. "A double Dewer's straight up, please."

At five-thirty, like soldiers, we marched up the steps, carrying roller-skates over our shoulders and into the Victorian house JR shared with three roommates. Greeting us at the door, he was more enthusiastic than ever. No one spoke as we marched past him. "We're going to have fun," he kept saying. Finally, realizing the group wasn't as committed as he expected, he shoved us into the living room, told us to have a seat and disappeared down the hall.

"This should help," he said, returning with a tray of water glasses filled half-way with Schnapps. While we drank he left and came back with a dish of Purple Barrel acid and another filled with Quaaludes. "Take half a hit of acid now," he suggested. "In fifteen or twenty minutes we'll take half a Lude. That'll calm us down and make us a lot more festive. We'll take the other halves later. We're going to have fun!" he shouted again as the group, all of whom had experience at self-medicating, did as they were told.

We sat around for the next half-hour talking about anything except what we were going to be doing that night, when suddenly it seemed like the lights got brighter in the room. Laughter started to break out, and JR appeared again "This way gentlemen," he announced, gesturing to the long hallway leading deeper into the flat. Like a mother hen leading her chicks to food, he led his now-willing troupe to the dressing rooms.

"I'm not shaving anything off," I shouted defiantly over the heads of my fellow inductees as we shuffled down the hall.

"No one's asking you to," a voice in the distance shouted back.

He ushered us into a dining room with card-tables full of make-up and a rack of white uniform dresses, colorful wigs and enormous white hats, each with a single black ribbon stripe indicating the highest rank of RN. "Your names are pinned to each uniform. Once you have yours, choose a wig off the rack and take a hat. I wasn't able to find white belts for everyone, so I got some white ball-fringe from a fabric store. I also couldn't find extra large white pantyhose, so we're going au natural tonight. You can leave your clothes here, but take some ID so if they find our bodies they'll know not to send us to the ladies morgue. Oh, and take some cash too. When you're dressed, line up and I'll do your makeup." Everyone turned, looked at him and frowned.

It wasn't long before the level of drug-induced enthusiasm and excitement in the room was palpable, and soon clothing was flying in every direction and there was no lack of suggestions on how to make things work. "I think we should safety-pin our hats on," one of the half-dressed bartenders suggested. "I'm going to use my own belt," another declared, to which JR demanded to know if it was white. "No, it's not white." a sarcastic reply shot back at him only to be returned with "Then wrap it in the ball-fringe to hide it." Moments later the group lined up for makeup, each a vision in white.

One of the first things a person who imbibes in the world of psychedelics learns is that nothing is more dangerous than looking at yourself in a mirror when you are tripping. That said, as each of us sat down to have our makeup done, we were confronted in the mirror with our new look, which was, to put it mildly, shocking. JR gave each of us a quick, once-over and suggested corrections if he wasn't pleased, then applied generous amounts of rouge and lipstick followed by large beauty spots and outrageous eyelashes. The process ended with a quick spritz of spray-adhesive and a handful of silver glitter thrown into our beards and moustaches. When the last of us was transformed he announced, "It's time for half a Quaalude now." Everyone obediently did as instructed. "In your pockets you'll find additional meds if you need them." His generosity was duly noted by the group.

"I think we're all going to want a roadie," he said retrieving a large cardboard box from under a table. He opened it and started to hand out smaller packages to the group. "I had enough money left to buy these enema bags. I also borrowed a case of vodka from the bar, so we can fill up here and have refreshments along the way." He pulled the white rubber bag out and extended the long tube and anal insert to arm's length, demonstrating how we could turn it on or off with a small metal clip. The moment resembled an airline attendant demonstrating the use of the oxygen mask before takeoff. Everyone mimicked him by extending their tubes to arms-length. Giggles turned into laughter and soon the kitchen was alive with people filling their bags with vodka. When it became apparent twelve bottles wasn't going to be enough, JR produced several bottles of gin from under the sink.

Things began to slow down considerably as the Ludes kicked in and mixed with the acid. We had each come with a pair of skates. Some of us owned our own while others had borrowed from friends. What should have been a quick stop at the living room to pick them up turned into forty minutes of sitting on the floor, trying to figure out whose belonged to whom. A great silence came over the room as some got sidetracked, intrigued by the pattern in the rug, while others seemed content to spend their time straightening its fringe and separating loops in the carpet to see what lay below. Others just sat there and spun the wheels on their skates. No one seemed to be in a particular hurry to go anywhere. Daylight turned into dark. "Damn it, I was worried this would happen," JR moaned standing in the doorway, his arms folded. One by one he pulled people to their feet making sure they had a pair, any pair, of roller-skates in their hands. "Let's not put them on now," he said pulling a half-laced skate off someone's foot, knowing there was a flight of twenty concrete stairs to go down on the way out of the house.

Outside, an old step-van with big lettering for Herman's Deli Salads waited to take the group down the steep hill to Castro and 18th so they could start on more level terrain. With everyone inside, mother JR announced it was time to put our skates on, and once again confusion reigned as skates were traded until the exchange seemed to please everyone. "Does everyone have a right and a left now?" he asked, but no one answered. The tightly focused group was limited to doing only one thing at a time, and at this moment it was putting on skates, not talking.

On Castro Street, Ernie from Cliff's Variety store was busy with the neighborhood kids. A long, flat-bed trailer parked in front of his store was decorated with bales of hay, carved pumpkins and lots of black and orange crepe paper. In a tradition that went back to when the neighborhood was filled with working Irish families, the judging of the best kid's costumes was well underway. A dwindling group of parents and grandparents clustered around and applauded loudly as each winner came to the stage. If one were able to look down from space, it would have appeared as though the children's party had been dropped into the middle of another planet. Scores of outlandishly costumed gay men and women filled the streets around it, oblivious to anything but their friends, yet there was a happy, touching, live-and-let-live attitude that existed, and both groups respected one another.

Before you saw them, you could hear people screaming with laughter and cheering. From the direction of Market Street, like the dancing packs of Chesterfield cigarettes on TV in the 1950's, a group of men dressed as the San Francisco skyline appeared. They wore amazingly detailed, lighted, towering cardboard costumes, some as high as fifteen feet tall. One was the Transamerica pyramid, another the Bank of America building, a Victorian house, a tower of the Golden Gate Bridge and even Coit Tower. They ran in tight formation through the crowd, suddenly stopping, and then violently shaking and tilting while screaming "*EARTHQUAKE, EARTHQUAKE!*" After the brief stop they ran on to the sound of much applause. Herman's Deli Salad truck careened around the corner of 18th and Castro and came to stop in front of Toad Hall.

No one inside the truck noticed it was no longer moving. Suddenly the back doors swung open and blinding lights from KRON's Channel 4 television cameras caught the group by surprise. "We're on, girls!" JR shouted, jumping out. He reached back inside and began pulling at the closest terrified nurse he could grab. "Pull your dress down! Don't show them your stuff," he shouted. A woman reporter shoved a microphone in his face and began interviewing but quickly disappeared in the confusion of fifteen nurses wearing roller-skates, wigs and hats that made each of them almost eight feet tall. JR pulled and shoved and in moments had everyone lined up facing the cameras. The group resembled deer frozen in car headlights. The rainbow of colors created by the synthetic wigs and glittered beards brought a hush over the crowds in the street - then applause and cheers rang out.   I spotted the open doors of Toad Hall and headed for cover. JR grabbed my waist and in seconds the roller derby train was up to full speed on its way into the bar. The disappointed reporter was left standing alone in the street. "Fantastic! Did you get that?" she asked her camera crew. "Did you get it? That's going to be our lead at eleven o'clock."

Noticing some of the group heading for barstools, JR shouted "Let's go! We're having fun now!" He grabbed my hands and put them on his waist and the group flew back out the doors, turned right and headed for The Midnight Sun. As we entered, the crowd broke into hoots and applause and David Ford, the bar owner, began counting and pouring fifteen shots. JR led the centipede through the crowd, allowing it to break formation only long enough to down our drinks before heading back outside.

It wasn't long before roller-skating through the Castro wasn't enough to keep the group challenged, so JR headed down Market Street toward the Civic Center. At City Hall we turned left onto Polk Street and uphill for the first time. Skating over streetcar tracks while turning presented another challenge, especially when the tracks went to the right and the group wanted to go to the left. The first time we made this maneuver, half of the nurses ended up going the wrong direction. As experience quickly taught, you wanted to be in the front or middle, but definitely not at the end. If, when turning, the front is going five-miles per hour, the guys on the end were going forty, which could lead to devastating consequences.

Huffing and puffing on the uphill climb, the nurses turned to their refreshment bags and soon long white rubber tubes were dangling from every pair of lips. There were a lot of gay bars on Polk Street. No one knew who decided we had to go into every one of them, but I'm sure it was JR. We only stopped long enough to rest and finish our drinks, but by the time we skated back down the Polk Street hill we were four nurses short. One of them fainted in the P.S. Restaurant, two of them picked up tricks at the Polk Gulch Saloon and one had to be left sitting on the steps of the Federal Building nursing a bloody knee because of a fatal mechanical failure.

"On to Folsom Street," JR shouted to the group behind him. Eventually small parts of our train broke away, bruised and bleeding or just too drunk and stoned to keep up with the rest. It was getting late and by the time we reached South of Market, it was just JR and me. We knew the bars and leather crowd on Folsom Street. For them, Halloween was just another night to dress in leather drag. No longer having enough members to be a train, as we skated into the Ramrod we went solo, throwing in a few pirouettes for good measure. Our friends in leather were not amused. But this was a test. We were pleased to realize our transformation into nurses was so complete, even with beards and moustaches intact, that we weren't recognized by anyone. We kept our mouths shut except to order beers in falsetto and kept skating, afraid of stopping long enough to be identified. We found comfort and appreciation in the non-leather, hippie patrons at The Stud and hung out there. I turned and JR was gone. It was almost two so I decided to start my lonely solo skate back to where my truck was parked in the Castro. Oddly enough no one seemed to look twice at a lonely bearded nurse roller skating up Market Street at two-thirty in the morning. San Franciscans are so jaded.

The Castro was deserted. The parking space where I left my truck was empty. The temporary no-parking sign told me it had been towed, but I knew I couldn't go to the Mission Police Station on acid, and after looking up the steep 18th Street incline going toward home, I decided it would be better to wait. I finished the last of the vodka in my bag, wishing I could fill it with hot coffee. *I'll go watch the sun come up in Dolores Park*, I thought to myself.

From the Castro to Dolores Park was downhill except for slight inclines between 18th and 19th streets. Once on 19th, the uphill climb between Castro and Henry Street could be tough, but after cresting the top, it was all downhill from there - severely downhill. I would have to be careful not to end up flying down the cement steps and onto the MUNI streetcar tracks. *Going down stairs is very difficult on skates.* I reminded myself.

It was all JR's fault, I thought again, picking three ants off my knee and tossing them to the sidewalk below.

It was almost sunup, the coldest time of the night. I shifted my weight to get comfortable and tried to figure out how I managed to climb this tree wearing a pair of roller skates and almost lost my balance bending over to look. I could see telltale marks in the bark on the trunk.

A man walking his three Rottweilers stopped on the sidewalk below me. "Morning," I said. He looked up, just shook his head and walked on.

He was wearing a brown leather jacket.

32

"Number Please"

No matter how much the guy sitting in the stall next to me tapped his foot, sex was the last thing on my mind. It was seven-thirty in the morning; I was taking a dump in Goodman's Lumber Yard on Bayshore and going over the list of what I needed to buy in my head. While washing my hands, someone I had watched getting off a motorcycle in the parking lot emerged for the other stall. I remembered wondering how he was going to carry 2x4s on his bike. Harry was a handsome man dressed in a well-worn motorcycle jacket, and it looked natural on him. His dark, almost black eyes were so intense there was no way he could hide being a Scorpio, which explained why he was horny at this hour of the morning. He had a full beard and very hairy arms, both attributes I admired. Yet there was something that just wasn't right. I found myself staring at him, and then noticed he was staring back. *Is it because his beard looks artificially dark?* I thought to myself. *That's not it.* Then I realized it was his hair. The sideburns were good, but the top of his head looked like someone had trimmed around a soup bowl, and the bangs hanging over his bushy eyebrows definitely didn't fit the masculine image of everything below them. "Good morning," I said, still staring at him in the mirror.

"Want to have breakfast?"

"I can't. I need to pick up some stuff and get to work."

"How about dinner then?"

"Sure." Something was pulling me to him and I knew better than to resist. He took out a card that told me he was a doctor, and asked me to call him that night.

Expecting to go out someplace to eat, I was surprised when he wanted to cook dinner. As soon as I finished the last bite, we were in bed. For a few days we followed a routine that consisted of meeting for something to eat then exhausting each other sexually. The strange thing about this new romance was he never wanted me to spend the night. There was always an affectionate "Good night. See you tomorrow?" But it made me feel cheap, like he had better things to do after I left. In the middle of one night I sat up in bed wide awake. *He wears a hairpiece.* I laughed at the thought and went back to sleep.

"What are you doing this weekend?" he asked as he picked up the dinner dishes.

"I don't have any plans, why?"

"Do you want to take a ride and visit some friends of mine up north? I think you'll like them."

~

"Number please." Alice said, shoving a plug into a hole on her switchboard and adjusting her headphones while she sorted mail and shoved letters into boxes. She could do all of this without leaving her chair.

"Hello, Alice, can you get me Sharon and Packy?"

"They're not home. I just saw them go by on their way into Gualala."

"Thanks, I'll try later."

"Stop and pick up your mail. I think the bathrobe you ordered from Sears came today. And there's a letter from your son in Oregon. Maybe he needs money again."

Alice knew everything about everyone. She could tell if the letter you received was good or bad news before you opened it. People loved her - and sometimes feared her - for it. She had been a fixture for decades in the tiny post office/telephone exchange in Annapolis, California. Not much more than a wide spot on a dirt road in 1901, years later the town still consisted of just the post office, the small Horicon school house, and an equally small general store with a gas pump where, on Fridays, they would sometimes have fresh chicken. If someone butchered a pig in town, there would be pork in the freezer. You could pump kerosene for your lamps with a hand-crank on top of a fifty-gallon barrel out back, and there was always cold beer in the refrigerator and plenty of gossip if you hung around the gas pump for half an hour or so.

By the mid 1950's, the Masonite Corporation had dragged out the last of the easy-to-get, old-growth redwoods from the forests surrounding the town. All that remained when they left was the dirt drag roads they had cut into the mountains, piles of slash, stumps and an assortment of small trees. Thankfully, it was impossible to clear-cut the area because of the rough terrain, so they also left a few, hard to get, old redwoods. Having no further interest in the thousands of acres they owned, they subdivided it into what became known as *Sonoma Forties*, 40-acre parcels of land the county designated for recreational use. They built a real estate office where the dirt road met the pavement and began to advertise.

There was no electricity, telephone or water, and because of the steep terrain, many of the places needed a four-wheel drive to reach them. Inside the small office there was an eager agent waiting to sell anyone who walked through the door their dream vacation property for as little as eight thousand dollars. It took a lot of imagination and determination to build on the land, but by the mid 1960's, the hippie generation fleeing San Francisco with copies of the Foxfire books tucked under their arms, arrived to establish their back-to-the land homesteads.

Although he wasn't a hippie, Harry's friend Lee saw the opportunity too and purchased a beautiful piece of land on Fuller Creek and started to build a cabin in the woods on top of three huge redwood stumps.

Crammed into the back of an old car with his brothers and sisters, Lee arrived in central California as a small child in the 1930's. Everything the family owned was either inside or on top. His dad was an Oakie carpenter who worked where he could find it and his mother raised her family on almost nothing during the Great Depression and dust bowl.

Lee was a seeker, a member of a miniscule group of human beings who emerged from their mothers' wombs with an urgent need for knowledge. He wasn't interested in going to college, and may not have had time to finish high school. No rote memorization for him, no useless things he didn't need to know. He absorbed the magazines he loved - *Popular Science* and *Popular Mechanics.* The universe fed his inquisitive mind whatever it demanded to know with a voracity that stunned people. His amazing ability to master anything mechanical continually pushed him. At the time we met, he was part of a team at Sloan Kettering, working to design machines that would someday let blind people see.

Lee could build or fix anything. When he needed water he hiked up the side of a mountain, found a spring, built a catch basin and ran pipe down to his house. When he wanted television, he hiked up another mountain dragging the materials he needed to build an antenna. He beamed the signal down using a microwave transmitter he built, not only to himself, but to all his neighbors living in the valleys, cracks and crevices of the mountains

that surrounded Annapolis. In the summertime, when
he wanted to swim, he'd damn up the creek behind his
house with logs and sheets of plywood covered in black
plastic. He knew everything about engines, and used a
diesel generator to charge banks of batteries and used the
heat the generator gave off to make hot water. Like magic,
he made living deep in the woods romantic, fun, and as
comfortable as city life.

Constantly on a mission, you could see it in his
eyes. He pushed his mind and body to their physical limits
without regard for their welfare. And when he occasionally
stopped, he slept, ate and thought about what he would do
next. Mister Wizard, as he became affectionately known,
also loved to drop a hit or two of acid with his friends on
weekends, have more than a few cocktails, do senseless,
silly things, and giggle a lot.

In addition to his motorcycle, Harry owned a classic
1950's Rolls Royce Phantom that he loved to tinker with.
"Let's take this on our trip to the country." He shoved
the dip-stick back in after checking the oil and closed
the hood. The car still turned heads wherever it went and
Harry looked oddly correct behind the wheel.

"Should I ride here?" I asked from the back seat.

"Do you see a chauffeur's hat? Get your ass up front
with me."

It was sixty-five miles from San Francisco to
Healdsburg on north-bound Highway 101 where we
turned off onto Dry Creek Road. For the next fifty miles
we were on a winding, narrow strip of blacktop barely

wide enough for two cars to pass. The problem was that large trucks with double trailers behind them filled with logs were still using the road. Meeting one on a blind curve demanded someone back up to a wide spot where they could pass. Size mattered, so it was always cars that did the backing. There were no gas stations, grocery stores and only a handful of houses as we drove through valleys framed by high mountains on either side. In Annapolis, we turned off the paved road and began a two-mile drive on steep, graded dirt roads. Lee's driveway was marked only by a steel ranch gate and a "No Trespassing" sign. He came out to open the gate, smiled and waved us in.

The tiny redwood cabin sat in a small clearing, cantilevered over a creek on one end. The kitchen stove was loaded with pots and pans that filled the house with smells that made my stomach rumble. There was a fire in the wood stove in the living room and the table was set for dinner. I felt like I never wanted to leave.

"Duane's visiting family back east, so it's just the three of us," he said, handing us frozen Margaritas, followed by giving me a quick tour of the cabin. "Why don't you show Lou around? Take a walk. I'll finish cooking and we'll have an early dinner when you come back."

The land was starting to heal from being logged. Fairy Circles of young trees were growing around the huge redwood stumps and the piles of slash were rotting into compost. Occasionally you'd spot a long, four-foot diameter log in the brush that had been left behind because it wasn't easy enough to drag out. All you could hear was the creek, the songs of birds and the wind high up in the trees. It seemed like it was almost sacred. "I can't believe this place," I told Harry.

"I knew you'd like it. I come up here whenever I can get away from the city." He kicked a stone down the dirt road.

~

"Life's pretty simple here," Lee said, refilling our glasses. "You get up when it gets light and go to bed when it gets dark. There's always a project, something to fix or something to build. Duane and I want to start building a big shop. I want a place where I can build cabinets and work on my electronics and Duane wants a room where he can work on his carvings." After dinner we sat around getting to know each other and I confessed my envy for what he was doing. "I'd be glad to help you build your shop," I said, hoping he wouldn't think I was being pushy.

"Are you serious? That would be great. Most San Francisco queens can't wait to get back to the bars and baths when they come up here. I'll make up a bed on the floor by the fire and you two can sleep out here."

"Sleep over?" Harry asked.

"I thought we were going to spend the weekend too," I said disappointed.

"Let's go back. I have things I could do in the city tomorrow."

Lee rolled his eyes and gave me a look that said; *don't give up so easily.* "It's because you're afraid I'll find out you wear that thing on your head, isn't it?" I knew that was the reason, and thought it was a perfect time to mention it with his ex-lover for moral support.

"You knew?" He looked shocked.

"Are you kidding? That's the worst thing I've ever seen."

"I paid a lot of money for this." He lifted up a corner.

"I've been trying to look under that since I met you. I think bald guys are handsome. You're an incredibly good looking man."

"Come on, it's time. Take it off and let me cut your hair," Lee said bringing out his clippers. In fifteen minutes Harry looked like a model out of GQ magazine.

"Wow! I knew you were under there." I hugged him and handed him a mirror. "I'm afraid I'll lose you to those boys in the city now," I said rubbing his beautiful bald head.

He picked up his hairpiece, opened the door of the wood stove and tossed it into fire. "Thanks, guys. I think I needed that."

From that day on, Harry never hid again.

33

Ballerinas With Beards

Ed was hung over when he arrived with his Alaskan sawmill to cut wood for Lee's shop. There was a good looking man under the layers of grease and grime that accumulate when one doesn't bathe. I stood watching as he set up his equipment to cut a twenty foot log left behind by Masonite. We needed more 2x12's to complete the shop floor, and this was how we would get them. Ed's chain saw was the biggest I had ever seen. The six foot long bar had a steel handle on the tip implying someone was going to be holding it while the saw was cutting. "That's your end," Ed said, pointing to the handle. "Keep your legs out of the way, and put your other hand behind your back. "As we cut, follow my lead as we walk down the log, but don't get ahead of me."

Easy for him to say. I thought. *He's going to be standing behind the motor where it's safe.*

It was a slow, messy process that covered both of us from head to foot in sawdust. It took almost twenty minutes per piece, but gradually a stack of four foot wide slabs two inches thick were piled next to us. On the fifth pass, the chain broke and flew at me. Ed hit the brake, but in a split second the chain wrapped itself around my right thigh three times. All I could hear was the sound of my heart pounding. We looked at each other, then at my leg. There was no blood and I didn't feel any pain, so I reached down, untangled the chain, and when I did, the pant leg of my overalls fell to the ground. My Levis weren't cut. "You're a lucky man," Ed said, pulling the bar out of the log. "And a good partner."

I almost fainted.

I had a dark ring bruise around my leg for several weeks.

Every Thursday afternoon for over two months, I left the city with Lee and Duane as soon as they finished work, and went to Annapolis to help them build their shop. We became good friends, and when the floor, walls and roof were up, Duane taught me how to split redwood shake shingles with an adz, a tool used by early settlers.

It was fun being with them; we worked hard and laughed hard too. On weekends, when unexpected friends arrived from the city empty-handed, Lee could take two cans of anything in the cupboard and make a feast for eight. He amazed me. One night over dinner he asked if I'd like to build a place of my own on their land. I was overwhelmed by the offer. "There's a sweet little spot up the creek and if you want, we'll give you a lifetime lease on it." The next day we hiked around and he showed me how we could run a waterline and I began to dream about life in the woods.

~

"It's incredible," I told Michael, as he put a beer on the bar for me. "I'm still having difficulty believing their offer. I don't have the money to buy the lumber, so if this happens, it's going to take a long time."

Michael had broken up with his partner, and was alone and lonely. "Why don't we do it together? I'll find a way to come up with the money. I need something to keep my mind off Gary." So the next weekend we went up together. When he met my new friends, saw the land and listened to my ideas, his eyes lit up and we both began dream. Lee and Duane put two names on the lease and we started planning our house on paper. A friend of Michael's offered to loan us the money, and we signed the note

for seven-thousand dollars.

Annapolis Mill arrived with the first truck load of lumber. For more than two weeks we took turns cutting sap wood off redwood logs with a chainsaw. It was a slow and tedious job, but we needed them for foundation posts.

A couple days into the work, Michael's eyes began to hurt. When he awoke one morning, his eyelids were dark red and swollen the size of golf balls. He looked like a fly but I didn't dare laugh as I poured the saline solution into them every three hours that the doctor prescribed.

Lee and Duane and friends from the city came to help us frame the house. We all loved to work naked, with nothing but a pair of sox, work boots and a tool belt. Before long Michael and I had tanned to the color of mahogany. When I stopped at the general store to buy beer and ice, Sharon started telling me, "If you get any darker, Packy won't serve you."

A time came when we began to feel like we were overstaying our welcome at Lee and Duane's. Michael mentioned his father had a small travel trailer that wasn't being used. Like my relationship with my own dad, Michael and his father Harry weren't close. When he found out his son was gay, communication between the two of them became awkward. But when Michael called to tell his father he had started building a cabin in the woods and needed his help, he couldn't wait to be a part of his son's life again. The next weekend he arrived pulling a small travel trailer. The truck was loaded with an old, gas Servel refrigerator, an Ashley wood stove, and a propane tank. Watching him embrace his son on the driveway brought tears to my eyes and memories of the morning my dad held me in his arms.

Harry Schoch became a real father to his son again, and in the process, also took me under his wing.

~

Every weekend as we drove up Highway 101, our trucks automatically turned off at the exit to Santa Rosa's biggest building supply. We arrived with lists of what we needed, knowing if we didn't have it in the back of our trucks when we arrived in Annapolis, there would be no place else to get it, and the weekend could be lost.

Michael's aunt Molly called. "I've got a stack of leaded glass windows we made for a restaurant that was never built. They've been sitting in the back room at the shop for years. Your dad said you guys could give them a good home." Michael picked them up, and we changed the window openings to fit them.

~

Sunday was always a day of rest. If we didn't have to drive back to San Francisco, we'd wake up, drop Acid and spend the day lying on the unfinished deck or hike down to Lee and Duane's to go swimming. There were

wild azaleas everywhere you walked along the creek, and I tucked one behind my ear. When Lee and Michael saw it, they disappeared and returned with more wildflowers, decorating me by shoving them in my beard and pockets.

The country was the perfect place to experience the life-changing details of nature on psychedelics. I spent entire days sitting by myself on a stump next to the creek watching fish swim upstream, or on my stomach, looking into the grass and the world of insects scurrying around, doing their chores. They lived in communities, held jobs, and each had its own responsibility. It was hard to fathom I could walk across the grass without knowing this.

One weekend when I was alone at the house, my puppy Buddy and I found an enormous redwood stump that had been hollowed out by fire. It had a hole on one side so we crawled in and didn't awake until the next morning when we heard Lee and Duane's calls.

"We've been looking everywhere for you. We were worried you got lost."

"We're not lost, we've been right here all night."

It was fall and soon the rains would begin. Michael arrived with a twenty-five pound bag of sweet pea seed and stood on the deck of the house tossing handfuls of it up into the banks of the creek. When they bloomed the next year, the banks were carpets of purple and red. With the glee of a small child, he stood there clapping his hands, shouting "More, More, More." He nicknamed the house "Oz" after our stint as *The Bush Sisters*. It was a happy, special place for both of us and for our friends.

Whenever there wasn't work for me in the city, I'd head for the mountains, often working eight or ten days on the house by myself. When I got lonely, I'd walk down the creek with my flashlight and have dinner with Lee and Duane. But there were times when I wanted to be with someone else.

My secret getaway was the Bottling Works, a tiny gay bar in the middle of an equally tiny wide spot in the road called Cazadero. There were two ways to get there; the fastest wasn't fast at all. It involved driving down Highway One along the steep cliffs above the ocean. The road followed the coastline as it snaked its way toward Jenner, where the Russian River met the ocean. The other choice, which I usually took on my way back, was an even slower road on the top of the mountains running parallel to the coast. It was dark, the road was narrow and you had to watch out for cattle, but there were no Highway Patrol cars if I'd been drinking.

Often I'd be the only customer in the Bottling Works. If I was lucky, Von would have taken the night off and Gerry would be behind the bar by himself and we would lust after each other. When the town's rednecks decided it was a good idea to burn the place to the ground,

I had to drive another twenty miles to The Rusty Nail on the other side of Guerneville.

~

Michael was busy in the city and Duane was someplace up north. Lee and I ate dinner together and he could tell I was restless. "I need a break," I confessed.

"Tomorrow is Halloween. Why don't we get dressed up and go to the Nail?"

"I don't know…"

"Oh, come on. Sometimes you're entirely too serious for your own good. You said you needed a break - well, here's your chance." He opened another cardboard box of Franzia Rosé wine and filled my glass.

"Excellent vintage, how many hours old do you think it is? Do we really need to go in costumes?"

"Of course, I've got all day tomorrow to come up with something. Leave it to me. We're going to have fun." When I heard those words I said "Do you know JR?" I was sure the next thing he would do was ask me for thirty dollars. The remark went over his head and he gave me a strange look.

The next day I called him every time I took a break, but he didn't answer. Eventually, I heard his voice on the radio calling me. "I just got back from town. I'm busy sewing. Be here at five o'clock. We'll have a few drinks before we leave."

When I walked through the door, Lee was putting away his sewing machine and the floor was covered in scraps. "So, who are we going to be tonight?"

"Why ballerinas with beards, of course. You'll be

Anna Nimity and I'll be Doris Vedonia". He brought out
two tutus with netting that stuck out two feet. One was
pink and the other was blue. "Since you're so butch, you
can have the blue one. You have no idea how hard it was
to find two sets of white dance tights in our sizes." From
a shopping bag on the sofa he pulled out two large silver
tiaras and placed one on my head. "We don't need wigs,
and because of your butchness, we'll wear our work boots."

"Good," I said amazed he had done it all so fast. *He
looks like a lumberjack, but under it all he's just a another
silly queen* I thought, smiling and shaking my head.

"Oh, by the way, you owe me thirty dollars."

~

After a few cocktails we decided it was best if
we got dressed before leaving. The netting on my tutu
was scratching the back of my legs and I couldn't get
comfortable on the seat of the truck. The plan was to make
our grand entrance into the Rusty Nail, then eventually
go back out and change into Levis for the rest of the
night.   But Gerald, a young hippie we knew from Tomales
Bay who made candles for the Renaissance Faire, had
other ideas. As we pulled into the parking lot, he was just
ahead of us in his beat-up Volkswagen bus. "Perfect!" he
screamed in delight, seeing our outfits. He was wearing a
wedding gown and it looked wonderful with his shoulder
length blond hair and long beard. "I've got something
for you." He pulled out a large package, loosely wrapped
in old tinfoil. When he opened it, inside there was more
than five-pounds of magic mushrooms. "Help yourselves,
gentlemen. We're going to have fun tonight."

Betty threw us out of her bar at two. Still in
our tutus and wet with sweat from the dance floor,
we stumbled into the back of Lee's van and slept until
morning. While changing my clothes, I found four pieces
of paper with names and phone numbers tucked into the
top of my tutu.

Apparently we were a hit.

34

City of Tears

In 1978 the flight crews on Pacific Southwest Airline were notorious for being fun people. The stewardesses in their bright orange and yellow mini-skirts, pill-box hats and their anything goes attitude had fun playing with their passengers and the passengers loved it. To keep costs low, the airline had no ticket counters; you simply went to the gate and got on the plane. Before takeoff, flight attendants came down the aisle taking credit cards or cash for the $16 one-way fare to Los Angeles.

When Mr. Magoo said, "It's the only way to fly," he never imagined a flight crew like the one my two friends would put together. Michael and Steve lived in a flat upstairs above Toad Hall. Not only had they survived the fires, they endured endless nightly hammering that began at two in the morning, and continued until 6 a.m. How they managed to sleep remains a mystery, but they did, and spent their nights dreaming up ways to make people laugh.

"Will you ever be finished with the bar?" Steve said on the sidewalk in front of Toad Hall. His arms were loaded with packages from a fabric store.

"Sorry, we're working as fast as we can. What are you up to now?"

"You know us, always something in the works to pay the rent. We've got a gig at a comedy club in L.A. and are flying down on Sunday, so you can make as much noise as you want."

"Funny, I'll be in L.A. too. I promised some friends in the Valley I'd help them tear out their kitchen."

Steve looked me up and down. "Why don't the three of us fly down together?"

"Sure, why not?"

"What size shoes do you wear?"

"Twelve in work boots, why?"

On Sunday they buzzed me in and stood waiting at the top of the stairs in perfect PSA stewardess uniforms. "What do you think? We added the fish net stockings and garter belts," Steve said, spinning around. "We've got a little something for you too." He handed me a dark suit, white shirt, black tie and a pair of black shoes. On the coat was a set of pilot's wings.

"Where'd you get this stuff?"

"We made ours and borrowed yours. Wait, I almost forgot the most important parts." He put a pair of dark sunglass on my face and handed me a captain's hat and a white cane with a red tip. "There, now you're complete." I laughed out loud, unbuckling my belt and dropping my pants. "We'll probably make the nightly news in San Francisco and L.A."

⁓

Tourists with cameras surrounded us as soon as we got out of the cab at the airport. With a stewardess on each arm, I tapped my cane as they guided me through the terminal. Steve whispered into my ear, and I wandered off and walked into a wall before being rescued to applause. A news crew waiting for the arrival of a foreign dignitary heard the noise and turned their camera our way. Steve and Michael gave a brief interview, including a plug for their appearance in Los Angeles, and when the reporter asked me for a comment, he was told "He's deaf too." The crowd grew so large that airport security arrived, but instead of harassing us, ran interference so we could get to the plane. I don't know how they knew it, but the entire crew, including the captain was waiting at the jet-way to greet us. The real stewardesses moved people out of the first row, and when we entered the cabin everyone laughed and applauded.

They gave Steve the microphone and in his best, breathless Marilyn Monroe voice, he did his impression of how to use the seat belts, oxygen masks, and pointed out the emergency exits. He did such a good job they didn't bother doing an official version. When we landed in Los Angeles, the captain came out of the cockpit and asked if he could borrow my white cane and sunglasses so he could walk off the plane and into the terminal with Steve on one arm and Michael on the other. I was momentarily demoted to copilot and followed behind. Some management from PSA asked if we would pose for a picture with them for their employee magazine. It was a time when flying was fun and carefree - before terrorism and all the security that came with it.

~

On Monday morning as I stood alone in a pile of plaster, broken kitchen cabinets and tangled wires, I sensed something wasn't right in the universe. There was a heavy feeling in my chest so I stopped working, fearing it might be something serious. Instead of hauling debris out to the dumpster, I sat down in front of the television, and as I did, the screen filled with a breaking news announcement and a picture that almost made my heart stop. A terrified looking Diane Feinstein stood at a microphone in San Francisco's City Hall:

> *"Today San Francisco has experienced a double tragedy of immense proportions. As President of the Board of Supervisors, it is my duty to inform you that both Mayor*

*Moscone and Supervisor Harvey Milk have
been shot and killed, ... and the suspect is
Supervisor Dan White."*

"This can't be happening," I shouted at the
television. My first thoughts were of Scott. *Where is he?
How can I reach him?* I began to panic. My next thought
was the irrational fear that Harvey would be angry with me
for not starting a project he had been hounding me to do.
I didn't touch the volume on the TV - my mind turned it
off. Then a picture of two men wheeling a stretcher with a
covered body strapped to it filled the screen. They stopped
in front of an open elevator and tipped the stretcher on
end to fit it in, as I had done myself many times. I could
tell by the weight, height and scruffy black dress shoes, it
was Harvey, and sobbed
uncontrollably. "I need to
get home."

Thirty-five years
later, I still cannot
remember what happened
during the rest of that day.
But I can still feel the
cold, hopelessness, anger,

City Hall Murders

**MOSCONE, MILK SLAIN
--DAN WHITE IS HELD**

San Francisco Chronicle

Mayor
Was Hit
4 Times

dread, sorrow, and numbness. If I close my eyes, clips from
the lost movies begin to play. They are in color with sounds
and smells, but parts of them are missing and some don't
play at all. I've buried those memories deep in that special
place I've used since my ambulance days.

Guilt: Harvey asked me to help with his campaigns,

but I wasn't political... I didn't have time... I was in survival mode, trying to find enough work to stay alive. He and Scott were good friends and recommended me to anyone who needed a carpenter. They gave me credibility when I had none. *Did I say thank you enough? Why didn't I help him like he helped me?*

There are no memories of the flight back to the city, not even going to the airport. One moment I was standing in a kitchen in Van Nuys, and the next, I was on the sidewalk, talking to Ray Herth in front of his real estate office on Castro Street. Another clip from the movie starts to play: I'm hugging him, asking if he knew where Scott was, but there's no audio so I can't hear what he's telling me.

And another: I am standing for a long time with my back against a wall, watching a small crowd of people on Castro Street getting larger and larger.

And another: People are standing alone in silence or talking quietly in small groups. Everyone is coming here because they know this is the place where the rest of their family will be tonight.

Harvey sensed someone would kill him. He even made a tape a year before Dan White did it, and the sound of his quiet, fatalistic voice on the recording rings in my ears:

> *"If a bullet should enter my brain,*
> *let that bullet destroy every closet door."*

A crowd of thirty or forty-thousand people carried candles and marched that night. I was among them. I remember the group was large when we left the Castro and at every intersection more people joined - gay people, straight people, old men and women carrying candles, weeping. At City Hall there were speeches, but the memory of what was said isn't there. Joan Baez sang "Amazing Grace" without any accompaniment. The rawness of her solo voice had a tone in it that begged people to hope and not despair, but there was no hope in the huge crowd that night. I suppose I could watch the videotape of it and put more details in here, but I can't do that yet. My own personal color movie plays in my head and that is all I can bear.

On Wednesday I stood in line at City Hall thinking; *It happened on a Monday. It was the 27th of November. It's 1978. He killed our mayor, shoulder, chest, and two in the head. He shot Harvey five times, twice in the head, hollow tip bullets. The police laughed when they heard the news.* An old woman bundled up in a white winter coat was sobbing behind me and being consoled by her daughter. Inside City Hall we walked past the caskets. That same night there was a memorial for Harvey at the Opera House. I was there in a dress circle seat, but that movie won't play yet. Maybe it never will.

⁓

On Monday, May 21, 1979, the eve of Harvey's 48th birthday, a jury in San Francisco announced their outrageous verdict of voluntary manslaughter for the premeditated murders of our Mayor, George Moscone and supervisor Harvey Milk. Dan White was sentenced to seven years and eight months in prison.

We were all astounded. Everyone who had struggled to control their outrage for six months, lost it and poured into the streets around the Castro. A chant of "*He got away with murder*" started, and as more people heard the news, the crowds grew larger and angrier. Harvey's friend Cleve Jones grabbed a megaphone and stood on Castro yelling "*Out of the bars and into the streets.*" A community of passive people the police felt certain would never be a problem, suddenly became a bloodthirsty angry mob ready to fight back with everything they had. Business owners up and down Castro Street came out and stood in front of their stores, not to protect them, but to support and join the outrage.

Ray Herth grabbed me by the arm. "I know you, Lou. Don't do anything stupid."

By the time the crowd reached the Civic Center it numbered over five thousand. Some members of the gay community, appealing for calm, stood waiting on the steps of City Hall, but police started beating them with clubs thinking they were part of the mob, and all hell broke loose. The beautiful doors into the building had their gold decorations torn off, and windows were smashed. More police arrived and began throwing tear gas into the crowd. The crowd responded by burning their cars, and soon a long line of police cruisers were in flames.

These same big macho cops had laughed and cheered inside the Hall of Justice on the day their buddy Dan White slaughtered the Mayor and Harvey with nine hollow point police bullets. Now they cowardly covered their badge numbers with tape and marched through the Castro, like the Gestapo, beating the shit out of people in retribution for making them look weak when confronted by an angry gay mob.

By the end of May in 1979 many in the gay community had retreated to lick their wounds and give themselves time to heal. I had become disillusioned with San Francisco but wasn't ready to resign myself to a life of solitude on a creek in Annapolis. I had some thinking to do.

Civil rights for gay San Franciscans weren't handed to them all at one time in a nice box with a pretty bow by the kind and gentle citizens of the city. In fact, quite the opposite was true. There were plenty of bigots in San Francisco at the turn of the century and into the 1970's who hated gay people and felt threatened by them. The popular political position, reinforced by an eager, corrupt police force, was to harass and entrap. They relished making life unbearable for homosexuals.

So how and why did San Francisco become so gay, open and accepting? It happened because a group of gay men and women who lived there finally had enough and began to fight back. And when they did, they started to win respect. And when that happened, more gay people came. The very thing San Francisco's public officials and police tried to get rid of grew into a presence they could no longer control with strong arm tactics. Gay people became a powerful voting base willing to fight for their right to live their lives openly.

The White Night Riot on May 21st, 1979 was the watershed moment when every gay man and woman in San Francisco said "Enough!" And we meant it not only for ourselves, but for gay men and women everywhere. From that night forward we would no longer allow ourselves to be threatened, beat-up or murdered by ignorant bigots no matter how powerful or connected they were. Whether with words or willpower and fists, we made it known that we would fight for our rights of inclusion in every phrase of the Constitution and Bill of Rights.

PART THREE

**Above the blue
and windy sea**

35

Redwoods
Make You Crazy

A tree known as the "Monarch of the Forest" stood more than 367 feet high and was 45 feet in circumference. At more than 3,300 years, it was the oldest tree in the area. Scientists said the night Christ was born, it was 17 feet in diameter.

As far as archeologists can trace, the Pomo people who still inhabit the Russian River valley in Sonoma County, California date back to 7,000 B.C. When walking along creeks in this area, mill-stones and hand-stones they used to grind acorns and seeds can still be found on huge rocks. After 1812 and the arrival of Russian fur traders who came down the California coast from what is now Alaska, life changed for the indigenous people. In a scenario repeated many times before in the Americas; Russians, Spanish missionaries and colonists arrived and brought with them diseases for which the Pomo people had no resistance, and soon only a fraction of them remained.

In 1849 the Federal Government homsteaded out the Russian River area; and it was settled by disillusioned forty-niners who had given up in the gold fields. It wasn't long before the last surviving Pomo natives were herded onto reservations. But the tribal shamans that the Pomo people used to heal their sicknesses had a secret they never shared with their captors. They knew that living in the shade and damp under redwood trees made people crazy. Perhaps this can explain a lot of the behavior and attitudes of early settlers and residents to this day.

San Francisco was always building and rebuilding after fires, getting larger each time, and the hunger for lumber was insatiable. Although the anything-goes attitude of the city was alive and well, San Francisco was becoming gentrified. Smart men built a narrow-gage railroad to move logs and lumber, and soon the huge forests of majestic redwood trees in Sonoma County began to fall and new mansions for the Lumber Barons were built on Nob Hill.

By the 1870's the men wielding axes and big hand saws had clear-cut vast areas of trees thousands of years old. The logging community that had become known as "Stumptown" changed its name when George Guerne, a young Swiss immigrant arrived. Seeing the area was almost logged-out, he bought land and built Guernewood Park, the first subdivision. As more cleared land became available, George's name would be used again, and the town of Guerneville appeared on the map. Francis Korbel and his brothers bought logging property near Guerneville and in 1882 began to make wine from their new vineyards.

As the trees disappeared, the narrow-gage railroad began to carry a different cargo - hundreds of summer refugees. Although San Francisco's climate was cool most

MONTESANO R. R. STATION, NEAR GUERNEVILLE, CAL.

of the time, late summer and early fall heat waves were intolerable before electricity. Rest and relaxation under the towering redwoods was a perk of wealth. Businessmen packed up their families and sent them off on ferries across the Bay where they took trains to Santa Rosa, then the Russian River. On weekends they joined their wives and children in cottages they'd built in the shady, cool canyons.

By the turn of the century, the river was a *happening place*. In the 1930's and 40's, Tommy Dorsey, Glenn Miller, Kay Kaiser and other big bands played under the stars and in huge wooden casinos, to packed audiences. But by the 1950's, most of the glitter had begun to fade, and by 1960 the area had almost become a ghost town. "*The River*" became a favorite hangout for

the biker crowd. They made themselves feel right at home
in the mold, mildew and rot, and scared away most of the
tourists. A few stubborn family resorts managed to hang
on and earned enough to eke out meager livings, but it
wasn't easy. By the mid-1970's things were ripe for change.

~

It was exceptionally warm for May when I left the
house that morning. Everyone was still numb and reeling
from the Dan White verdict, not to mention the riots and
police brutality in the Castro that followed. Halfway to the
door I went back and put my checkbook in my pocket. I
had no idea where I was going. Before I knew it, my truck
was driving north across the Golden Gate Bridge. I saw the
Sausalito exit and felt no urge to turn off, realizing I had
decided to go shopping for someplace to live. Apparently
my mind had decided it was best not to tell me this earlier.
Memories of Halloween with Lee at The Rusty Nail
gave me a taste of what life might be like on the Russian
River. It was definitely slower than the city, but not as
remote or lonely as the cabin in Annapolis. It felt like
a place where I might regroup and find a way to digest
what had just happened - and still be around gay people.
I drove through downtown Guerneville without stopping.
Something was pulling me so I let it guide the way. The
tiny Guernewood Park post office caught my eye, so I
pulled off the road and parked under an old, faded sign
that barely read: "Ginger's Rancho Resort." But Ginger's
was nowhere to be seen. I took a walk following a trail
through the brush down toward the river. And then,
tucked in the shade under large redwood trees and among

huge ferns, I stumbled onto it. The cabins were gone. All
that was left was a dilapidated old building with a rotten
wood porch and a roof covered in a couple feet of branches
and leaves. *This must have been the Rancho part*, I
thought to myself. Cut-out plywood letters *"B A R"* hung
from the eves; the letter "A" sseemed to be struggling to
stay attached. It looked haunted, but then I noticed lights
inside and the open front door.

Ginger stood behind her bar like she was expecting
me, at least I thought it was Ginger because her hair
was orange. "Do you know where I can find a real estate
office?" I asked.

"Why there's one right next to the post office,
darlin', Don and Bob should be in there. They'll take good
care of you." Her ratted hair bobbed around as she washed
glasses. There were enough suds in the sink for a bubble
bath. "Want a beer?" She held up a cold Heinekens.

"Not really, but thanks." I felt guilty getting
information but not buying anything. She looked lonely,
like she wanted me to stay.

"They're nice boys, real honest." She popped the
cap off the beer she just offered me and took a long swig.
"Welcome to the river. I hope you find a place," she said,
wiping her mouth on her sleeve.

I had parked less than thirty feet from the office
but never noticed it. Not having any real estate business
at the moment, the oddly-matched couple who looked
like Oliver Hardy and Frodo, busied themselves playing
Monopoly. "Are you guys Don and Bob?"

"That'd be us." The bigger one got up from his chair

bumping the table and knocking his hotel off Park Place. I couldn't stop wondering what it looked like when they had sex and chuckled as I shook their hands. "I'm looking for something cute and small that needs work, but has good bones," I said, not really having thought about what I wanted before opening my mouth.

"Oh, you mean cheap." The short one began thumbing through index cards on his desk. "Do you care if it floods?"

"Well yes, of course."

"Just asking; that's where most of the real cheap stuff is, but I do have something I think you'll like, and it's right around the corner."

"Will it flood?"

"Anything can flood if we have one of those hundred-year storms, but it's higher than most so it shouldn't get water inside with our regular winter rains."

The three of us took a five-minute walk to a cute, two-car, garage-sized cottage half a block away on Riverside Drive. It had a yard big enough to park my truck and was across the street from houses on the river. "No one's lived in it for awhile so you'll need to clean it up." Walking around the house I noticed the roof looked new and was glad to see no problems. When the agent unlocked the front door, the knotty pine living room with a vaulted ceiling and a red-brick fireplace right out of the 1930's, instantaly told me *this is it, you're home!* I swallowed. *Don't look too eager*, I reminded myself, cancelling my urge to say "*SOLD*", and began snooping around. The little kitchen and dinette looked out onto the front yard. Off the living room there was a bathroom with a tiled stall shower and a bedroom with a large closet and enough room for a queen-sized bed.

"Because it's under big redwoods it'll be nice and cool in the summertime."

There's nothing here a little work can't fix. "What are they asking for this?" I said trying to appear aloof.

"Thirty thousand, but they'll carry a note for fifteen years at six percent with seven thousand down."

"Sold!" I spit out, losing control and throwing aloofness to the wind. And in less than fifteen minutes I became a homeowner on the Russian River in Guerneville, California. I signed the contract and wrote the check for the down payment without a second thought. Since there was no bank financing, I was given the keys that weekend.

~

In 1905, a year before the big earthquake in San Francisco, the Murphy family opened the largest vacation operation along the Russian River. Murphy's Ranch Resort sat on the edge of downtown Guerneville. In 1977, after more than seventy-five years, the family decided it was time to sell. Peter Pender, a world-class bridge player, and wealthy gay man had heard rumors the Russian River was about to be the next gay Mecca, so he purchased Murphy's. He spent a chunk of his fortune transforming the 15 acres of dilapidated dance halls, restaurants, pool and cabins into what he chose to call "Fife's." Peter knew how to do things, sparing no expense to do them right and to keep them that way. His new resort was incredibly successful with the gay community and was packed from the moment it opened. Fife's became a key part of an opening salvo that started a new "gold rush." As in San Francisco a few years earlier, tired houses, Main Street businesses, and struggling family resorts gradually began to sell. Enthusiastic gay men and women who saw the potential were ready to transform the town with the same talents they had used to bring the Castro back to life, and they had the money to make it happen.

There was a not-so-subtle undercurrent of resentment by the old timers. Soon it seemed every other building in town was a real estate office, and the established realtors were angry about the new competition. The ones who ultimately survived and prospered learned to keep their opinions of what was happening to their town to themselves.

Actor Fred MacMurray owned a ranch along the Russian River where he spent time raising prize Angus cattle when he wasn't busy making movies. By 1976 homophobic Fred had his fill of the emerging gay scene and began harassing people whenever they passed near his property while canoeing or while they sunbathed on the banks along the river. In 1996 he finally sold his ranch to Gallo brothers who soon planted vineyards.

It was dusk and getting difficult to see when I walked through Fife's gates looking for the bar. In the distance I saw a hunchbacked old man carrying a long pole with a flame on the end of it. Warren was lighting torches along the paths as he had done every night since childhood for the Murphy family. He worked his way toward me and when he was close enough I asked for directions. It was a warm evening but Warren was bundled in a shirt, sweater and jacket. Not interested in starting a conversation, he grunted and pointed his lighted stick in the direction I needed to go. I had no idea then that this old man and I would become the best of friends. He was a great storyteller, and his tales about growing up on the river could have filled volumes.

The bar was empty except for the bartender and one person sitting at the far end. I took a stool next to him and introduced myself, not realizing I was talking to the owner. For more than an hour, Peter Pender told his version of what was happening on the Russian River and painted a picture of the place I was going to call home. His voice never changed, and I could feel his optimism as he encouraged me to become a part of the gay business community. "Why don't you come back tomorrow morning? We'll have breakfast, then I'll take you around and introduce you to the players in town." His generous invitation surprised me.

Our tour of river society started with breakfast at Pat's, a downtown institution. When we sat down the owners, Rich and Donna Hines, came over to greet us and Peter made the introductions. It was obvious they wanted to know anyone he did. He shocked me by telling them I was thinking of opening a business in town. The next stop was the only building in Guerneville with any architectural value, a tiny, powder-blue bank built in the 1930's with Palladium windows and classic ornamentation. As we walked through the door, two people greeted us. Erv Hanson was the president of Centennial Saving and

Loan Association, although you'd never suspect it. He was dressed like a Texan ready to go to the rodeo in his open-collar western shirt, big gold beltbuckle and snakeskin cowboy boots. Beverly Haines, his second in command, exuded enough confidence and no-nonsense banker image for the both of them and we were greeted like VIPs. "Any friend of Peter's is a friend of ours," Erv said, shaking my hand too hard. In seconds they insisted on first names only.

For the rest of the morning we made the rounds and met every business owner in town. I felt like visiting royalty, and the importance of Peter making the introductions was priceless. On the way back to Fife's we passed a tiny building that looked like an abandoned railroad station. I couldn't resist looking into the window to see what was inside. It was being used as an office by an alarm company. "See, this is what I mean. There are opportunities all over the place," Peter said peering into the window with me.

"I'd like to know more about this."

"I know who owns it. If you want, I can give him a call and see if he wants to rent or sell it."

Peter Pender's Fife's Resort was clearly his toy and he treated it that way. Under his ownership, it grew and improved with his every whim. He was having fun and really didn't care about profitability. It gave the town an air of quality and success that it badly needed.

As word spread about what was happening seventy miles to the north, people began to move from San Francisco to the River. Randy Shilts discovered he could continue to write and live outside the city. Leonard Matlovich, tired of being the poster boy for the gay movement, put the cover of Time Magazine behind him and opted for a lower profile life, opening Stumptown Annie's, Guerneville's first pizza parlor. The next spring, my artist friend David arrived to start looking for work as a bartender.

~

Kathy Korbel stood behind the bar at The Rusty Nail. She could tell I couldn't see. "Over here," she called, and I followed her voice to a barstool. I was on my way back with a truck full of lumber and building supplies and stopped for a quick beer. When my pupils dilated enough to see in the darkness, I noticed Dave Peterson and Ron sitting across the bar. "What are you two doing here? Aren't you supposed to be on the ship?" They came over and joined me. "Moe's having a pig roast. Didn't you get an invitation?" Dave pulled a piece of paper out of his pocket and handed it to me.

"I didn't know Moe had a place here. I just moved to the river and haven't had time to tell anyone yet. My invitation is probably sitting in San Francisco."

"Everyone you met at Gordon and Jack's party on Elizabeth Street is going to be there." They finished their beer and got up to leave. Dave pulled on my arm. "Come on... Follow us. It's just down the road a couple miles toward Guerneville."

"Now?"

"The party started an hour ago."

The fields along the driveway were full of pickup trucks, motorcycles, cars and campers. Moe's house was a modest but elegant Craftsman bungalow with a huge barn and enough acreage to farm. When his cute Italian boyfriend Danny wasn't working as a DJ spinning records, Moe kept him busy on a tractor mowing lawns and gardening.

On the hilltop above Moe's house was a white colonial mansion that had become a local landmark. Brad and his lover Ron were Texas boys. And like their state, where everything is big, their home above the Russian River was no exception. Almost a full-scale version of Tara from "Gone with the Wind," their house was complete in every detail from the huge columns out front to the big winding stairway inside. By contrast, tucked around the corner and behind Moe's place, another Ron from San Francisco and his friend Lynn shared a mobile home. Friends but not lovers, the two were always the life of the party.

David shoved a beer in my hand and Moe hugged me. "Dave just told me you moved up here."

"I thought I needed a break from the city, but by the look of things, I think the whole city is here."

"The pig has been in the pit for three hours. We should eat by nine or so," Mo said, grabbing a basket out of Danny's hands. "Here take one of these." He shoved a hit of acid in my mouth, then David's and Ron's. "Don't fall into the pit with the pig," he warned, laughing and walking away.

Inside the barn, fresh straw covered the dirt floor
and strings of red and blue lights were draped from
side to side. At one end Danny had set up his expensive
turntables, amplifiers and huge speakers on a table. Stacks
of albums surrounded him and he was busy doing his
favorite thing - playing music. At the other end, just inside
the door, a long table with plates and silverware awaited
the arrival of the pig.

After dark, people moved inside. Drunk and stoned,
no one seemed interested in eating, and soon everyone
was dancing in the red and blue glow. Danny played
with two strobe lights, giving the barn and everyone in it
the appearance of being in an old black and white silent
movie.

I heard someone say "It's not done yet," referring
to the pig. It was after eleven and people began to sit in
the straw and shirts came off on the dance floor. As if in
a dream, I was being shoved, along with another person,
into the back of a Datsun 240Z, and was almost crushed
when the hatchback slammed shut. I think I remember a
ride back to The Rusty Nail. A bartender kept asking if I
wanted anything to drink. Too stoned to answer, I listened
to what was going on, hearing it like the sound was
coming through a tin-can walkie-talkie. I don't know how
long we were there, or if we really were there at all.

No one announced it, but sometime around two
thirty the pig appeared in the middle of the big table.
People began to circle it in silence, and eventually someone
had the courage to reach over and pull a piece off. Like a
scene out of "Lord of the Flies", everyone began pulling

and eating with bare hands. The stack of dinner plates, silverware and napkins sat unused. Sometime around four or five the music stopped and Danny disappeared. Moe hadn't been seen for hours. People began to break into smaller groups and disappear, but no cars or trucks were leaving.

Dave pulled me into the house to look for a place to lie down. There were people sleeping everywhere, even in the bathtub and shower. It was interesting to note there was no sex going on, just fully clothed bodies of very large men scattered everywhere. Moe and Dan were in their king-sized bed but so were four other people and two dogs. All eight of them were snoring. We found a closet with no one in it and curled up on the floor. It was cold, and Dave's body heat wasn't enough so I started hunting for a blanket. Stopping to use the bathroom, I stepped over a person on the floor with his arms wrapped around the toilet bowl. There was a full laundry hamper in the corner so I took it with me, dumped its contents on top of us, snuggled up to Dave and went to sleep.

Roosters crowed but no one heard them. The sun came up, but no one stirred. My fingers were stuck together with pig fat. There was a boot next to my hand and I tried to focus on the grease-covered Levis above it. Dave was staring down at me holding two cups of coffee. "Good morning, bright eyes," he said handing me a cup. "Rise and shine. We're the only two living creatures in the house." I followed him outside onto the porch, then took a leak against a redwood tree, holding onto it for balance. "I need a shower. Shit, what a party."

By noon everyone was wandering around like zombies. A long line waited for showers, and people used whatever soap or detergent they could find to degrease themselves.

Inside the barn two cats were busy tearing at the lonely fly-covered carcass sitting on the table, and a Banty hen sat brooding on a newly-laid egg on Danny's expensive DJ setup. All of his albums were coated in a half-inch thick mixture of congealed fat, straw and dirt. Thankfully, he was still asleep with Moe and the two dogs when we left.

Cars and trucks snaked down the road heading back toward San Francisco, but I turned the other way toward my new home in Guerneville.

Everyone thought they probably had had a wonderful time.

36

Hexagon Whores

Just off the beaten path near Guerneville, along the edge of a tiny lake in a 2,700 acre stand of old redwoods, there is a forty-foot tall concrete statue of an owl. The land and the bird are owned by an all-male, invitation-only, private membership club started in 1872 by Henry Edwards, a stage actor from New York City. Each summer for two weeks, it is home to artists, musicians and some of the most powerful men in the world. Membership has included every Republican - and some Democratic - U.S. President since 1923. Cabinet officials, CEOs of some of the largest corporations and financial institutions in the world, including the Federal Reserve, come here to meet and play.

Perhaps President Richard Nixon, a member since 1953, best described the Bohemian Grove during one of his rants on the Watergate tapes:

*"The Bohemian Grove, that I attend from
time to time – the Easterners and the
others come there – but it is the most faggy
goddamn thing you could ever imagine, that
San Francisco crowd that goes in there; it's
just terrible! I mean I won't shake hands with
anybody from San Francisco."*

The club motto - *"Weaving Spiders Come Not
Here"* is set in stone in the club's San Francisco building
at Taylor and Post Streets. It implies that members are
to leave all their business deals outside. But the towering
grove of ancient trees has been witness to conversations
that have changed the course of world history, including
one meeting for the Manhattan Project in September 1942
that led to the atom bomb and the end of the Second
World War.

~

At the stoplight in Guerneville a right turn will put
you on Armstrong Woods Road, a flat, straight patch of
blacktop, rare for these parts where roads tend to snake
and bend alongside rivers and through mountains. At the
end is the entrance into Armstrong Woods State Park and
a beautiful stand of very old redwood trees.

Just a few feet from the park entrance is a site that
once held a significant piece of Russian River history.
Inspired by the Bauhaus movement and Frank Lloyd
Wright's Taliesin, Gordon Herr and his wife Jane created
Pond Farm in 1939 on a ranch they purchased above
Armstrong Woods State Reserve. Gordon called his idea

"*..a sustainable sanctuary for artists away from a world gone amuck.*" In 1948 he expanded on his dream using design concepts many people felt were pure futurism, and built The Hexagon House on property next to the park entrance. It was used as a meeting place, school and gallery to showcase the Pond Farm artists' work. Six huge Douglass fir poles that were cut nearby were used to make the interior core of the building. They were pulled into position using a winch mounted on an old truck. Redwood shake shingles were cut by hand and the building was finished with fieldstone floors. When the Pond Farm workshops fell apart in 1953, most of the resident artists left.

By the 1960's the beautiful old hexagon building had gone through several owners, including a brief stint as a Chinese restaurant. Eventually two gay men, Rex and his partner Perry, purchased it and turned it back into an art gallery and restaurant. They were excellent chefs, and soon their success created a need for more accommodations so they added a separate motel building near the cabins.

For years, scores of multi-million dollar private jets have converged on the tarmac at Sonoma County's tiny airport. Long lines of stretch limousines with black windows containing Presidents, foreign leaders and Hollywood's "A" list snaked as quietly as they could through Guerneville for the kickoff of "Grove Week". Because of its hidden location and excellent food, the Bohemians took over the Hexagon House whenever they were in town. It was the perfect place for the rich and famous to escape their tents and rustic living and sneak back into civilization for a few hours each night. Just off the large hexagon dining room, Betty Hutton could sometimes be found entertaining her friends at a baby grand piano in the tiny bar with a big stone fireplace.

Every year before the Bohemians got to town, all the rooms were reserved by one of Hollywood's oldest comedians and filled with the most beautiful hookers he could find for his famous friends.

~

In 1975 Carl Bruno and Gene Arnez, sensing Guerneville was about to become the west coast version of Fire Island and Provincetown, moved to the river and bought the Hexagon House. They added a huge room to the main building that became a disco and cabaret, hosting entertainers like Wayland Flowers and his foul-mouthed puppet, Madam, singer Sharon McKnight and gay drag comedian Charles Pierce. On summer weekends, much to the chagrin of the neighbors, as many as five-thousand people crowded the property, parking their cars in long lines along Armstrong Woods Road that stretched two miles back toward town.

Gene and Carl wanted to keep a first-class dining experience, but felt they needed new blood. In 1977 they hired chefs Bill Walls and his partner Rick

Cook to run the restaurant. The Hexagon House became The Woods, and with the name change, the Bohemians relented to the gay invastion and retreated to their tents at The Grove.

~

The last of Hollywood's silent film stars had almost untraceable credentials, and Maria de Cordova was no exception. She was in her nineties and weighed no more than a delicate caged bird. During her career she had married well, into a cosmetic fortune. Her doting husband, a contemporary of Max Factor and renowned Hollywood makeup artist, lived to make his wife look beautiful. Transplanted from Los Angeles, widowed Maria now lived with her nephew Gene and his lover Carl in their new Russian River restaurant and resort. Her life consisted of rising late to begin getting ready for an eight o'clock dinner. Before allowing herself to be seen by anyone but her nephew, she underwent a makeup ritual that began each day at three in the afternoon and involved burning a wine cork and using it for eye shadow. Long pieces of surgical tape pulled winkles from her face, neck and eyes. The tapes were attached behind her ears where she hid them under her wig. The technique produced a look of being permanently surprised, and while the effect was somewhat youthful looking, it stretched her skin so tight she couldn't smile or blink. Maria made a precarious trip down the wooden steps from her upstairs room and held court nightly in the towering Hexagon House dining room. She always sat alone; the loud tapping of a spoon against her wine glass was a signal to the waiters that it was almost empty. She spoke to no one, but if you passed her table you could imagine her saying "I'm ready for my close up, Mr. DeMille."

On Thanksgiving Day in 1979, I was a new face in town and found myself having dinner at the Hexagon House with my two new boyfriends. I don't remember how this happened, but I do know that everyone seemed to be getting along and no one was jealous or upset. While we ate, a handsome man in a chef's uniform with a beautiful smile, naturally curly auburn hair and nice moustache periodically appeared in the dining room to check a pot of soup at the waiters' station. He kept appearing and disappearing, each time looking longer in our direction. I wasn't sure who was being watched, but knew it was someone in our group. Finally he came to our table and asked if we were enjoying our food. We locked eyes for a moment, long enough for my two friends to notice. Later that night Bill and I met again at The Rusty Nail and I found out more about how "checking the soup" had become a familiar cruising routine for both him and his partner Rick.

"Are you in a relationship?"

"Not really. We've been together for thirteen years, but Rick's gone his way and I've gone mine. We still live together but that's about it."

Been there, done that, I thought to myself, still stinging from that night in Saugatuck. "I need to go."

For the next month Bill and I continued to bump into each other in the bars and although I fought it, we began to spend time together. I started to fall in love with him but knew how that could end. "Look, this isn't going to work," I told him one night in the bar. "You're still in a relationship and I don't want to get in the middle. We need to stop this." Without giving him time to answer, I headed home upset, but knowing I was doing the right thing.

Someone was knocking on the door and when I opened it, Bill was standing there. "Go home. We can't do this anymore."

"Let me come in."

"Go home. You have a lover."

"Please let me come in."

"No."

"I have to pee. Let me use the bathroom and I'll leave."

I opened the door.

He never left.

~

Over the next year we remodeled the little cottage on Riverside Drive, adding two new bedrooms. Bev Haines at Centennial Savings and Loan approved the loan without even asking for an application. Mortgage rates were 19%, signaling tough times ahead for the river. The little railroad depot on Main Street near the entrance to Fife's became Guerneville Station, an imitation of the Castro's "All American Boy." We sold Levis, flannel shirts, Acme work boots, and tons of printed T-shirts with sayings like "Mouth of the River" and "This is No Ordinary Housewife You're Dealing With." Beverly wanted to invest, but we managed to do it without her money.

Peter Pender encouraged us to open the town's first laundromat. We found the perfect location, but the old woman who owned the building demanded astronomical rent because we were gay. When I went to complain to my friend Bev, she insisted on negotiating the lease, but only if she could give us the money and be our partner. Around that time our friend Steve Pizzo, the editor of the Russian River News, started telling us what he thought was going on in the savings and loan industry, warning us of a pending doomsday scenario. Something had been worrying us about Beverly's no-questions-asked, always-open checkbook, so we decided to give ourselves some time to think about the laundromat idea.

Straight business owners welcomed new gay merchants with open arms - until they became more successful. Gay people coming to the river wanted the best accommodations they could find, shunning many straight resorts because they hadn't been upgraded in years, and because they were made to feel unwelcome. As the number of gays arriving exceeded the number of straight families with children, owners of family resorts became even more upset.

Tiny Guerneville Station continued on a successful path with both straight and gay customers, but we put everything back into the business. We also discovered we weren't cut out for the confinement of standing behind a cash register seven days a week. At Peter's urging I became involved in local politics, and later that year, not realizing the significance of it, became the first openly gay president of a Chamber of Commerce in the United

States. As prestigious as the title sounded, I was hated by most straight business owners because I was gay, and worse still I was called a turncoat by my gay brothers and sisters because they felt I should be doing more to promote their gay businesses.

No one complained so long as the sun was shining

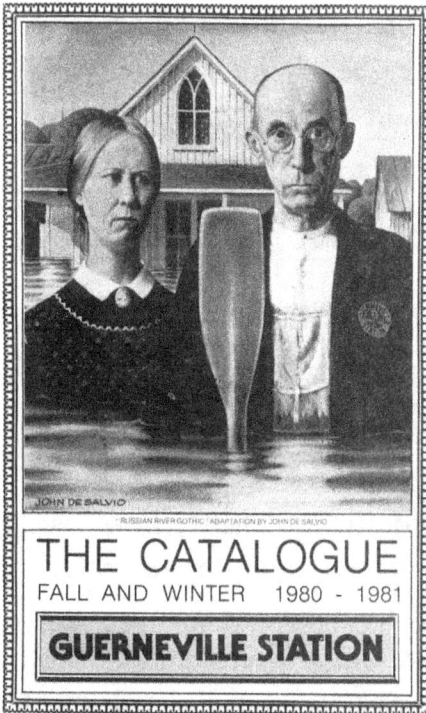

JOHN DE SALVIO

RUSSIAN RIVER GOTHIC "ADAPTATION BY JOHN DE SALVIO

THE CATALOGUE
FALL AND WINTER   1980 - 1981

GUERNEVILLE STATION

and the crowds were coming. But the Russian River was a resort area with a definite season, and when summer ended, so did everyone's income. The Chamber did what it could to stimulate winter business, but once Halloween, Thanksgiving, Christmas and New Years were over, you could roll a bowling ball down Main Street and not hit anyone until spring. If you hadn't put enough of the summer profits away, winter could be a horribly depressing time.

During the cold, wet, dead month of February, to brighten the spirits of the locals and business owners, the Chamber sponsored the first annual "Hard Times Ball". It was supposed to be a fun evening of dressing up in hobo costumes, dancing and eating one-cent Mulligan Stew. Bill worked for three days making the food, but the night of the event we discovered that I was the only thing about to be stewed. "Why aren't you at the meeting?" Gladys, a local realtor, asked.

"What meeting?"

"The one that's going on at the Chamber office."

"There's no meeting going on."

Her husband, Monty, the manager of the local Safeway food store and past-president of the Chamber, shot an angry look at his wife. "Yes there is," Gladys continued, defying her husband's evil eye. 'It's something about you."

"What the hell's going on, Monty?"

"Randy and some of the other rednecks in town are saying you went to the County and filed secret funding requests to get advertising money to promote only gay businesses on the river. Did you?"

"Of course not. You know better than that. Why didn't any of you tell me this?" It seemed like Bill and I were the only people in the room who didn't know. We had worked ourselves into exhaustion getting ready for the party. I'd been drinking since noon and lost it. "I've been busting my ass trying to make things better for all of us. Some of the gay businesses won't even talk to me because I refused to put them first, and this is the thanks I get." People rushed to console me but I couldn't stop crying.

"They ought to put a statue of you in the middle of town," Leonard said, trying to cheer me up.

"The only statue I want is one with my pants around my ankles, bent over so all of them can kiss my ass. I'm through. They can find themselves another whipping boy." Bill and I packed up our things and left. The next day I went to the Chamber office and demanded to see proof of what they accused me of doing, but none could be produced because it didn't exist. My resignation proved not to be in vain. The last hardcore group of fanatical, gay-hating rednecks and their failing businesses were finally shoved out of power in the Chamber by people who had been their friends for decades. I felt vindicated, but retreated from local politics. For all the time and effort spent and the negative impact it had on our own business, I would have been ahead of the game if I'd just written a check for twenty-thousand dollars to the Chamber and not gotten involved.

Bev Haines continued to offer us financing tied to partnerships for anything we wanted to do, but thanks to Steve's warnings we didn't take the money.

By 1983 some of our friends were starting to get sick, first Randy Shilts, then Leonard Matlovich and then my artist friend David.

It was only a hint of what was to come.

～

Later, in 1985, two years after Bill and I left the river, Centennial Savings and Loan collapsed. Federal regulators found $165 million dollars were missing.

Beverly Haines didn't know when to stop and was found guilty of embezzling $1.6 million dollars in a check-kiting scheme she ran while authorities were in the building closing it. She got a five-year prison sentence, but only served two months of it.

After two earlier attempts at suicide, on July 30,

1987 Erv Hanson was found dead in bed, apparently of natural causes, the day before he had to begin answering to the Justice Department.

The $165 million dollars that went missing was never found, and no one spent more than a month in jail because of it.

The most architecturally significant building in Guerneville, the cute little powder-blue bank building with big Palladian windows, sat empty for years, the landscaping overgrown and the fancy white Austrian curtains inside the windows rotting.

My friend Steve Pizzo and his associates wrote a highly aclaimed book about it in 1991 called, "Inside Job - The Looting of America's Savings and Loans."

37

Changes in Attitudes

"Wind blows like hell up here during the winter storms. You guys better buy yourselves some trucker's cord, drive some steel fence posts in the ground and tie this thing down or you'll end up in Healdsburg some night." Rich Noonan unhooked his tow-truck from the small, used travel trailer he had just hauled up the side of a mountain. Before today, we had been living ordinary lives in our cottage with a big fireplace near the river. Guerneville Station was doing great. The community had adopted it as

their favorite clothing store and tourists loved our printed T-shirts, buying them eight and ten at a time. Bill was still cooking at The Woods and life was good.

Earlier that spring we had found a wonderful piece of land on McCray Ridge that separated the Russian River from the vineyards inland. We used the equity from the house to borrow the down payment. We had plans and were about to start building our dream home, but things came to a screeching halt. It was August, 1981. The recession was severe; people stopped spending and business fell off sharply. The bank kept calling to tell us we could start using the money in the construction loan they had approved, but we knew if we began to build we wouldn't have the money to pay back the loan. And that's how two men and a big mutt of a dog ended up living in a 17' travel trailer on a mountain top eighty miles north of San Francisco.

Like the cabin in Annapolis, we were definitely off the grid. There was no electricity, so we used a solar panel, a car radio and a tiny 12-volt TV for entertainment. We put in a well and used a diesel generator to pump our water. To stay connected with the outside world and each other, we used Citizen Band radios, and put one in our truck, one in the store and another in the trailer. Surprisingly, things were pretty good in spite of the limited space. Our spirits were high and we kept planning and dreaming. It's hard to believe we spent almost two years in that tiny trailer waiting for things to get better, but by 1983 we realized things weren't going to change any time soon.

I had grown up on the Great Lakes in Michigan where my dad always had a small fishing boat. After finishing high school, I was lucky enough to go on a weekend sail with friends in Bermuda, ending up as crew on my first and only ocean sail from Bermuda to Antigua in the West Indies. It was the trip of a lifetime for me. Bill had never been on a sailboat, but listened endlessly as I relived my trip. One day, while sitting in the trailer watching him cook dinner, for no reason I blurted out, "Why don't we go sailing?" Bill of course thought I meant a sailing vacation, and as he has always done since the day we met, agreed without hesitation. I could tell what he was thinking by the sound of his voice and added: "No, I mean, why don't we sell everything, buy a boat and go sailing?"

"Sailing where?" He put down the half cabbage he was slicing into coleslaw and sat down beside me.

"Hell, I don't know, but it'd be better than sitting here. I don't want to wait anymore, do you?"

"I don't know how to sail."

"We could go back to school and take some courses." With those few words, and the many conversations that followed, we started to make life-changing decisions - to walk away from stalled old dreams and start new ones.

There was a boat show in Alameda near San Francisco, so we bought our first boat shoes and spent a day in the tradeshow tents gathering resources for things we would need. At the booth for the College of Alameda School of Nautical Sciences, a part of the California university system, we signed up for classes in coastal piloting, seamanship and celestial navigation. We took two full semesters while we kept planning. Of course we looked at boats, first in Alameda and then at shows in Long Beach, Fort Lauderdale and Miami.

We realized we liked traditional-looking boats, and that helped narrow the search. The phrase "sticker shock" lived up to its name, but since we were just shopping we denied reality; but at the same time we looked at older used boats in hopes of finding something affordable. There was beautiful "Eagle", a 64' Mason ketch in Long Beach, but she too was pricey and needed lots of work. In the Bay Area we found a large ketch that had just returned from the South Pacific, but she had been used up and needed everything before it would be safe to take her out again. There was one thing about her we both loved. On the stern, directly above the transom, there was a stainless steel framework that did nothing but support a toilet seat. The thought of sitting there and letting everything fly was somehow exciting to both of us. The thought that you'd never have to worry about a plugged-up marine toilet was no doubt the reason behind the practical design. But, I DID worry about sharks.

I knew that if I was going to get Bill hooked, I would need to get him into warm water. We'd save the blustery San Francisco Bay for later. Cold and wet is no way to convince anyone to go sailing. While looking at boats in Florida, we booked a charter with a dealer in Tarpon Springs, but storms made that trip impossible. With time running out and no sign of a change in weather, we jumped on a flight to St. Thomas, found a young couple in Red Hook with a forty-foot boat and went sailing for two days in warm Caribbean waters. It worked. Bill was convinced. Happy from spending time in St. Thomas, we flew home to the cold, wet Bay Area with sunburns and continued our boat shopping and school.

In the East Bay we found a beautiful Hans Christian that had everything anyone could want in a cruising sailboat. The beautiful interiors were teak, and the entire boat emanated quality and craftsmanship. The galley had marble counter tops and the floor plan made sense for onboard living. We met the local dealer and were invited to join him for a sea trial in San Francisco Bay. Of course the winds were blowing hard and it was foggy and cold. The broker had all the canvas up and the boat heeled over dramatically. I watched as Bill took the wheel, trying to read how he felt about the conditions and was amazed that he seemed not only at ease with the angle of our sailing, but curious about every aspect of the boat's abilities. The expression on his face said he wasn't a fair weather sailor, and I smiled with pride.

The trip back to our mountain-top trailer was a quiet one. Neither of us wanted to be the first to start a conversation about the truth of what we could really afford. The new boat was fantastic and far beyond our reach financially. Even if it was affordable, by the time we got it ready to go cruising, it wouldn't be. As we undressed and climbed into bed that night our disappointment was palpable.

Sunday morning we woke up feeling better, but

still not wanting to talk about the obvious. We went into town, picked up the Sunday San Francisco Chronicle and got our usual booth at Pat's for breakfast. I handed the comic section and Sunday magazine to Bill and went to the classifieds to look at "boats for sale". There was an ad for Edgewater Yachts in Sausalito filled with tiny, black and white photos of boats they had listed. My eyes stopped in the middle of the second row and I pulled the paper closer to my face. "Look at this," I said, shoving the page across the table, covering what Bill was reading. The boat in the photo had many of the features we were looking for. "Look at the price."

Edgewater Yachts were known for selling older "*character*" boats that had seen better days. There were a few fiberglass boats in the photos, but most were made of wood. Before making a trip to see it, we had to remind ourselves that whatever we saw was going to need a lot of work, as well as a thorough survey by someone who knew old wood boats. "What do you think?" I asked, pulling the page back for another look.

"It could be junk, but I think we should call and go take a look." We finished breakfast and headed for Sausalito.

When we walked into the office an older man, who looked more like he was going to play golf than go sailing, looked up from his newspaper and shoved a set of keys attached to bright yellow float across his desk. "She's the second boat on the right." *No hard sell from this guy*, I thought.

The first thing we saw was the transom - peeling

varnish surrounded two ornate pirate-ship windows. Below the windows, the hailing port of San Francisco was missing some letters. Above the windows another plaque read "Providence." We

turned to each other and mirrored a look that was half smile and half disappointment.

The dictionary's definition of "Providence" is "*The divine foreseeing care and guidance of God and nature over the creatures of the earth.*" Not a bad name we thought. "Quite a come-down from what we've been looking at," I admitted to Bill. "Do you want to see more, or should we just leave?"

"We're here, why not check it out?" We stepped onto the boat and unlocked the door leading into the forward cabin. The boat smelled musty but was roomy. A neat little galley was to the left and a built-in refrigerator was on the right. A pair of single berths sat behind two small sofas with a folding dining table on the centerline. In the bow there was a toilet and chain locker, but no shower. We climbed back up the ladder to the pilot house to check the steering controls and lifted the floor hatch to take a look at the engine. The three-cylinder Detroit diesel looked good at first glance and the bilges had some, but not much water in them. Thinking we had seen it all and still fighting our disappointment, we stepped back onto the dock and started to walk away. Passing the stern we turned to look at the big transom windows again and realized we had missed half of the boat's interior.

We both gasped the moment the door opened into "Providence's" aft cabin. The beamy, pumpkin-seed shape of the hull created a large, dramatic space in the stern of the boat. There was a pair of berths connected by a "U" shaped sofa. A big teak skylight let in plenty of sun and made the space feel huge. Along one side, there was a small head, but again, no shower. But the real treasure of the aft cabin was the tiny stainless-steel and soapstone fireplace that was tucked into a corner. It was a pirate ship if we'd ever seen one and we smiled. "It's a cartoon," Bill said laughing out loud, "with a fireplace!"

We locked the boat up and headed back to the office to return the keys. About half-way there we stopped, turned around, walked back to the boat and just stood there. Scanning the decks and looking up the masts, I shook my head and said, "Naaa."

We started walking back to the office, stopped again, looked at each other and smiled.

"Why not?" I asked Bill.

"Why not, indeed," he said under his breath.

38

Buckets of Piss

We set about the work of saving an old boat. Over the next few weeks we moved onboard what few possessions we had kept and made "Providence" our home. Before we realized the scope of our decision, everything we owned was sitting inside and an overwhelming feeling of *what the hell have we done* swept over us. It felt like we were living inside a beautiful wood china cabinet as we bumped around the boat putting things away. For the first few days we seldom went outside except to take the long walk up the dock to use the bathroom and shower. The life-changing decisions we had made so easily were just starting to hit home.

While familiar with how to live in tight quarters from our time in the trailer, we now had to adjust to level changes and the curves of the hull surrounding us. Although tied to a dock, the boat was constantly moving. There were strange noises; the lapping of water against the side and the sound the wind made as it whistled through the rigging. But soon they became part of our subconscious and we didn't hear them unless they changed. The smell of mildew and neglect began to disappear as we cleaned and Bill began cooking meals in the galley.

Days, weeks and months slipped away in a haze of question-asking, hard manual labor, and check writing.

Our friends Mark and Mary, John and Linda, Phil and David and others stopped by to visit and occasionally stayed to help us for a few days.

After we finished work on the decks, the boat was hauled out of the water so we could work on the bottom and paint the hull. John and his wife Linda, who designed a line of women's fashions, agreed to help us make all new upholstery and cushions for the inside of the boat, as well as sailcovers, cushions and deck-awnings for the outside. As things were crossed off the list, new things were added, and after a while we began to see that "Providence" was coming back to life.

Our hands were like raw hamburger from the

chemicals we used, and fatigue was slowing us down. Not having taken a day off since starting work in the boatyard, our tempers grew short and we started to pray for rain so we'd have an excuse to rest. Living inside the boat while it was out of the water was a challenge. At night we would avoid trips to the bathroom by using a five-gallon plastic paint bucket. There were countless mornings of carrying the sloshing bucket of piss down the ladder to dump it in the men's room, and that was getting old. Finally clouds appeared and it started to rain.

The first day we stayed in our bunks catching up on sleep, nursing our sore hands and reading the latest issue of "Latitude 38", a free, monthly Bay Area sailing magazine. Our favorite section was "*Changes in Latitude*" where sailors around the world reported what they were experiencing, offering tips and suggestions to others who would follow.

The second day of rain we woke to a sharp jolt and loud bang like a car hitting the boat, and we ran up on deck to see what was going on. Yard workers were scurrying around boats in the rain, checking steel stands that hold vessels upright. "We just had an earthquake," one of them shouted. "I'm going to tie your stands together." He disappeared under our boat with rope in his hands and we came down the ladder to help. Deciding we could do nothing about another earthquake if it happened, we cleaned ourselves up and headed for San Francisco for a day off in the city.

Fresh mussels and fried calamari at Scoma's on Fisherman's Wharf were always Bill's favorites so we started there and had a leisurely lunch. Several cocktails later, we decided to walk around the Wharf in the rain. Later that afternoon we headed south of Market to a few of our favorite old haunts where we managed to get shit-faced drunk. For no reason other than exhaustion and being reminded of what a normal life was like, we began to pick on each other and before we knew it, were in a shouting match. As we headed for the Bay Bridge and the boat yard, Bill complained: "I never wanted this god-damn much work." He blamed me for pushing him to the point of exhaustion.

"I'm pretty damn tired too. This wasn't just my idea you know," I defended myself, knowing it *was* just my idea that started all of this. For the next forty minutes we shouted at each other while I drove. "Let's just sell it then. I never meant to push you into something you didn't want to do." There was only silence in response as we pulled into the boat yard.

The next morning I slept in, sure that we had made another life-changing decision in our anger. I awoke to the sounds of scraping on the hull, got dressed and went outside to find Bill back at work on the transom, albeit with quite a hangover. Without saying a word I found the aspirin bottle, then my brushes, and went to work below him on the first coat of bottom paint. We didn't speak to each other for a full day. When I broke the silence to ask him if he still wanted to sell the boat and call it quits, he answered shaking his head no. "Let's finish what we've started."

39

Changes in Latitudes

At dusk on Friday we stood in the parking lot and watched my beat-up, red Chevy pickup disappear down the road.

On Saturday morning, September 15, 1984, three days before Bill's birthday, and after sixteen months of work, "Providence" left her berth at Sanford Wood in Richmond, slipped under the Golden Gate Bridge, turned left avoiding the rough waters of the infamous "*Potato Patch*" and headed south in the Pacific Ocean. It was the beginning of a five-year journey into the unknown. Below on the table was the first chart of what would be many, and we began to plot our course down the California coast toward Mexico and the Panama Canal. We made a solemn promise never to let a schedule decide when we had to be somewhere, vowing to be only fair weather sailors.

Going south is easy. Generally the swells and winds are behind you, so "Providence" port-hopped down the coastline stopping anywhere the spirit moved us.

We anchored in front of Pebble Beach and hiked across the golf course to visit the town of Monterey, ducked into the tiny harbor at San Simeon and visited Hearst Castle, then tracked down the Monarch butterfly migration and made some engine repairs in Morrow Bay.

At San Luis Obispo we anchored with other boats and waited for the wind and seas to calm before going around dangerous Point Conception.

And on a beautiful sunny day we discovered what Santa Ana winds can do to a sailboat, and got the crap kicked out of us for a couple hours before ducking into protected Santa Barbara harbor.

We sailed past the Santa Monica pier, and I saw Will Roger's Beach and the Friendship Bar where I had met Hans. At Marina Del Rey in Los Angeles, Bill's friend Rick came to see the boat and took us to Disneyland.

By December we had worked our way down the California coast and decided to stop for the holidays. Our families joined us for whale-watching trips around

San Diego's Point Loma and we made preparations to leave for Mexico in the New Year.

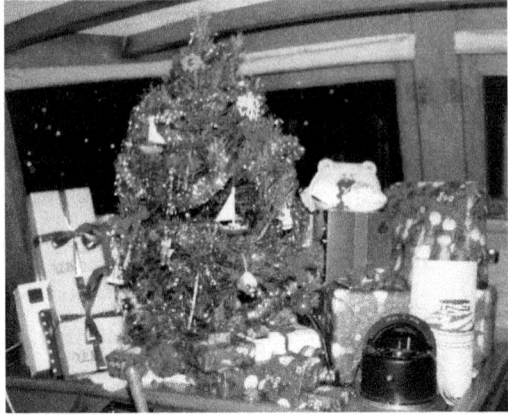

On a beautiful January afternoon we left San Diego Bay and turned south toward Ensenada Mexico. The weather turned cold and foggy, and we wished for the radar that we didn't have the money to buy so we could see what was around us. Bundled up in long underwear and foul-weather gear, and knowing we were in busy shipping lanes, we strained our eyes and rang our bell through the night in hopes of not being run over by a container ship.

About half-way down the Baja Peninsula the fog disappeared and so did the cold. Suddenly it was 80 degrees and sunny and we were wearing shorts and T-shirts. Pooped from our first overnight sail, we anchored behind Cedros Island and decided to have a cocktail before getting some sleep. Suddenly, a furry head with big whiskers and inquisitive eyes popped up over the side of the boat. The sea lion seemed to be as curious about us as we were about him.

The next day we watched whales mating in groups of three in the warm Baja waters, and in Cabo San Lucas the dinghy we bought before we left because it was unsinkable, sank with us and our groceries.

Early one morning, as we motored through the Sea of Cortez, we found ourselves in the middle of thousands of manta rays sunning themselves on top of water that looked like glass.

On an island like a moonscape we picked buckets of chocolate clams off a beach inside what was left of a million-year-old volcanic crater.

At dusk in San Blas, after capsizing our dinghy in the surf, filling the outboard with seawater, and having to fight off clouds of mosquitoes, we joined a group of locals riding in the back of a dump truck full of rocks into the tiny town.

By the time we reached Puerto Vallarta, we were sixteen-hundred miles from San Francisco, but not from our friends. We ran into Brad and Ron, the Texans who owned the big house like Tara on the Russian River. Brad looked like a ghost. They were in Mexico so he could check into a clinic that claimed to have a cure for the new "gay cancer."

While we were anchored in front of the gay beach,

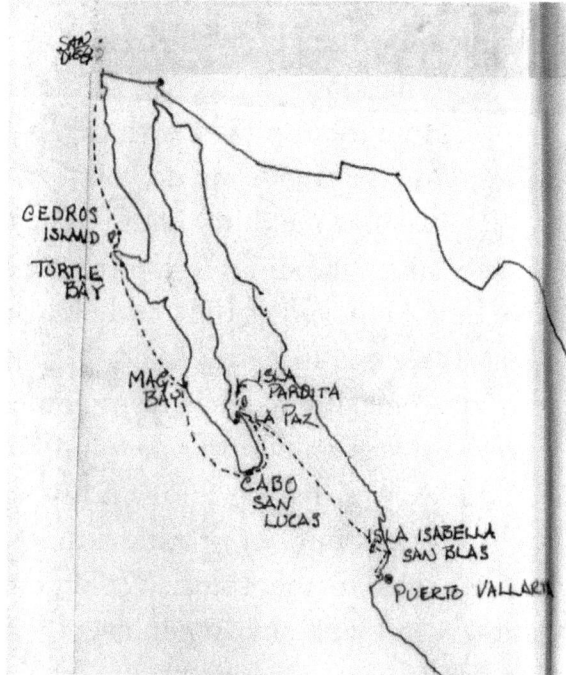

my friend JR swam out to get a better look at the boat and was surprised to find it was ours. We hauled him aboard for cocktails and caught up on Castro gossip.

"I love your pirate ship and have an idea," he said, looking at his friends on the beach.

"What now?" I groaned cautiously.

"How about pirates with water-wings?"

"You never give up, do you?"

"Just give me thirty damn dollars and I'll take care of everything," he smiled. "Don't worry, we're going to have fun!" I looked at Bill and he just rolled his eyes.

It seemed like a week didn't go by before running into someone else we knew from home. We stayed in Puerto Vallarta for almost nine months. The first few because we were having so much fun, and the rest because we had to wait out our first hurricane season before it was safe to go further south. We left one morning in the darkness and were almost run over by an arriving cruise ship whose captain wasn't paying attention.

～

A year had passed, and we spent our second Christmas on the boat in Manzanillo, and New Year's Eve at anchor in Zihuatanejo Bay, watching the fireworks.

In Acapulco the marine radio operator told us she had calls for yacht Providence and Bill's brother Frank, in Florida, and Danny Marsh, a gay bartender friend from The Pendulum in San Francisco, each called to tell us they were flying down to join the crew.

We took on fuel and water at Puerto Madero, a tiny Mexican port town tucked against the border

with Guatemala, and left late in the day with two other
sailboats. It was a beautiful breezy afternoon as we sailed
out of Mexican waters toward Costa Rica. Having been
warned of the political conditions in Guatemala, El
Salvador and Nicaragua, and hearing stories of people who
had been arrested and lost their boats for being too close
to shore, we plotted a course due south. As the coastline
of Central America fell back to the east, we soon found
ourselves six-hundred miles off shore.

By sunset the breeze had stopped and we motored
in calm water. The VHF radio came to life with the voice
of Bonnie on "Faith", one of the boats in the group. "My,
that looks dark and foreboding," she said, referring to a
line of black clouds crossing the full moon ahead of us.
We could see moonlight on the water on other side of the
clouds and it looked peaceful enough, still her words made
a chill run up my spine.

By dawn we had gone through the gates of hell.

Huge waves, some forty feet high, driven by
hurricane-force winds called a "Papagayo" gave us a lesson
on how powerful the Pacific Ocean can be. For four days
and nights we rode a roller coaster of huge swells and
wind waves, chugging slowly up one side and then surfing
down the other, turning in the bottom of the trough so
we wouldn't punch our bowsprit into the next wave and
flip the boat. We kept a small sail up, but it did little good
except to steady the boat. The wind was coming at us from
the direction we needed to go, so the only thing pushing
us forward was our small diesel engine. We lost sight of
the two boats we had left port with, but occasionally heard

them on the radio.

On the second day there were distress calls from a Russian freighter trying to get to Nicaragua. It sank in the storm. Later that day we heard from Phil on the other boat traveling with us. They were taking on water from someplace under their engine. He, his wife and young son were scared. We heard nothing more from them. None of us had slept. At one point Danny was thrown across the cabin and his ribcage was black and blue. A Vietnam vet, he had equilibrium problems caused by Agent Orange that we didn't know about, so we tied him in his bunk and he spent the rest of the passage there, eating Lomotil to calm his gut. Bill, Frank and I took turns steering in one-hour shifts.

On the third day our engine began losing oil pressure and at one point stopped, but Frank managed to get it running again. We kept adding oil, but it didn't help give the engine power and we worried about losing the only thing moving us toward where we needed to go. Later, we met three young Canadians who got so afraid they decided to turn and put the storm behind them. They were blown a thousand miles out to sea, ran out of food and water but were saved by a lucky encounter with a Mexican fishing boat and eventually towed back to shore.

On the fourth day I began to hallucinate and had convinced myself that if I went to sleep the boat would sink and we would all die. But the reality was that Bill and Frank had everything under control. I went below, tied myself in my bunk and drifted off for what seemed like days. Four hours later I awoke wearing a fur hat. When I reached up it was Benecia, our cat. She had her belly firmly pressed against the top of my head and her legs wrapped around each side of my cheeks to hang on. The weather hadn't changed, but I felt refreshed and could think rationally again.

One of the first things you learn about sailing is never come into a strange port at night. We heard from Bonnie on the other boat. They were anchored at Playa del Coco, a small bay in Costa Rica just below the border of Nicaragua, "We asked a man on shore to leave his porch light on for you. If you follow it you won't hit the rocks." I thought to myself, *if we hit the rocks at least I can step off this fucking boat and walk to dry land.*

At dawn I could see our friends' boats in the anchorage. Everyone made it. We untied Danny and he traded stories with Bonnie, who sported a black-eye after being thrown against a porthole. Phil borrowed our underwater epoxy to fix the leak below his engine, and a group of Costa Rican men came out to our boat and pulled our engine apart. We had broken a valve stem that had fallen into a piston. It was a miracle Frank had managed to keep it running. They bundled up the huge cast iron head in a blanket, and Danny and I took a bus to San Jose to have it machined. While waiting, we found the only gay bar and in town and got drunk.

After two months instead of one, Frank left the boat and went back to Florida. Gail, a friend from the Russian River, flew down and joined Bill, Danny and I for the next part of the trip.

Somewhere after Playa del Coco we crossed a line and suddenly were in the hot, steamy tropics. In Golfito, our last port in Costa Rica, we heard about a one-legged American expat who had married a Costa Rican woman and ran a make-shift bar called Captain Tom's Paradise. While there, Bill got bit by what we learned later were sand flies. We were ready to leave for Panama in the morning, but overnight what had looked like mosquito bites had turned pitch black and had grown to the size of dimes. By noon two of the bites were the size of quarters and one of them erupted. "I've got AIDS," he cried.

"Don't be silly! Something growing this fast isn't AIDS. I don't know what it is, but I do know we need to get you to a doctor." At the local hospital they gave him shots and pills to take and told us we should wait and not leave. Apparently the sand flies inject a parasite that causes the problem and it can be serious. By morning the bites weren't growing and had a dull appearance, so we pulled up anchor and headed toward Panama.

We stopped at a small island with a fishing camp and went ashore to see if they had any ice or beer to sell. "Do you guys have someone on your boat that is sick?" the man running the camp asked. "If you need it, we have a sea-plane and can fly him back to Golfito." He had received a call from the doctor telling him to look out for us.

"He's OK now, but thanks for asking and please say thank you to the doctor who called you." We took our ice and beer back to the boat and the next morning headed for the Panama Canal.

~

For centuries, ships' captains have kept logs and notes about places they visited and how they got there. They recorded weather and wind conditions along with information about good anchorages and things that could be helpful to those who followed. The U.S. government continues to do this in the form of books for mariners called "Sailing Directions." For getting to the Panama Canal, the book warns that you'll experience gusty winds coming off the land as you sail along the coast. The winds form large rolling swells that prevent a boat from making the left turn to head toward the canal entrance. They tell you to be patient and that gradually the winds will begin to shift and allow you to turn up toward where you want to go.

By the second day of being heeled over at a 45-degree angle and rolling in big swells, we were convinced that, like it or not, we were going to South America. It was uncomfortable sailing but not dangerous.

A large pod of Killer Whales kept pace with us. They loved playing in the big swell, occasionally coming close to the boat. As promised, the winds finally began to shift and we gradually turned north weaving our way through the Las Perlas Islands before reaching the entrance to the canal.

We made a brief stop on Tobago Island and watched as a huge, 130-foot tuna boat unloaded its catch. The captain and his very nelly first mate were the only other gay people we had seen in months. We exchanged "*It takes one to know one*" looks while smiling at each other.

~

On Sunday, April 26, 1987 we picked up a mooring buoy at the Balboa Yacht Club and started the paperwork to go through the canal. Noriega was still in command of Panama and the country was a dangerous place. Our taxi

driver kept a pistol under a newspaper on the seat next to him. At a stop light, a man selling fruit approached the cab. The driver shouted for us to roll up the windows as he uncovered his gun, making sure the man approaching saw it.

The following Thursday, our Panamanian advisor, Huge, boarded the boat and we began our canal transit. Inside the first set of locks, we were rafted-up to two other sailboats. Since our fifty-six foot length made us the largest, we had one on each side and would do the steering for everyone. On our starboard (right) side, a small steel sailboat from Belgium, battered and beaten with a coconut growing on deck, had two very skinny young men, and a French woman onboard. On our port (left) side, we had a pristine fiberglass sailboat with a distinguished looking man in his fifties, his wife and two young couples onboard. They looked like military people. Gail took our video camera and made it her job to film everything. She quickly became infatuated with one of the Navy husbands whose balls continually fell out the leg of his shorts when he crouched down, so she spent much her time photographing them instead of what was going on with the trip.

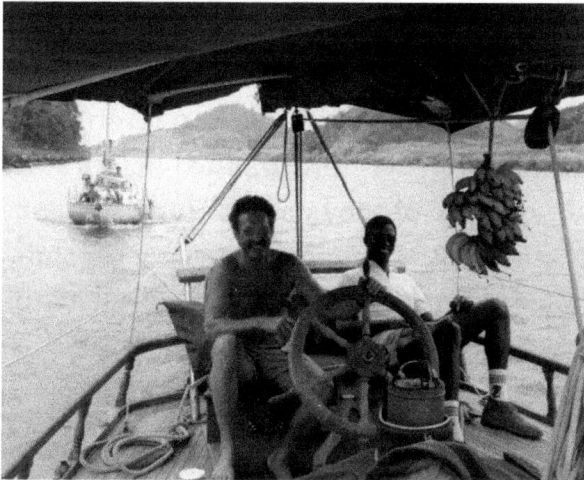

After finishing the locks on the Pacific side, we unhooked from the other boats to motor down the

Guillard Cut, a fifty-mile long, man-made waterway. Our Belgium friends' engine wouldn't start, so we towed them and spent the night in a beautiful freshwater lake near the last set of locks.

At ten in the morning our advisor returned with news that people had started rioting and burning cars in the streets of Panama City. We rafted up again to begin the trip through the last set of locks that would put us into the Caribbean. During morning greetings, we found that "Mofti", the fiberglass sailboat tied to our port side, was indeed filled with Navy people, and that Dick, the distinguished man who stood behind her wheel - and who I had been skippering through the locks - was the head of the Navy's Southern Command. With three locks to go, I wished no one had told me this.

By the time we untied, we had all become good friends. Gail traded sea stories with the French woman about how she learned to put a Tampax in while standing on her head when sailing in rough weather. To return the favor her new friend showed her how to pinch herself so she could pee off the side of the boat like a man. We spent a few nights at the rustic Panama Canal Yacht Club, grocery shopped and went to the Colombian consulate to get our visas to visit the island of San Andreas.

By the time we left the Panama Canal Zone, we had traveled over 3,700 miles from San Francisco.

40

Sailing Backwards

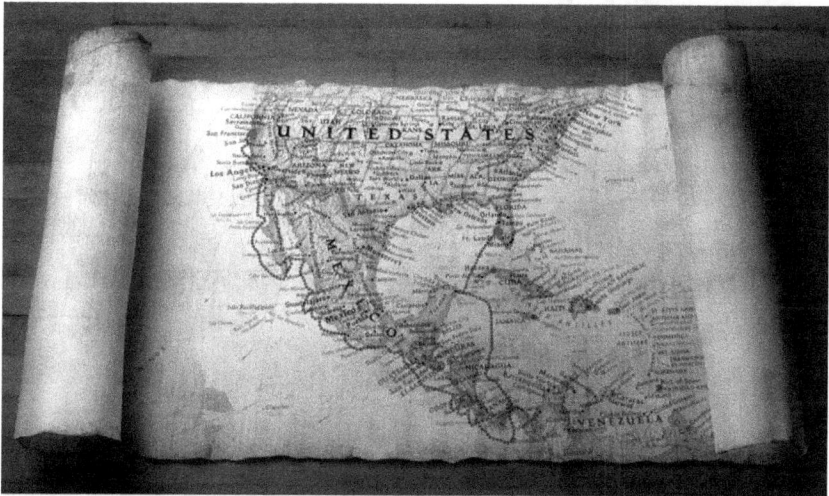

It was raining and the seas were choppy as we came out of the Canal Zone. Instead of going north, we made a right turn and tucked into Portobello where, in the 1600's, the Spaniards stacked in warehouses the gold and silver they looted from the Mayans and Aztecs before loading it onto ships to take it to Spain. Legend says that in 1502, Christopher Columbus gave this place the name "Puerto Bello", which means "Beautiful Port." The Spanish treasure fleet made the port safe by building fortifications to protect it from attacks by pirates.

We hiked around the walls of the old fortress looking at the abandoned bronze canons in the constant drizzle. An enormous tree filled with different types of orchids caught our attention and we wished we could take some plants with us.

Whenever we went for a walk, Bill always found nails, odd rocks and things on the road, so it was no surprise when he bent over and picked up a tiny silver *quarter-real* off the cobblestone street in Portobello that had probably been laying there for more than three hundred years.

We grew tired of waiting for the rains to stop and watching mold grow on the ceiling of the boat, so we headed north toward the Colombian island of San Andres.

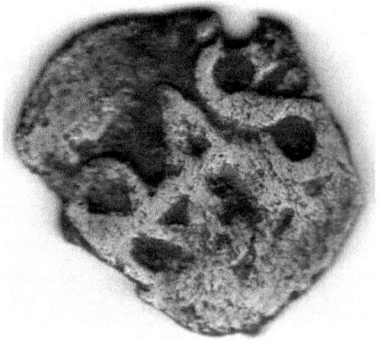

Sailing at night, we could see commercial jets making the approach to the island so we didn't need to plot a course. As we got closer, we saw lighted navigation buoys, but they were difficult to distinguish against the lights on shore, so we decided to wait until sunup before going in, and anchored just outside the channel. I slept in the pilot house, and at dawn I could see a large freighter with its bow resting on a coral reef only a few hundred yards from our boat. Smoke was still coming out of the stack and the deck was filled with new cars. *Bad luck*, I thought to myself, grateful we didn't try to find our way into port in the dark. We stayed for almost a month on the little resort island, but it was getting late and hurricane season was just around the corner.

We sailed past Isla Providencia, and by the time we reached Swan Island we were tired and wanted to sleep. Sailing Directions told us there was a good anchorage there and we decided to stop, but as we approached we heard gun shots and bullets began to ricochet off the water near us. We turned away and continued sailing toward Cozumel. Years later we would learn that Oliver North was secretly training his Contra forces there to use in Central America with weapons President Reagan later denied knowing about.

Our arrival in Cozumel was another night landfall, but seas were flat and there was no wind, so we watched the depth sounder until it indicated we were in twenty feet of water, then anchored. Just to make sure we would stay put, we dropped all three hundred feet of anchor chain before going to sleep. In the morning I turned on the depth finder and it said we were in two *hundred* feet of water, not twenty. I walked out onto the bowsprit and looked down at our anchor resting in white sand on the bottom. I had never seen water so clear.

We had been living on the boat for over four years, and were tired. Feeding ourselves and taking care of the boat on six hundred and twenty-two dollars a month was getting more difficult. We had plenty of time to think while waiting for money to arrive and decided to sell the boat in Florida, get jobs and become real people again. While we waited, we began to sell off things we didn't think we would need for the last leg of the trip. We watched people carried away our hand-held VHF radio, our small Honda gas generator, our old charts, and finally our trusty wind generator that had kept our batteries charged when we were anchored. On Wednesday, July 15, 1987, we crossed the north end of the reef around Isla Mujeres, departed Mexican waters and headed into the Gulf of Mexico toward Florida. Winds were light, so we motored through the night. At six in the morning, our water pump broke, and because it ran directly off the engine, not on belts, we had to shut the motor off and sail. We were in waters crowded with oil tankers, and were about to be introduced to the "loop

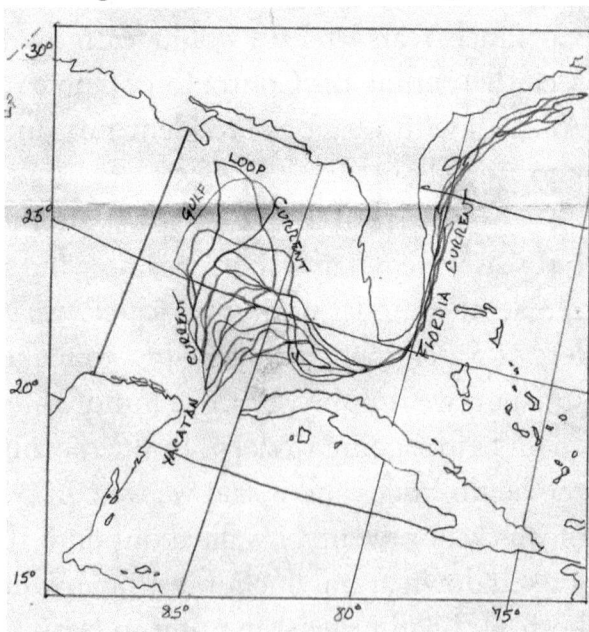

current" and would spend almost nine days making a
passage that should have taken three.

It was July and there were thunderstorms all around
us. At times we had plenty of wind to sail and it felt like
we were making good progress until Bill noticed small fish
alongside the boat going faster than we were. We plotted
our positions on the SatNav and found we were actually
sailing backwards! The strong currents that came up
between Mexico and Cuba extended far into the Gulf then
looped back down around the tip of Florida. They were
pulling us backward. Just as fast as the winds came up that
would allow us to sail, they disappeared, leaving us drifting
in the currents on a glass-like sea. We had provisioned
for a week and had plenty of water, so thought we were
in no danger. We stuck with the watch schedule Bill had
made before we left Mexico, and to keep our families from
getting worried, we radioed the Coast Guard to report our
position and asked them to call Bill's brother Frank and let
him know we were OK.

Waterspouts - tornados over water - would appear
and disappear leaving gusty winds that we would use to
sail and make headway. I finished my morning watch and
had climbed into bed when I heard Bill's voice through the
open skylight above me. "Lou, can you come up here?"
Danny was asleep in his bunk and snoring. Bill handed
me the binoculars and pointed to a ship on the horizon
coming from Texas. It was a gigantic oil tanker, so loaded
the sides of it were barely visible above the water. "It looks
like it's heading right for us," he said, reaching to take
the glasses back from me. I went down below and began

calling the captain on the radio, but there was no answer.

"Captain, this is the skipper of the sailboat in front of you. We have no engine and no wind to sail and are not able to move out of your way." My message was met with silence. I tried another channel and also received no response. For the next twenty minutes, I radioed as the ship got closer and closer to us. Feeling desperate, I went below and woke Danny, telling him to get the big yellow plastic bag we kept in the locker and to bring it up on deck. Inside were our abandon ship supplies of food, water, flashlights and flares. I put in my black satchel with the ship's papers and our passports. "Put it in the dinghy". I told him, knowing that we wouldn't stand a chance of living if this behemoth hit us.

When the ship was less than a football field away, I watched as someone stepped out of a door and onto the flying bridge. He was looking at us through binoculars as I radioed again. There was still no answer. Seconds later I saw the ship turn slightly away from us. It passed our boat by less than a hundred feet.

I knew our batteries were almost dead, and because I had sold the little Honda generator, we had no way to charge them. I feared we would lose our radio and our navigation lights and could be run down by another tanker in the darkness.

Later that day we spotted a tug boat hauling a barge behind it heading in our direction. I made contact with Vince, the captain, and told him our story. He slowed down to a standstill, nudged the barge full of liquid asphalt where he wanted it, then accepted a bridle we made by tying our anchor lines together and attached us to the back of the barge. He invited us onboard into the air-conditioned tug where we met the crew: Scott, the cook, and Jim, a tall, good-looking man with a very friendly face who turned out to be gay. They gave us ice and cold beers and Danny got some cigarettes before we went back to our boat for the ride into Tampa Bay.

The ad in the St. Petersburg Times read:

56' Hugh Angleman - designed solid teak ketch
For sale or trade for Florida real estate.

Bud was a retired military man with Vietnam battle scars to prove it. His wife Mary was a writer and bird lover who knew Audubon's books inside out and backwards. We didn't know it when we met, but we were to fall in love with both of them.

As they approached the boat I could tell by the way Bud was gesturing that "Providence" was everything he ever wanted. We sat and talked, mostly about our trip, and in twenty minutes we had an offer to trade the boat for an old six-unit, wood apartment building with a mortgage in downtown St. Petersburg.

We gave it some thought, and a week later Bill, carrying our cat Benecia, and I walked down the dock for the last time. We didn't look back. We had traveled more than 5,300 miles since the beginning of our voyage and felt happy knowing the boat was in good hands and would go on to fulfill someone else's dreams.

We moved into one of the apartments on Sixth Street and began to get our land legs back. Our cat moved into a closet and wouldn't come out for days except to eat and drink at night. After a few weeks, Benecia became a loving, affectionate cat for the first time. We didn't know it then, but she hated that damn boat and the five years she had spent on it.

Bill found work as a chef in an elegant private dining club. With my good typing skills, I became a "*Kelly Girl*" and worked temporary jobs. We gave Florida a try, but were homesick. Life without a dream was depressing, so we sold the apartment building at a loss, paid off the mortgage, packed up what few belongings we had accumulated, and headed west, back to San Francisco.

41

Roaming No More

At eight o'clock in the evening I switched on the television in my friends' home in High Point, North Carolina. October 17th, 1989 was the day we had all been waiting for - the beginning of the Bay Bridge World Series. The first game between the San Francisco Giants and the Oakland A's was about to start, and I wasn't there. The image from the Goodyear blimp high above Candlestick Park of a stadium packed with thousands of fans made me homesick and I felt cheated. As I sat down the picture suddenly began to shake, got snowy, and went black. *Shit*, I thought to myself. *Damn TV*. Before I could get up to kick it, the shot of Candlestick Park returned, but a crawl line ran over and over again across the bottom of the screen, reading: "San Francisco is experiencing a major earthquake." It was 5:04 p.m. in California. Realizing my hand was resting on the telephone, I dialed our number but each time I tried, a "Circuit busy, try your call again later" message confirmed what I was seeing on TV. I dialed the operator. "Can you help me? I live in San Francisco and can't get through." Before the male voice could tell me what I already knew, I stopped him. "I'm really concerned. I know my partner Bill is at home and I just want to make sure he's OK," I said, trusting a hunch that I had a gay operator on the other end of the phone. Like magic my new boyfriend went into action.

"Whatever you do, don't hang up or what I'm about to try will all fall apart. It may take awhile, but stay on the line with me. Just listen but don't speak." For what seemed like an eternity I could hear him calling one operator after another in adjacent states, and with each connection he got closer to California. Finally he managed to get a San Francisco operator on the line and suddenly I heard Bill's voice.

"Thank You!" I said loudly, hoping the operator was still on.

"I'm happy I was able to help and glad he's OK." And before I could get his name he was gone, probably being reprimanded for spending too much time helping me.

"Are you alright?"

"Yea, I think so. It was quite a ride. The big mirror in the bathroom came crashing down, but I don't think anything else is broken. There's no electricity right now, but I can see lights down below in the Castro." The little Victorian house on Corbett Street we had rented from Alberta's son was built before the big earthquake in 1906, and although it was on the side of a steep Twin Peak's hill and the back was supported by four, very skinny redwood posts, it had just managed to ride out another major earthquake. "The house shook so bad the front door was jammed and I couldn't get out at first. I finally got it open and stood on the sidewalk until the shaking stopped. I think I said, "Shit" really loud because I could hear someone uphill from me say "Indeed". "What a welcome back to San Francisco, eh? Please come home as soon as you can."

It was 1989 and we had been gone for over five years. It seemed like two. The realization that our decision to go sailing had saved our lives hadn't hit us yet, but would soon be driven home as we watched the AIDS crisis take our friends and the people we loved.

Before we left on our trip, my kind and gentle artist friend David got sick. Everyone at the bar where he worked in Guerneville raised money and bought him a ticket to go see his Mom while he was still well enough to do it. When he called to tell her he was dying of AIDS and wanted to come, she told him she didn't have a son and hung up. A small group of us went to see the road production of "Dream Girls" in San Francisco. During the performance David and I sat holding hands. We both knew he was dying. Holding hands wasn't enough so I took his and slid it into the pocket of my Levis, where it stayed for the rest of the show. His friends Jerry and Bill took him to their home, and on Easter Sunday, April 22nd, 1984 he died. As he wanted, he was cremated. Men from the company who rented the hospital bed arrived to pick it up in surgical masks and yellow hazmat suits. They dragged it out of the house into the street and pressure washed it with disinfectants before putting it into their truck. When we returned from our trip, we completed the last of David's wishes and had a party in San Francisco, divided his ashes among us, filling our Levis. I put them in the same pocket where his hand had been while we watched "Dream Girls." We went to his favorite bars, scattering them a little at a time on the floor among the crowds without being noticed.

Leonard Matlovich died on June 22, 1988, the year before we reached Florida on the boat. He wanted to be buried in Arlington National Cemetery, but because he had been dishonorably discharged from the Army for being gay, he ended up buying a plot in the Congressional Cemetery in Washington, D.C. With the help of his friends on the Russian River, his grave is marked with a large, black stone with pink triangles that reads; "*When I was in the military, they gave me a medal for killing two men, and a discharge for loving one.*"

Joel Coleman was my friend and a San Francisco treasure. He loved to take visitors on walking tours of his city. He knew where every obscure historical detail was hidden, including the gold fire plug that was one of the only working hydrants in 1906 after the earthquake. By using it, the Fire Department was able to save everything above 19th Street from the fires. Joel was always there for his friends and family, but the day I went to visit him at San Francisco General he was alone in his room, unconscious and tossing in his bed. As I sat with him I noticed a drawer full of unopened cards. His nurse stuck her head in the room and said, "Stay awhile, nobody comes anymore." So I sat there, held his hand, opened each card, and read them to him. Before I left, I told him it was OK to go now if he wanted to. He died that night.

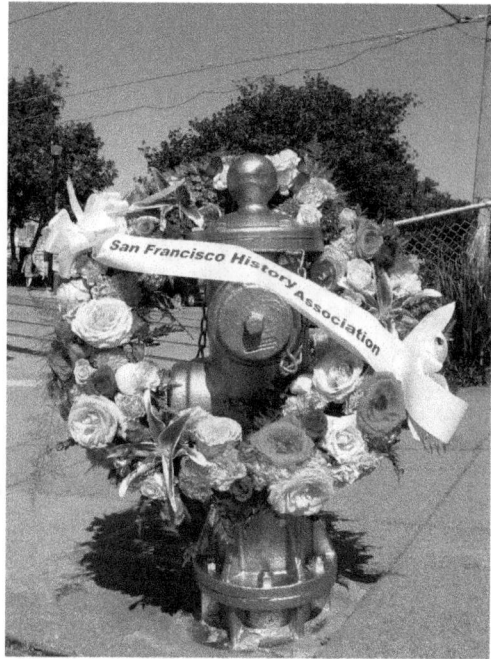

Bill's first love and partner for more than thirteen years, Rick Cook, died on April 5, 1990 in Los Angeles. He was a talented, cordon bleu chef. For his entire life he had

waited to inherit the wealth of his mother's estate, but by the time he received it, he was too sick to enjoy his windfall. On his death bed he rewrote his Will, leaving half of it to his friend Jade who lived down the hall and took care of him in the last months of his life. He left the other half to friends, including enough money for Bill and me to put a down payment on the only home we would ever own in San Francisco.

My kind and gentle friend, Randy Shilts, who wrote "The Mayor of Castro Street" & "And The Band Played On" about the AIDS epidemic, left us on February 17, 1994. He's buried in a beautiful little cemetery on a hill, under the redwood trees in Guerneville, California.

On the morning of February 26, 1994, the phone next to my bed rang. It was Chuck calling to tell me that Michael was gone. To paraphrase what he wrote in his partner's obituary: It wasn't an easy passage because while he wanted to be free of the pain and humiliation of incapacitation, he also wanted to take care of me and his friends. Once everyone promised to look after each other, he found peace.

At Michael's memorial in the beautiful garden he created for Jim Hormel at his home, I felt a tap on my shoulder and an arm around my waist. It was Scott. We spent the time together reminiscing about Michael and the good times. When we said goodbye that day, we both knew we'd never see each other again. He died less than a year later on February 4, 1995.

And on Sunday, February 13, 2005, as if to bring everything full circle, Hans, the master of disguise and the man who taught me the value of a foreskin, died. He had morphed one final time and was living in a remote part of Humbolt County, where he and his partner Glen grew marijuana quasi-legally for a living, selling whatever they didn't smoke to medical marijuana dispensaries in San Francisco. He called late in the afternoon two days before to say goodbye, to tell me how much he loved me, and to ask Bill and me to keep a loving eye on Glen for him.

~

A few years later I thought I'd sit down and write a list of everyone I have known and loved and lost to AIDS. I wanted to carry that list in my pocket while I marched in the Pride parade in San Francisco. As I wrote the one hundred and first name, I stopped and cried.

"How many slams in an old screen door?
Depends on how loud you shut it.

How many slices in bread?
Depends how thin you cut it.

How much good inside a day?
Depends on how you live 'em.

How much love inside a friend?
Depends on how much you give 'em."

- *Shel Silverstein*

"First they ignore you,
then they laugh at you,
then they fight you,
then you win."
     - Ghandi

On the morning of Wednesday, June 26, 2013
The Supreme Court of the United States announced two
landmark decisions affecting gay people in the USA.

The opinion in United States v. Windsor
holding that Section 3 of the Defense of
Marriage Act is unconstitutional
- and -
The opinion in Hollingsworth v. Perry
holding that petitioners lacked standing to
appear from the district court's order.

❦

On
Friday, June 26th, 2015
at 10:05 AM Eastern Time
The Supreme Court of the United States
Declared Same-Sex Marriage Legal in All 50 States
ending decades of discrimination and heartbreak.

José Sarria

Empress José I
by the grace of God, Widow of Norton I
Emperor of the United States
& Protector of Mexico
Departed this life at 7:02 in the morning, August 19, 2013

ʚ̃ɞ

"United we stand - divided they catch us one by one."

December 12, 1922 - August 19, 2013

José & Michelle play the Palace of Fine Arts
(inset: José & Michelle at Jose's 90th birthday party)

Epilogue

At 5 p.m., on February 28, 2013, a helicopter carrying Pope Benedict XVI, who had been strapped into his seat by his weeping "trusted secretary," Archbishop Georg Gaenswein, lifted off from a hill in the Vatican. It would carry them to Castel Gandolfo, where at 8:00 p.m. that night, with only 17 days' notice to the world's 1.16 billion Catholics, the 265th pontiff of the Roman Catholic Church resigned the powers of St. Peter, the first to do so in almost 600 years. The red shoes of Peter would be filled by another's feet.

As one of his last official acts as Pope, Joseph Ratzinger sealed the 600-page report that he had ordered three of his Cardinals to prepare, making sure it would be only for the eyes of his successor and no one else. In it, many people speculate, are the details that expose his relationship with Gaenswein. In effect, he had been outed by his own clergy.

According to the Vatican, Benedict's handsome male companion will continue to live and spend nights with him.

On February 27th, 2013, noted columnist Andrew Sullivan wrote in his blog, "The Dish":

> *"This man – clearly in some kind of love with Ratzinger (and vice-versa) will now be working for the new Pope as secretary in the day and spending the nights with the Pope Emeritus. This is not the Vatican. It's Melrose Place."*

The subliminal, but almost audible, final message from His Holiness Benedict XVI to LGBT people everywhere seems to be *"Do as I say, not as I do."*

Afterword

On Thanksgiving Day in 2016, Bill and I will celebrate thirty-seven years of life, love, happiness and adventures together. Neither of us has the answer to the question of why we were spared.

On our deaths, all rights to this book will pass
to the James C. Hormel Gay & Lesbian Center at the
San Francisco Public Library.

Acknowledgements

Writing a book is always a collaborative effort. In my quest for accuracy, information and encouragement, I have people to thank.

Bill Walls, who filled in many blanks, is a patient sounding board full of ideas, and knows how to put a writer's ego where it needs to be - out of the writing - and is one hell of an editor. We walked many parts of this journey in our real lives, now we've walked them together again. I love you.

To Rich Petersen, thank you for your tireless editing and proofreading.

Thank you, José Sarria. Although you didn't live to see this book's completion, thanks to your memory, wit and help in the phone calls during the writing, people everywhere will get to know about you, your courage and tenacity. Thanks for helping me get it right. You are truly are a San Francisco treasure and no accounts of our LGBT history would be accurate without the long list of your many contributions.

To Tony Ross who kept a watchful eye over José, making sure he has had everything he needed right up to the end. You have provided so much help and so many introductions, you can take credit for the real magic in this book.

Danny Nicoletta, your generosity in introducing me to Marc Cohn so I could get permission to use my favorite photo of Scott and Harvey is deeply appreciated. You've done so much to preserve the faces of gay history with your own camera.

Tony Onorati, Brian Benamati and Rich Stadtmiller, your photos of Michelle, Bella and José are precious treasures. Thank you for sharing them with the rest of the world through my book.

Phyllis Christopher, photographer extraordinaire; your beautiful photo of Randy Shilts lets his soul shine through your camera lens.

And to everyone who generously shared their photographs and histories for this effort, I can't say thank you enough. You helped bring this story to life by putting faces on people and places that deserve to be remembered.

My deepest gratitude goes to every WikipediA contributor. Thank you for your dedication to continually update content in this fantastic living encyclopedia.

Rolando Mafnas and Alberto Downing, your excitement and enthusiasm about this book and your encouragement to share stories of the 1970's in San Francisco inspired me more than you'll ever know.

Thank you, Jim Hormel, for your generosity to make sure the San Francisco Public Library included a special Gay and Lesbian Center in its new building . Generations of our brothers and sisters will always have a public legacy because of you and the people who contributed to the cause you championed.

Other books by Lou Kief

In All the Silent Manliness

Print Edition ISBN: 978-1-94565552-3-8
Electronic Editions ISBN: 978-0-9831935-0-0

Doing Retail Right

Tips & Inspiration
from
Lou Kief & Bill Walls

Print Edition ISBN: 978-0-9831935-7-9
Electronic Editions ISBN: 978-0-9831935-1-7

Appendix

San Francisco LGBT Historical Timeline Pre-1980

Special thanks to Edwin Jones for his permission
to use historical data he researched, collected and posted
on his blog GayDads.Blogspot.com

The infamous Barbary Coast in San Francisco
Is the first Gay Neighborhood

San Francisco has a reputation as a progressive, accepting city of its gay and lesbian citizens. This was not always the case. Although LGBT people have been finding their way to the City from the beginning, it has been a long, hard struggle to get to where it is today. Here is the best historical timeline of important gay and lesbian events and milestones in San Francisco history from 1849 to 1979.

1849: The California Gold Rush propels the small pueblo village of San Francisco, population of about 500 to over 20,000 inhabitants the first year. One source cites a 50-1 male-to-female ratio. Men will continue to outnumber women for the next 100 years.

Patty Wagon of male undesirables
In the Gold Rush days

1850's: Reacting to pressure from morally concerned citizens, local officials wage the first of many anti-vice campaigns that often target homosexuals. Subsequent intense raids occur in the 1870's, 1910's and 1950's. The highly publicized raids and anti-vice campaigns have the effect of branding San Francisco as the go-to place for adventure seeking homosexuals.

1875: Drag (male and female), cross-dressing, and female impersonation are sewn into the fabric of city life dating back to the Gold Rush. Female impersonator **Paul Vernon**, in his lacy gowns and Goldilocks wigs, performs to acclaim before largely male audiences and becomes one of the young city's first celebrity cross-dressing vaudevillians.

1898: A military investigation reports of rampant male homosexual prostitution among soldiers mustering at San Francisco's Presidio during the Spanish-American War.

Late 1800's: The first gay neighborhood in San Francisco is located in the infamous Barbary Coast that now overlaps North Beach and the Financial District.

1903: **Charles Warren Stoddard**, a member of San Francisco's literary elite and a pioneering California writer, publishes the homoerotic and autobiographically novel, "For the Pleasure of His Company: An Affair of the Misty City."

1907: **Alice B. Toklas** (born in San Francisco, 1877) and **Gertrude Stein** (family home in Oakland) both grew up in the Bay Area. They meet in Paris in 1907 and become one of LGBT history's most well known lesbian couples and have iconic status in the history of both twentieth-century literature and lesbian culture.

1908: City officials close the "Dash," the city's earliest known gay bar located at 574 Pacific Street in the red-light district of the Barbary Coast. A police report describes cross-dressing male entertainers dancing on tabletops with customers performing oral sex on them beneath their upraised skirts.

1919: **Bothwell Browne**, who grew up in SF, becomes one of the top performers in the vaudeville circuit, as well as a local favorite, with exotic and seductive female impersonations. After starring on Broadway and in a Max Sennett silent film, Browne headlines the Palace Theater in NY, the most prestigious booking in vaudeville. When vaudeville stopped booking female impersonators, he continues his career in SF as a dance instructor.

1929: "Finocchio's" opens in North Beach as a speakeasy at 406 Stockton St. In 1936 the police raid the club and arrest five female impersonators, including the owners because the Police Chief 'declared war' on lewd entertainers. It soon moves to 506 Broadway and become less a gay bar and more the premier female impersonation cabaret and a destination point for tourists from all around the world. It closes in 1999.

1930's: The gay neighborhoods in the city are now found along the waterfront, lower Market Street, and the long-gone boarding house district South of Market where the Moscone Convention Center and Yerba Buena Center for the Arts now stand.

1931: **Magnus Hirschfield**, the German Jewish leader of the Scientific Humanitarian Committee for the legal rights of German homosexuals, visits the city. He denounces both the Comstock Law, which "gave the Post Office the power to decide what was obscene," and Prohibition.

1933: With the repeal of Prohibition, a number of gay bars quickly open in the Tenderloin. The area remains the epicenter of gay bar culture into the 1960s.

1933: The first two explicitly gay male bathhouses open in SF: "Jack's Turkish Baths" and "Third Street Baths." The last gay bathhouse in SF, "21st Street Baths," closes in 1987.

1936: "Mona's 440 Club", the first lesbian bar in America, opens in North Beach. It features waitresses and female performers wearing tuxedos. Like "Finocchio's," it becomes popular with the tourist crowd.

1940's: During WWII, San Francisco becomes something of a dumping ground for homosexuals dishonorably discharged from military service. In addition, many gay war veterans opt to stay in SF rather than return home. In the late 1940s, a local newspaper describes this demographic trend with the sensationalistic headline, "Homos Invade S. F.!"

1947: California becomes the first state in the US to have a sex offender registration program. It requires all persons convicted under California law for sexual crimes, including sodomy and oral copulation, since 1944 to register as sex offenders. The law is used to target homosexuals.

1949: The "Black Cat Café" at 710 Montgomery St. is raided as part of a police and Alcohol Beverage Control Commission (ABC) crackdown on nightspots 'featuring lascivious entertainment and catering to lewd persons.' Police arrest ten people, hold seven for vagrancy, and prosecute three. Gay Beat poet Allen Ginsberg describes the Black Cat as "the best gay bar in America. It was totally open, bohemian, San Francisco... and everybody went there, heterosexual and homosexual.... All the gay screaming queens would come, the heterosexual gray flannel suit types, longshoremen. All the poets went there."

1949: California State Penal Code classifies sodomy (anal and male-male sex of any kind) as a felony. The maximum prison sentence for sodomy is doubled from 10 to 20 years. Another code for oral copulation insures a sentence of up to one year in jail for consensual oral sex.

1950's: San Francisco police raids on bars and public meeting places intensifies. Undercover agents pose as homosexuals to entrap them. Using broad legal interpretations, people are arrested for same-sex kissing, touching and dancing. In 1955, cross-gender behavior and dress are construed as illegal. The aggressive and often hostile attacks on gay bars pushes politics into the bars, and the bars become part of the gay liberation movement.

1950's: The Beat Generation and the San Francisco Renaissance of poets and writers flourish and intermingle with the gay bars and homophile activists in North Beach. Many of the Beats are homosexual or bisexual, including **Allen Ginsberg, Jack Kerouac, Jack Spicer, Robert Duncan,** and **Robin Blaser**. Both Beats and gays challenge the conformist pressures of the 50's and early 60's. Gays begin to view themselves as nonconformists rather than mentally ill rebels.

1951: The State Board of Equalization suspends the Black Cat bar's liquor license indefinitely. In response owner **Sol Stoumen** takes the state to court. The California Supreme Court in **Stoumen v. Reilly** rules that "in order to establish 'good cause' for suspension of plaintiff's license, something more must be shown than that many of his patrons were homosexuals and that they used his restaurant and bar as a meeting place." This is one of the earliest legal affirmations of the rights of gay people in the United States. The court qualifies its opinion, however, by stating that ABC might still close gay bars with "proof of the commission of illegal or immoral acts on the premises." Even after that ruling gay bars are regularly busted for flimsy excuses. Gay bathhouses are perilous as well because they could be raided and the patrons brought up on sexual deviancy charges and be required to register as a sex offender.

1954: The San Francisco Examiner editorializes: "There must be sustained action by the police and the district attorney to stop the influx of homosexuals. Too many taverns cater to them openly. Only police action can drive them out of the city...before the situation so deteriorates that San Francisco finds itself as the complete haven for undesirables."

1954: **Douglass Cross** and his lover, **George Cory**, write "I Left My Heart in San Francisco." Tony Bennett first sings it in 1961 at the Fairmont's Venetian Room.

1955: State legislature passes Section 24200(e) of the Business and Professional Code in an attempt to skirt the 1951 state Supreme Court decision in **Stoumen v Reilly**. The code addition provides that a license might be suspended or revoked if the premises "are a resort for illegal possessors or users of narcotics, prostitutes, pimps, panderers, or sexual perverts."

1956: The Mattachine Society, founded by Harry Hay in Los Angeles a couple years before, moves its national headquarters to San Francisco under the new leadership of Hal Call. The society is the earliest, sustaining, gay liberation organization in the US. Its charter calls for creating a service and welfare organization devoted to challenging anti-gay discrimination and building a gay community.

Del Martin & Phyllis Lyon

1956: **Del Martin** and **Phyllis Lyon** along with three other lesbian couples establish the Daughters of Bilitis (DOB), the first lesbian rights organization in the US. They also publish the monthly magazine The Ladder.

1957: Police confiscate copies of "Howl and Other Poems" by **Allen Ginsberg** and arrest City Lights bookstore owner **Lawrence Ferlinghetti** on obscenity charges. The charges are overturned in a landmark free expression case.

1958: The first leather bar, "Why Not?", opens in the Tenderloin. Others soon follow in the South of Market area.

1959: Park Merced, one of the largest planned neighborhoods of high-rise apartments towers and low-rise garden apartments in SF, refuses to rent to single men (homosexuals) or African Americans.

1960's: Homosexuals are still harassed, intimidated, and arrested for congregating in bars, parks, or other public spaces. It is routine for beat cops and vice squad officers to entrap, beat and blackmail gay men.

1960: A "gayola" scandal erupts when it is discovered that a state alcohol-board officials and some local cops had taken bribes from gay bars. The scandal results in increased police harassment of gay bars but also sparks pleas for tolerance from religious and city officials. The "gayola" trial ends in the acquittal of the officers.

1961: Police raid the "Tay-Bush Inn" at Taylor and Bush. It is the largest gay bar raid in San Francisco history. 103 patrons are sent in seven patrol wagons to city jail and arrested on 'lewd behavior' charges. San Francisco Examiner publishes the names, addresses, occupations and employers of all arrested. One municipal judge calls the city a "Parisian pansy's paradise" and threatens stiff penalties for any homosexuals brought before him.

1961(Sept 11): Public TV station KQED broadcasts The Rejected, the first made-for-television documentary about homosexuality on American TV. Mattachine Society president **Hal Call** is one of three gay spokesmen. The program is critically and popularly well received. This is in contrast to nearly all mainstream local and national media coverage of gays and lesbians. Well into 1990's, LGBT people are portrayed in the media as deviant, immoral, mentally ill, or criminal. Demeaning stereotypes are reinforced and gays and lesbians are assumed to be inherently inferior.

1961: **José Sarria**, a war vet and a Mexican-American drag entertainer who also waited tables at the "Black Cat Café," runs as an openly gay candidate for San Francisco's Board of Supervisors in order to call attention to police harassment of gay-friendly establishments. He does not win, but he receives 5,600 votes, comes in 9th out of a field of 32 candidates, and demonstrates that a gay vote could be a significant voting block.

1961: The League for Civil Education (LCE), organized by **Guy Strait** and **José Sarria**, distributes the first gay tabloid in SF, Citizen News. It features gossipy news on bar culture and police impropriety.

1961: **Lou Hogan**, who was a successful drag performer (**Sonia Pavijev**) in the 1920's, writes a number of books under various pen names: "The Scarlet Pansy", a novel of gay love in 1932; the first gay detective novel, "The Gay Detective" (aka "Rough Trade") in 1961; and a compendium of camp cuisine, "The Gay Cookbook" in 1965. He is also a chef and columnist for Gourmet Magazine.

1962: The Tavern Guild (co-founded by **José Sarria**), an association of gay bar owners and liquor wholesalers, forms in response to police harassment of gay bars and gay people. The Guild retains a lawyer and bail bondsman for anyone arrested in or near a gay bar, and it publishes a brochure on how to deal with being arrested or harassed by police. It eventually becomes a political force in local politics. It is the first gay business association in the US and lasts until 1995. **Phil Doganiero, Bill Plath** and **Darryl Glied** are its first leaders.

1963: The first gay bar in the Castro, "Missouri Mule," opens at 2348 Market St. Recent gay bars that have operated in this space include "Detour", "Jet" and now "Trigger."

1963 The "Black Cat Café" finally closes. The bar's legacy is that it broke the barriers that prevented overtly gay bars from existing freely and affirmed the right of homosexuals to assemble.

1964: Life magazine publishes a malicious story identifying San Francisco as the "Gay Capital" of the US. The article's tone is accusatory and leads to an outcry against the homosexuals infesting California. The unintentional effect is that thousands of gay people pour into California now that they know where to go.

1964: The Society for Individual Rights (SIR) is founded by **William Beardemphl, Jim Foster, Bill Plath, José Sarria**, and others in response to police raids and harassment focuses on building a visible gay community. It sponsors drag shows, dinners, bridge clubs, bowling leagues, softball games, field trips, art classes, and meditation groups. It also produces a slick, professional monthly magazine Vector.

1964: "The Big Glass" on Fillmore Street opens. It is the first black-owned and African-American-oriented gay bar in the city.

1964: Ted McIlvenna, a social worker at Glide Memorial Church, organizes the Council on Religion and the Homosexual (CRH) to fight homophobia within mainline churches.

1965 (Jan. 1): The police raid a benefit for CRH sponsored by several homophile groups including SIR, Tavern Guild, Mattachine Society and Daughters of Bilitis. Outside California Hall on 625

Polk Street, police snap pictures as the 600 attendees, including a number of clergymen and their wives, as they arrive or leave the event in a blatant attempt to intimidate. Police are still in the habit of making arrests for same-sex touching in bars and urge cancellation of the dance. When police demand entry into the hall,

The ministers who sponsored the benefit. [from left] Rev. Lewis Durham, Rev. Cecil Williams, Canon Robert Cromey, Rev. Fred Bird, Rev. Charles Lewis, Rev. Clarence Colwell and Rev. Ted McIlvenna.

Incidents at a Homosexual Benefit

Angry Ministers Rip Police

three CRH-attorneys explain that under California law, the event is a private party and they cannot enter unless they have bought tickets. The lawyers are then arrested, as is a ticket-taker, on charges of obstructing an officer. The cases go to trial with support from the ACLU. All are acquitted.

1964: **José Sarria** declares himself "Empress José I, The Widow Norton" and founds the Imperial Court System, which grows to become an international association and one of the largest LGBT charity organizations.

Mid-60's: Three distinct gay enclaves reside in SF. The gay commercial center is on Polk Street with bars and restaurants catering to the white-collar, professional gays. The Tenderloin is a mix of bars, restaurants, and residential hotels that catered to the gay poor and sexually marginal, such as transvestites and male hustlers. The South of Market is home to bathhouses, sex clubs and the leather subculture.

1965: Thirty people picket Grace Cathedral to protest punitive actions taken against **Rev. Canon Robert Cromey** for his involvement in the Council on Religion and the Homosexual.

Compton's Cafeteria Riot

1966 (August): The Compton's Cafeteria Riot occurs in the Tenderloin at 101 Taylor Street at Turk. This incident is one of the first recorded transgender riots in US history, preceding the more famous 1969 Stonewall Riots in NYC. Transgender patrons riot against police oppression at the popular all-night restaurant. It marks another turning point in the local LGBT movement.

1966: SIR opens the first gay community center in the US. It is located in the South of Market area on 6th St.

1966: The North American Conference of Homophile Organizations holds its first national convention of gay and lesbian groups in San Francisco.

1969: Tower Records fires **Frank Denaro**, believing him to be gay. The newly formed Committee for Homosexual Freedom (CHF) pickets the store for several weeks until Denaro is reinstated. CHF, a splinter group of SIR and founded by **Leo Laurence** and **Dale Whittington**, runs similar pickets of Safeway stores, Macy's, States Steamship Company, San Francisco Examiner, and the Federal Building.

Gay Power

1969 (Oct 31): The purple handprint becomes a local symbol of gay liberation, after the San Francisco Examiner dumps purple ink on members of the Gay Liberation Front and the Society for Individual Rights. The groups were protesting another in a series of news articles disparaging the LGBT community. When the police are called in, the cops storm through the crowd clubbing the protestors.

1969 (Dec 31): The Cockettes, a psychedelic drag queen troupe, perform for the first time at the Palace Theatre on Union and Columbus in the North Beach. The collective is conceived by Hibiscus and will inspire the glitter rock era and the campy show extravaganzas of the 70's. Notable members include disco singer **Sylvester**, drag performer **Divine** and musical director **Scrumbly Koldewyn**.

1970's: The Castro District comes of age as a gay center following the "Summer of Love" in the neighboring Haight-Ashbury District that saw a large influx of youth. Many local gays move to the Castro around 1970 from the prominently gay Polk Gulch neighborhood. Major economic draw is affordable housing. Large Victorian homes are available at low rents or available for purchase for low down payments when their former middle-class owners were fleeing to the suburbs. It is the first major gay neighborhood that does not develop from a Bohemian or vice enclave or from an artsy/entertainment district.

1970: A small "gay-in" is held in Golden Gate Park. This is the first event resembling the modern San Francisco Pride celebration.

1970: Rev. Howard Wells organizes the Metropolitan Community Church of San Francisco. MCC is a leading force in the development of Queer Theology.

1971 (Apr 1): **Bob Ross** and **Paul Bentley** co-found the Bay Area Reporter -- a free weekly gay newspaper. It is the oldest-continuously published, and one of the largest LGBT newspapers in the US.

1971: San Francisco police arrest more than 2,800 men on public sex charges while NYC only arrests 63 during the same time. The old Irish/Italian Catholic politicians and police continue fighting the perceived moral erosion of the city. SF Public Health Department estimates the gay population in 1971 to be 90,000. In 1977, the gay population grows to 120,000; and in 1978, to 150,000 or 20% of the city. By the mid-70's, San Francisco and the Castro neighborhood, the city-within-a-city, surpasses New York City and Amsterdam as the gay urban center.

1971: Activists couple **Del Martin** and **Phyllis Lyon** along with **Jim Foster** from SIR organizes the "Alice B. Toklas

LGBT Democratic Club." This political action committee is the first organization for gay Democrats in the US. The club will consistently take more conservative political stances than its chief rival, the "San Francisco Gay Democratic Club" that starts in five years.

1972: The San Francisco Gay Pride Parade is first held. It becomes the largest gathering of LGBT people and allies in the nation with over a million people attending.

1972: San Francisco becomes one of the first cities in United States to pass a homosexual rights ordinance. The law prohibits employment discrimination based on sexual orientation in the public sector and prohibits companies that have contracts with the city from discriminating based on sexual orientation.

1972: City College of San Francisco offers first Gay Literature course in the country.

1972: **Jim Foster** is given a prime time TV spot speaking at the '72 Democratic National Convention after helping to secure George McGovern the first position on the California Democratic primary ballot. He and fellow delegate **Madeline Davis** are the first openly LGBT people ever to address a national party convention.

1972: **Harvey Milk** moves from NYC to the Castro and opens his camera store at 575 Castro Street.

1973: Two lesbians, **Mary Ellen Cunha** and **Peggy Coleman**, open the Castro bar, "Twin Peaks Tavern." It is the first gay bar with clear plate-glass windows facing the street.

1973 (Dec 15): The American Psychiatric Association removes homosexuality from its diagnostic list of mental disorders. The passage of the resolution "cures" millions of gays and lesbians across America.

1974: Castro Street Fair begins and becomes the city's longest-running street fair. **Harvey Milk**, and the local merchant group he leads, the Castro Valley Association, promotes it.

1974: The Gay Community Softball League starts its first competitive season with sponsorship from eight gay bars and a gym. The word "gay" is soon dropped because several players have corporate careers and are fearful of being outed and losing their jobs. In an effort to de-escalate tensions between the police and the gay community, the championship team plays the police. "Twin Peaks Tavern" beats the police 9 to 4.

1974: Frontrunners, now international LGBT running and walking group, kicks off its first chapter in SF. It is inspired by **Patricia Nell Warren**'s bestselling gay novel "The Front Runner," a love story exploring issues relating to homosexuals in American sports.

1974 (Labor Day): Tensions between the gay community and the police come to a head when a man is beaten and arrested while walking down Castro Street. Police reinforcements suddenly appear, their badge numbers hidden, and beat dozens of gay men. Fourteen are arrested and charged with obstructing a sidewalk. **Harvey Milk** dubs them the "Castro 14", and a $1.375 million lawsuit is filed against the police.

Mid 1970's: Gay and lesbian activists are forming multiracial coalitions including Third World Gay Caucus and Black And Third World Lesbians. Several racially specific gay organizations are started: Gay American Indians, Black Gay Caucus, Gay Latino Alliance, and Gay Asian Support Group.

1975: **Tom Ammiano** becomes the first public school teacher in San Francisco to make his sexual orientation a matter of public knowledge. With **Ron Lanza** and **Hank Wilson, Ammiano** co-founds the Gay Teachers Coalition and lobby against discrimination for gay teachers in the city schools.

1975: A number of activists including **Howard Wallace, Hank Wilson, Jane Sica, Chris Perry, Jim Gordon, Claude Wynne**, and **Tom Ammiano** initiate an organization called Bay-Area Gay Liberation (BAGL). Its aims are to advance lesbian and gay liberation by reaching out to potential allies within the labor movement, the feminist movement and movements of people of color and national minorities.

1975: Two straight Teamster union organizers approach gay community leaders **Howard Wallace** of BAGL and **Harvey Milk** about supporting the Coors beer boycott. **Wallace** and **Milk** agree, if the Teamsters would agree to promote the hiring of openly gay truck drivers. With the Teamsters consent, the Coors boycott took off in the City, and spread nationally. In California, the market share of Coors dropped from 40 percent to 14 percent. Facing this boycott, Coors stopped asking its applicants about their sexuality.

1975 (Sept. 22): **Oliver Sipple,** a decorated US Marine and Vietnam War veteran, foils an assassination attempt on **President Gerald Ford** by **Sara Jane Moore** outside the St. Francis Hotel. The subsequent public revelation that **Sipple** is gay turns the news story into a cause célèbre for gay activists.

1975: California becomes the 12th state to decriminalize consensual sodomy in a bill sponsored by **Willie Brown** and **George Moscone** and signed by **Governor Jerry Brown**. Besides repealing the law against consensual sodomy, it also repeals laws against oral copulation by homosexual, unmarried, and married heterosexual couples.

1976: Believing that the existing "Alice B. Toklas LGBT Democratic Club" will never support him in his political aspirations, **Harvey Milk** co-founds the "San Francisco Gay Democratic Club" in the wake of his unsuccessful 1976 campaign for the California State Assembly. Activists **Harry Britt, Hank Wilson, Dick Pabich, Jim Rivaldo** and first club president **Chris Perry** join **Milk** in forming the club.

1976: **Armistead Maupin's** "Tales of the City" begins its serialized run in the San Francisco Chronicle.

1976: The Butterfly Brigade (an offshoot of BAGL) works the Castro neighborhood in the evenings to make the streets safe. Armed with whistles, note cards to record license plates, and portable CB radios, the 30-strong brigade lays out a walkie-talkie network of security. This is in response to the street beatings of over 40 gay men the previous year.

1976: The motorcycle club, Dykes on Bikes, makes it first appearance at the Gay Pride Parade.

Supervisor Harvey Milk & San Francisco
Mayor George Moscone

1977: **Harvey Milk** is elected city supervisor, becoming the third openly gay American elected to public office and the first in California. Milk serves almost 11 months in office and is responsible for passing a stringent gay rights ordinance for the city. Article 33 of the SF Police Code prohibits discrimination in employment, housing, and public accommodations based on sexual orientation in the private sector.

1977: Sha'ar Zahav, a progressive Reform Jewish synagogue, opens for people of all sexual identities.

1977: Theatre Rhinoceros, founded by **Lanny Baugniet** and his partner **Allan B. Estes, Jr.**, is the first gay theater company to employ actors under a professional seasonal agreement.

1977: The San Francisco International Lesbian and Gay Film Festival (now known as Frameline Film Festival) premieres. It is the oldest continuing lesbian and gay film festival in the world. Founding members include **Daniel Nicoletta, David Waggoner, Hank Wilson,** and **Marc Huestis**.

1977: Lesbian activists **Donna Hitchens** and **Roberta Achtenberg**, as well as others, create the National Center for Lesbian Rights (NCLR). It is a public interest law firm that advocates for equitable policies affecting the LGBT community.

1978: Artist **Gilbert Baker** designs the Rainbow or Gay Pride Flag. It first flies at the San Francisco Gay Freedom Day Parade in June 1978.

1978 (Nov 7): Proposition 6, the Briggs Initiative, is defeated with tepid support from **Governor Reagan** and **President Carter**. **Harvey Milk** spearheads the campaign in the state with **Hank Wilson** and **Tom Ammiano**. If the ballot initiative had passed, it would have barred gays, and those who support gay rights, from teaching in public schools. The initiative is the first failure in a movement that started with the successful campaign headed by **Anita Bryant** and her organization Save Our Children in Dade

County, Florida to repeal a local gay rights ordinance.

1978 (Nov. 27): Former Supervisor **Dan White** assassinates Supervisor **Harvey Milk** and **Mayor George Moscone**. Despite his short career in politics, **Milk** becomes an icon in San Francisco and a martyr in the gay community.

1978: Gay music pioneer **Jon Reed Sims** starts the San Francisco Lesbian/Gay Freedom Band and the San Francisco Gay Men's Chorus in 1978. He creates the Lesbian/Gay Chorus of San Francisco in 1980. The San Francisco Gay Men's Chorus, the world's first openly gay chorus, sings its first public performance at an impromptu memorial for slain **Mayor Moscone** and **Supervisor Milk**.

1978: **Rabbi Allen Bennet** allows himself to be outed in the San Francisco Examiner, making him the first openly gay rabbi.

1979: Bay Times (originally called Coming Up!) begins publishing as a free weekly LGBT newspaper.

1979: The Sisters of Perpetual Indulgence arises as a charity, protest, and street performance organization that uses drag and Catholic imagery to call attention to sexual intolerance and to satirize issues of gender and morality.

1979 (March 11): **Sylvester**, the flamboyant soul and disco singer known as the "Queen of Disco", sells out the War Memorial Opera House. **Mayor Dianne Feinstein** awards him with the key to the city and proclaims March 11 to be "Sylvester Day".

1979 (May 21): The White Night Riots follow **Dan White's** acquittal of first-degree murder charges and conviction on lesser charges of voluntary manslaughter. Hundreds of people march to city hall to vent the injustice. A riot ensues with broken windows and torched police cars. The spontaneous actions lead to a retaliatory police raid on a Castro gay bar, the "Elephant Walk" (now "Harvey's Restaurant and Bar"), two miles away and hours after the City Hall disturbance. Police in riot gear beat many patrons. Two-dozen arrests are made during the raid, and several people later sue the police. In the following days, gay leaders refuse to apologize for the events of that night. The gay community begins to flex increase political power in the City. In response to a campaign promise, **Mayor Dianne Feinstein** appoints a pro-gay Chief of Police, who increases recruitment of gays in the police force and eases tensions.

Much of the 1980's and 1990's focuses on grim and relentless imprint of AIDS as it marches across the city and the nation. As thousands die, AIDS becomes the focus of LGBT people who participate in organizations, marches, and vigils to stop the spread of the disease and increase the availability of treatments for people living with AIDS.

The late 1990's and 2000's sees the incremental expansion of civil rights for LGBT individuals, but same-sex couples' rights become an increasingly controversial topic, with referenda and judicial cases on same-sex marriage jousting for constitutional finality.

Timeline References:

"Gay by the Bay: A History of Queer Culture in the San Francisco Bay Area," by Susan Stryker, Jim Van Buskirk

"Out in the Castro," edited by Winston Leyland
"Queer Sites: Gay Urban Histories Since 1600," by David Higgs

"Wide Open Town - A history of Queer San Francisco to 1965," by Nan Alamilla Boyd

Fact Sources:

http://wikipedia.org
http://glbtq.com - glbtq encyclopedia)

http://gayinsacramento.com/Chron1-Calif-page.htm
(Gay Chronicles)

http://www.glapn.org/sodomylaws/sensibilities/california.htm
(Sodomy Laws)

http://outhistory.org/
(OutHistory)

http://foundsf.org/index.php?title=Category:Gay_and_Lesbian
(FoundSF)

http://thecastro.net/index.html#index
(Uncle Donald's Castro Street)

http://www.sanfranciscogay.com/
 (Gay San Francisco)

http://focusfeatures.com/article/why_is_san_francisco_so_gay_
(Why Is San Francisco So Gay?)

SAN FRANCISCO
Gay Bars – Restaurants & Businesses
1908 to 1996

This list is not complete or necessarily accurate to the letter. It was compiled by many persons, with special thanks to Vic at the Community Thrift Store and the one and only Marlow, bartender at Uncle Bert's. I ran across the list while researching and made every effort to reach the contact listed on the web page, but all phone numbers and addresses are no longer good. I include it here in good faith to help preserve it for posterity and to put into perspective just how many gay establishments (700 or more) San Francisco has hosted over the years. Please take note of how many on this list were started in 1960's and 70's.

CinchSF.com:
Gay-Bar-History
http://cinchsf.com/wp-content/uploads/2012/01/SF-Gay-Bar-History-Log.pdf

A

Abby Room – Atherton Hotel	685 Ellis St.	1970
A Little More	702 15th St	
Academy	2166 Market St.	1982
Accident		
Adler Place	12 Adler Place	

Adobe	Eddy & Jones	1939
After Dark	936 Montgomery	1974
Agenda	1st Street & Market	
Alamo Square Saloon	600 Filmore St.	
Alfie's	2140 Market St.	1973
Alibi		
Alley Cat	330 Mason St.	1971
Alta Plaza	2301 Filmore St.	
Alvin's	59 2nd. Street	
Alvin's	692 Geary Street	
Ambassador	101 Eddy Street	1972
Ambush		
1351 Harrison Street	1974	
Amelia's	Valencia Street	1990
Andromeda	1550 California Street	
Ann's	440 Broadway	
Anxious Asp	Green Street	
Anxious Asp	Haight Street	
Art's Cavern	878 Valencia Street	
Asylum		
Aunt Charlies	133 Turk Street	

B

Bachelors Club	3481 18th. Street	1972
Back Stage		
Back Street		
Badlands	4121 18th. Street	1974
BAJ	131 Bay Street	1964
Balcony	2166 Market Street	

Ba's Corner
Ballroom
Bar "D"
Barbary Coast   312 Columbus Avenue   1974
Barrell House   17th & Florida Streets
Barrell House   Embarcadero
Bay Brick Inn   1190 Folsom Street
Bear Hollow   440 Castro Street
Bear   440 Castro Street
Burton's   Market Street
Buzzby's   1436 Polk Street   1974
Buzz's Southside   6th Street

C

Caberet   936 Montgomery Street   1972
Caborra's Place   California Street   1974
Cadell Place   524 Union Street   1970
Café, The   2367 Market Street   1991
Café Akimbo   116 Maiden Lane, 3rd. Floor 1995
Café Biarritz   Broadway & Kearny Streets
Café San Marcos   2367 Market Street
Caffe Monda   2032 Polk Street   1994
Cal-Hyde   California & Hyde Streets
CallBoard Garden   Polk Street
Call's
Camelia's Room
Campus   1551 Mission Street
Candle Light Room
Capri   1326 Grant Avenue   1972
Cardi's   2166 Market Street

Carnival Blue	179 Eddy Street	
Carriage Inn		
Casa de Dristal	1021 Post Street	1973
Casey's Frontier	1145 Folsom Street	1972
Castaways		
Castro Cabana		
Castro & 19th Streets		
Castro Café	484 Castro Street	1974
Castro Station	456 Castro Street	1975
Cavanaugh's	Mission Street	
Cave		
Cellar		
Chains		
Chances R		
Chaps	11th & Folsom Streets	
Charpe's Grill	131 Gough Street	
Checker Club		
Cheek-to-Cheek	1550 California Street	1976
Chez Chou Chou		
Chez Mollet	527 Bryant Street	
Chez Jacques	Broadway Street	
Chi Chi Club	Broadway Street	
Chicago Saloon	200 Capp Street	1975
Chick's Caboose	Jones & Turk Streets	
Chill's Chops	Embarcadero next to YMCA	
Chris's Fog Horn	Market Street	
Chris's Seafood	Mission & 4th Street	
Chuckie's		
Chukker's	Turk Street	
Church Street Station	2100 Market Street	

Cinch	1723 Polk Street	
Cissy's Saloon	1590 Folsom Street	1974
City, The	936 Montgomery Street	
City Dump	506 Castro Street	1974
Cloud 7	2360 Polk Street	1962
Clover Club	Mission & 30th Street	
Club, The	718 14th. Street	
Club Dori	427 Presidio Avenue	1964
Club Elite		
Club Malibu	3395 Mission Street	1994
Club Rendezvous	567 Sutter Street	1970
Cock & Bull		
Cockring		
Cocktails	201 9th Street	1993
Coffee Don's	22nd & Valencia Streets	1974
Commuter Club		
Company	1319 California Street	
Connie's Why Not	878 Valencia Street	1972
Copper Kettle		
Copper Lantern	Grant Avenue	1953
Corner, The	1898 Folsom Street	1970
Corner Drug Store	Masonic & Haight Streets	
Corner Grocery Bar	4048 18th Street	1974
Corner Longhorn Saloon	1898 Folsom Street	1971
Corner Outlook	2100 Market Street	
Corner Zoo	2100 Market Street	
Corral, The	2140 Market Street	1988
Country Club	2742 17th Street	1972
Covered Wagon	278 11th Street & Folsom	1972

Cow Palace Saloon	1347 Folsom Street	1972
Crossroads	Stewart & Mission Streets	1966
Crystal Bowl	Market Street	1953
Crystal Chandelier		
Crystal Pistal	842 Valencia Street	1989
Curtain Call	456 Geary Street	1972

D

D'Oak Room	Divisadero & Oak Streets	1966
DJ's		
Daddy's	440 Castro Street	1995
Dalt Club	Turk Street	1963
Dance Your Ass Off	Larkin & Ellis Streets	
Dario's		
Dash, The	Barbary Coast Area	1908
Dead End	582 Folsom Street	1970
Deluxe	1511 Haight Street	
Depot		
Detour	2348 Market Street	
Devil's Herd	853 Valencia Street	
Dial Club		
Diamond Sutra Café	537 Diamond Street	1972
Dick's at the Beach	La Playa & Judah	1986
Different Strokes	1550 California Street	1976
Dirty Dick's		
Dirty Sally's		
Dog Patch Saloon		
Dolan's	Suttor & Stockton Streets	1953
Don's Coffee Shop	Leavenworth & Pine Streets	

Down Under		
Dreamland	715 Harrison Street	
Duo	4049 18th Street	
Duste's	16th & Market Streets	
Dutch Café Club	888 McAlister Street	1967

E

Eagle Creek Saloon	1884 Market Street	
Early Bird	1723 Polk Street	1970
Ebb Tide		
Eclipse	1548 Polk Street	1994
Edge, The	4149 18th Street	1991
Edgewater		
Eichelberger's	2742 17th Street	
Eighth Day		
El Rio	3158 Mission Street	1985
Eleanor's	3309 Mission Street	1978
Elephant Walk	500 Castro Street	
Elite, The		1972
Emerald Isle		
Emperor Norton's Folly	2155 Polk Street	
End Up	401 6th Street	1974
Ensign Club	Embarcadero & Market	
Este Noche	3079 16th Street	
Ethel's		
Exit, The		1972

F

Fairmont Grocery	

Fanny's	4230 18th. Street	1974
Fantasy	330 Mason Street	1969
Fantasy	Geary Street	
Fat Albert's	O'Farrell Street	
Fat Fairy's Grill	1558 Haight Street	1974
FeBe's	1501 Folsom Street	1970
Festus	4149 18th Street	1975
Fez, The	Turk Street	
Fickle Fox	842 Valencia Street	1970
Finale	Geary Street	
Finocchio's	506 Broadway	1936
Fireside	1319 California Street	1966
Five Twenty-Seven	527 Bryant Street	1970
Folsom Prison	1898 Folsom Street	1974
Force		
Four Leaf Clover	3346 Mission Street	
Francine's	4149 18th Street	
Frank's	Broadway Street	
Fred's Cellar		
French Quarter Bar & Grill	201 9th Street	1994
Frisco Disco	60 6th Street	1976
Frolic Room	141 Mason Street	1970
Front, The	Front & Jackson Streets	1959
Frontier (Casey's)	1145 Folsom Street	1972
Full Moon	1550 California Street	

G

Gallagher's Gold Room	939 Geary Street	
Galleon, The	718 14th Street	1975

Gangway	841 Larkin Street	1972
Garden of Earthly Delights	1808 Market Street	
Gas Station Bar	6th & Folsom Streets	
Gaslight #1	Townsend Street	
Gaslight #2	Pine Street	
Gaslight Disco & Show Bar	647 Valencia Street	
Gate, The	1093 Pine Street	
Gay 20's Speakeasy		
Gay 90's		
Gaylord's	Polk & Broadway Streets	
George & Gordy's		
Gilded Cage	Ellis Street	
Gilmore's	1068 Ryde Street	1979
Giner's Too	43 6th Street	
Ginger's	100 Eddy Street	
Ginger's Trois	246 Kearny Street	
Giraffe, The	1131 Polk Street	1977
Gladwin's	2217 Market Street	
Glass Clipper		
Gold Coast		
Gold Eagle	1601 Market Street	1972
Gold Room	939 Geary Street	
Gold Street	56 Gold Street	1970
Golden Cask	Haight Street	1962
Golden Door	233 Ellis Street	1971
Golden Eagle	California & front Streets	
Golden Eagle	Embarcadero Center #2	1980
Golden Rivet	9th St. Mission & Howard	

Gordon's Saloon	1750 Polk Street	
Gordon's	840 Samsome Street	1952
Gordon's	Jones Street	1976
Graffiti	942 Valencia Street	
Greco's	1335 Grant Avenue	1969
Gretta's Wooden Horse	622 Pine Street	
Grub Stake Grill	1525 Pine Street	
Grub Stake	Turk & Mason Streets	
Gus's Pub	Haight Street	1974

H

Hamburger Mary's	Turk & Mason Streets	
Hamburger Mary's	12th & Folsom Streets	
Handball Express	6th & Harrison Streets	
Handle Bar	California near Hyde Street	1962
Hans Off	199 Valencia Street	1972
Harry Ho's Landmark	45 Turk Street	
Harvey's	500 Castro Street	1996
Haven, The	7th & Mission Streets	1974
Havoc House	Polk Street	
Head Hunters	Embarcadero & Mission	
Headquarters	469 Castro Street	1992
Here's Now	11050 Market Street	1970
Hideaway, The	438 Eddy Street	
Hideaway (Church St. Station)	2100 Market Street	
High Chaparral	2140 Market Street	1987
Highland		
HobNob	700 Geary Street	1974
Hole In The Wall	289 9th Street	1994

Hole In The Wall
Hombre   2448 Market Street
Honey Bucket   4146 18th. Street
Hook & Ladder   1035 Post Street
Pumping
Horny Owl   741 O'Farrell Street   1973
Hot House   1548 Polk Street   1973
House of Harmony   1312 Polk Street
Hula Hut
Hungry Hole
Hunks   1160 Polk Street
Huntington Hotel   Nob Hill   1943

I

I Beam Disco   1748 Haight Street
I Do Know   4186 18th Street   1960's
Images
In-B-Tween   1347 Folsom Street   1971
Inn Debt   1390 California Street   1972
Ivy's   398 Hayes Street

J

J-Line   Church & 30th Streets
JJ's   2225 Filmore Street
JP's
Jack's   Embarcadero & Sacramento
Jackaroo   Mission Street
Jackhammer   290 Sanchez Street   1994
Jackie D's   147 Mason Street

Jackie D's	301 Turk Street	
Jackson's Bar & Restaurant	2237 Powell Street	1963
Jackson's	Jones Street	1976
Jack's Waterfront	Front & Jackson Streets	1960's
Jacques	California Street	
Dim Dolan's	Sutter Street Garage Area	1950's
Josie's Cabaret	3583 16th Street	
Jumping Frog	Polk & Broadway Streets	1960's
Just For You	1453 18th Street	

K

Katie's Opera Bar	1441 Grant Avenue	1965
Kelly's Saloon	3489 20th Street	1971
Keno's	Bush Street	
Keno's	47 Golden Gate & Market	1950's
Kimo's	1351 Polk Street	
Kito's		
Kitty's at The Cavern	601 Eddy Street	
Kiwi		
Kokpit	301 Turk Street	1970

L

La India Bonita	3089 16th Street	
La Cave	1469 Sutter Street	1972
La Cucaracha	Market & Castro Streets	
Landmark	45 Turk Street	1970
Larriat		
Last Resort		

Latex Lily's Saloon	29 Stevenson (3rd & Market)	1971
LeBouef	Washington (El Cortex Hotel)	1971
Le Club		
Le Domino	2742 17th Street	
Le Disque	1840 Haight Street	
Le Piano Zinc	708 14th Street	
Leather Neck		
Lena's Burger Basket		
Lenny's 36 Club		1954
Leonardas	16 Leland Avenue	1970
Leticia's	2223 Market Street	
Latreen	8th St Howard & Mission	
Liberty Inn	863 Bush Street	1974
Libra	1884 Market Street	1970
Lily's Saloon	4 Valencia Street	1987
Line Up	398 7th Street	
Lion Pub	2062 Divisadero Street	1971
Lions Lair	410 Brannan Street	1971
Lip's Wooden Horse	622 Polk Street	
Living End	3349 18th Street	
Lo Bill's	1st & Mission Streets	
Lone Star Saloon	1354 Harrison Street	1984
Lonely Bull	471 Turk Street	1970
Lotie's	Market Street	
Lucky Club	1801 Haight Street	1970
Lucky Spot	Post & Polk Streets	1969
Lumber Yard	979 Folsom Street	1974
Lupann's Café	4072 18th Street	1986

Lupe's Echo

M

Ma Tante Sumi Restaurant	4243 18th Street	
Magic Garden	1840 Haight Street	1971
Main Street		
Male Box		
Mama Billy's	1498 Pine Street	
Mammy Plesant's		
Man's Country		
Manhandler	1840 Haight Street	1972
Maple Leaf	1548 Polk Street	1968
Marlena's	488 Hayes Street	1993
Mary's Tower	1500 Grant Avenue	1960
Mason Club	Mason & Eddy Streets	
Masque	1160 Polk Street	
Maude's Study	937 Cole Street	1966
Maurice's	57 Powell Street	1957
McDonalds Pub	11088 Market Street	1992
McDonalds Pub	34 7th Street	1996
Meat Rack		
Mecca	2029 Market Street	1996
Meet Market		
Men's Room	2988 18th Street	1976
Metro	2100 Market Street	
Midnight Sun	4067 Castro Street	1997
Midnight Sun	506 Castro Street	1971
Milky Way	645 Geary Street	1972
Mind Shaft	2140 Market Street	1974

Mint, The	1942 Market Street	1969
Miss Moffett's	853 Valencia Street	1970
Miss Smith's Tea Room	1353 Grant Avenue	1950's
Missouri Mule	2348 Market Street	1964
Mistake	3988 18th Street	1971
Moby Dick's	4049 18th Street	
Mocambo	1160 Polk Street	1972
Mona's 440	440 Broadway	
Moth & Flame	California & Hyde Streets	1959
Mother G's		
Motherlode	1002 Post Street	
Mouse House #1		
Mouse House #2		
Mr. B's	2nd Street	1963
Mr. B's	6th Street	
Music Hall	Larkin Street	1970
My Place	1225 Folsom Street	1991
My Room	209 Stevenson Street	1970
Market	90 Market Street	1960's

N

N'Touch	1548 Polk Street	1970
Naked Grape	2097 Market Street	1972
Neal's Kitchen		
NeUie's	17th Street	
Nellie's	4th & Mission Streets	
Neon chicken	4063 18th Street	1974
Nevada Club		
New Bell Saloon	1203 Polk Street	1971
Nickelodeon	Mason Street	

Night Cap	499 O'Farrell Street	1972
Night Shift	469 Castro Street	1994
Ninty Market	90 Market Street	
Nob Hill	Polk Street	1958
No Name	1347 Folsom Street	1974
Noah's Ark	524 Union Street	1971
Norse Cover	434 Castro Street	
Nothing Special	469 Castro Street	1971
Number's	Filmore Street	
Nights	335 Jones Street	1970

O

Oak Room	St Francis Hotel	1960's
Off The Beaten Path	18th Street	
Off The Levee	527 Bryant Street	
Oil Can Harry's	Larkin & Ellis Streets	1976
Oil Can Harry's	1312 Polk Street	
Old Crow	926 Market Street	1950's
Old Mission Inn		
Old Rick's Gold Room	939 Geary Street	
Old Spaghetti Factory	Grant Avenue	1956
Olive Oil's	Pier 50 China Basin	
Olympus		
On The Levee	987 Embarcadero Street	1963
One-Eighty-One Club	181 Eddy Street	1954
Opera Club	621 Gough Street	
Opus I	Montgomery & Pacific Streets	
Opus II		
Original Jackson's	2237 Powell Street	1975

Orion
Orpheum Circus   1184 Market Street   1970
Our House
Our Kitchen
Our Place
Outer Limits   853 Valencia Street
Overpass   488 Hayes Street

P

P.S. Piano Bar   1121 Polk Street   1970
& Restaurant
Pacific Exchange   225 Filmore Street
Page One   431 Natoma Street   1971
Pandora's Box   3041 Geary Blvd.
Paper Doll   524 Union Street   1953
Paradise
Paradox
Park Beverage Company
Partner's   1035 Post Street
Party Club
Patio Café   531 Castro Street
Patio Exchange   531 Castro Street
Patsey's   2348 Market Street
Patty's Pub   Haight Street
Patty's Pub   Post Street   1977
Paul's Saloon
Pearl's   (Behind Gilded Cage)   1960's
Peg's Place   4737 Geary Blvd.   1972
Peke Place   180 golden Gate Avenue   1972
Pendulum   4146 18th Street   1970

People's Place		
Pepperment West		
Peter Pan	45 Turk Street	
Peter Pan	Taylor Street	
Petri's Caoara	161 California Street	1972
Phillip's French Quarter	201 9TH Street	1994
Phoenix	482 Castro Street	
Phoenix	Folsom Street	
Phoenix, The	1035 Post Street	1974
Phone booth	11398 S. Van Ness Avenue	1974
Pic & Pan	Ellis Street	1966
Pilsner Inn	225 church Street	
Pines, The	1093 Pine Street	
Pink Cloud		
Pink Octopus		
Pipeline	4149 18th Street	
Playland		
Plunge		
Poke's Place		
Polk Along	1548 Polk Street	1971
Polk Gulch Saloon	1100 Polk Street	1971
Polk Rendezvous	1303 Polk Street	
Polk Street Connection		
Polynesian Mary's	154 McAllister Street	
Poopie's	1500 Grant Avenue	1950's
Powerhouse	1347 Folsom Street	1995
Previews	Geary Street	
Primrose Kane		
Prizm	482 Castro Street	1980's
Purple Pickle	2223 Market Street	1972

Q

Q.T.	1312 Polk Street & Clay	1960's
Quake	1748 Haight Street	
Quarry	17th & Florida	1974
Queen Mary's Pub	133 Turk Street	
Question Mark	Haight Street	

R

Rafters	1035 Polk Street	
Rag's	4th Street	
Rainbow Cattle Company	199 Valencia Street	1974
Rainbow Grocery	Larkin & O'Farrell	1972
Ramrod	1225 Folsom Street	1970
Rams Head	117 Taylor Street	
Ray's	289 9th Street	
Rawhide II	280 7th Street	
Rear End	14th & Market Street	1974
Red Balloon	Kearny Street	
Red Eye Saloon	335 Jones Street	
Red Lantern	180 Golden Gate Avenue	1974
Red Lion		
Red Lizard		
Red Star Saloon	1145 Folsom Street	1974
Reflections	1160 Polk Street	1988
Rendezvous	567 Sutter Street	1971
Rendezvous	Polk Street	
Renegade	1548 Polk Street	1985
ResErection	567 Sutter Street	1974
Rick's Cavalcade	Hyde Street	

Ride-On	1010 Bryant Street	
Riff Raff	621 Gough Street	1970
Road Runner club	499 O'Farrell Street	1974
Rock Bottom Saloon		
Rocket Club	230 Leavenworth Street	1954
Romeno's	Haight Street	
Round Up	298 6th Street	1970
Royal Palace	335 Jones Street	1970's
Rusty Nail		

S

Saddle Tramp Saloon		
Salina's Parlor		
Salley's		
San Francisco Bay		
Sanctuary	1601 Market Street	1974
Sandy's Saloon	946 Samsome Street	
S.F. Eagle	398 12th Street	1981
S.F. Motorwerks	4 Valencia Street	
Sarah Gooda's	Geary Street	
Sausage Factory	517 Castro Street	1972
Savoy Tivoli	1438 Grant Street	1963
Savoni"s Nite Cap	699 O'Farrell Street	
Scandals	162 Turk Street	
Score Board	Mason Street	
Score U	147 Mason Street	1974
Scott's Pit	10 Sanchez Street	1972
Scott's Potato	10 Sanchez Street	
Sea Cow	Stewart & Mission Streets	1960's

Season's	1160 Polk Street	
Seven Eighteen Club	718 14th Street	
Sha-Boom		
Shapes		
Shed, The	3520 16th Street	1972
Shep's	527 Montgomery Street	1965
Shutter's, The	709 Larkin Street at Ellis	1952
Silver Dollar	Eddy Street	1950's
Silver Rail	Market & 6th Street	1952
Silver rose		
Silver Slipper		
Silver Trumpet		
Slot, The	Folsom Street	
Small World		
Smoke House	1695 Polk Street at Clay	
Sound of Music	162 Turk Street	1970
Soup Kettle	643 Clay Street	1971
South of the Slot		
Speakeasy	2742 17th Street at Florida	1968
Special, The Nothing	469 Castro Street	
Splatter's	Mission Street	
Spur	Folsom & 11th Streets	
Spur Club	Turk Street	
Stables	1123 Folsom Street	
Stained Glass		
Stallion, The	749 Polk Street	1978
Starlight Room	1121 Market Street	
Stud, The	1535 Folsom Street	1970
Stud, The	399 Ninth Street	

Submarine Room	438 Eddy Street	1963
Sundown		
Sunshine Saloon		
Susie Q		
Sutter's Mill	10 Mark Lane	
Sutter's Mill	77 Battery Street	1986
Sutter's Mill	315 Bush Street	1969
Sutter's Mill	Market Street	
Sutter's Mill	Mission Street	
Swallow, The	1750 Polk Street	
Sweetlips' A Saloon	O'Farrell Street	1979

T

Talk of the Town	702 15th Street	
Tattoo Lagoon		
Tay-Bush	Taylor & Bush Streets	1960's
Teddy Bears	131 Gough Street	1985
Tender Trap		
The 8th Day		
The Arena	399 9th Street	
The Brig	1347 Folsom Street	
The Cave	280 7th Street	
The Caverns		
The City	Harrison Street	
The Dude		
The Number 3	18th & Valencia Streets	
The RNET	Bush Street	
The Shed	Market Street	1973
The Spirit	Divisadero & Fulton Streets	1973

The Web	9th St.bet Mission & Howard	
The Woodshed Theatre Club		
Tiffany's	1990 Market Street	1974
Tin Angel	1290 Battery Street & Embarcadero	
Toad Hall	482 Castro Street	1972
Tommy's	North Beach near Broadway	1954
Tool Box	4th & Harrison Streets	1962
Top Drawer		
Top Hat	1423 Market Street	
Tortuga	335 Jones Street	
Totie's	743 Larkin Street	1971
Two Eighty Five	Ellis Street	
Two Two Two	Turk & Hyde Streets	
Tower Lounge	1488 Pine Street	1970
Transfer, The	198 Church Street	1983
Trapp, The	72 Eddy Street	1960's
Travel Agency		
TRAX	1437 Haight Street	
Tree House	1884 Market Street	1972
Trench	6th Street bet Market & Mission	
Trinity Place	Bush Street	
Trinity Place	Trinity Place	1970's
Tracadero Transfer	520 4th Street	
Trolley	30th & church Streets	1970
Tropics	990 Post Street	1972

Truck Stop	Church & Market Streets	1974
Turf Club	76 6th Street	
Turn Table		
Tuxedo Junction		
Twilight	456 Castro Street	1971
Twin Peaks Tavern	401 Castro Street	1972
Two Turtles	741 O'Farrell Street	
Tycon's	1450 Lombard Street	1971

U

Uncle Bert's Place	4086 18th Street	1988
Uncle Billy's Scoreboard	147 Mason Street	1960's
Uncle Sam's		
Underground		
Union Square	484 Geary Street	1972
Up & Coming	18th & Collingwood Streets	
Upper Warehouse	1551 Mission Blvd	1952

V

Via Vai	1203 Polk Street	1960's
Victoria's Corner		
Villa's	510 Brannan Street	1972
Villa Caprice		
Village Pub	4086 18th Street	1977
Village, The	901 Columbus	1972

W

Wagon Wheel	1st Street off Mission

Wagon's, The	917 Folsom Street	1985
Warehouse	333 11th Street	1986
Water Front	128 The Embarcadero	1970's
Watergate West		
Watering Hole II		
Watering Hole II	1145 Folsom Street	
Web	1965 Polk Street	1965
White Swallow, The	1750 Polk Street	
Whatever's Right	Haight Street	1965
Who Cares	Haight Street	1956
Why Not	Ellis Street	
Wild Goose	1488 Pine Street	1972
Wild Side West	424 Cortland Avenue	
Wilde Oscar	59 2nd Street	1971
Windjammer	645 Geary Blvd.	1974
Wood Shed	1601 Market Street	1974
Wooden Horse	622 Polk Street	

Y

Yacht Club, The	2155 Polk Street	1962
Yerba Buena Village	Taylor & Washington	

Z

Zell's	
Zoo	3600 Market Street

Sources
By Chapter

We Two Boys Together Clinging
> Photo: Walt Whitman - Public Domain

Oscar Wilde Visits San Francisco
> Photo Oscar Wilde - Public Domain

Author's Notes
> Photo: Anna Kief
> - Author's personal collection

1   Brown Leather Jacket

2   I'll Cut Your Ears Off
> Photo: Author's home
> - Author's personal collection
> Photo: Author in tricycle 1947
> - Author's personal collection

3   Hold Your Nose
> Photo: Media Hotel
> - Mount Clemens Public Library
> The Detroit News:
> Mt. Clemens, 'Bath City of America' – July 24, 1999
> By Pat Zacharias and Vivian Baulch
> WikipediA: Mount Clemens, Michigan

4   The Magic Milton Show

5   A Sense of Duty

6   Merry Little Christmas

- June 26, 2964
Found SF: Folsom Street: The Miracle Mile
WikipediA: Charles (Chuck) Arnett
Photo: Michael Keller - The ruins of the Tool Box in
1971. Chuck Arnett's Mural
Leather-Folk: Radical Sex, People, Politics, and Practice
By: Mark Thompson, Editor
Artist Chuck Arnett: His Life/Our Times
By Jack Fritscher

Photo: Empress I, The Widow Norton
- With Permission José Sarria
WikipediA: José Sarria
WikipediA: Imperial Court System
Photo: Empress II Bella & Her Boys
Photo: Gene Bache (Empress II Bella)
Photos Courtesy of Brian Benamati & Tony Onorati, OnoratiDesign, Inc.
Photo: - Empress Doris X & elephant 1975 Parade
- Author's personal collection

30   Lions & Tigers & Bears
WikipediA: Japantown, San Francisco
History is tucked away in this Japantown theater
By Natasha Chen - Out of the Fog
Photo: Wizard of Oz float #1
 - Author's personal collection
Photo: Wizard of Oz float #2
 - Author's personal collection
Photo: Oz Medal - Author's personal collection
SFGate: Herb Caen: Bay Area rapid typewriter

31   Sunrise in The City
World Travel List:
Get Your Ghoul On – Halloween in Five U.S. Cities

32   "Number Please"
The Press Democrat:
Annapolis shutters its post office, town center
By: Chris Smith
Photo: Annapolis Post Office
- Author's personal collection

33   Ballerinas with Beards
Photo: Michael Schoch & Lou Kief
 - Author's personal collection

Photo: Annapolis "Oz" Cottage #1
- Author's personal collection
Photo: Flower Child
- Author's personal collection
Photo: Annapolis "Oz" Cottage #2
- Author's personal collection

34   City of Tears
Photo: Michael Daly & Steve Miller
Mike Foundation:
Photo: SF Chronicle Headlines - Chronicle Publishing
Encyclopedia of World Biography: Harvey Milk bio
KQED: Harvey Milk, Hero and Martyr
The Dan White (Harvey Milk Murder) Trial (1979)
– by: Cindi Ernst
WikipediA: Moscone-Milk assassinations
WikipediA: Harvey Milk
WikipediA: White Night riots

35   Redwoods Make You Crazy
WikipediA: Pomo people
kstrom.net: Pomo People Brief History
RussianRiverTravel.com:
Armstrong Redwoods State Park
Redwoodhikes.com:
Armstrong Redwoods State Natural Reserve
Photo: Guerneville circa 1860 - Public Domain
GayRussianRiver.com:
Big Bottom (No seriously that's what it was called)
The Bay Area Reporter:
Russian River resorts ready for summer
WikipediA: Leonard Matlovich

36   Hexagon Whores
WikipediA: Bohemian Grove
The Press Democrat: Gaye LeBaron – July 22, 1979

Pond Farm Artists gathered at Hexagon House in 1949
WikipediA: Max Factor, Sr.
WikipediA: Pond Farm
Photo: Bill Walls & Rick Cook
- Author's personal collection
WikipediA: Fred MacMurray
Graphic: Russian River Gothic
- Courtesy John DeSalvio, www.desalvio.net
Los Angeles Times: The State – September 09, 1986
Centennial Savings & Loan

37   Changes in Attitudes
Photo: Lou Kief & Bill Walls
- Author's personal collection
Photo: Yacht Providence
- Author's personal collection

38   Buckets of Piss
Photo: Friends of Providence
- Author's personal collection

39   Changes in Latitudes
Photo: Providence Golden Gate
- Author's personal collection
Photo: Providence Christmas
- Author's personal collection
Photo: Map of Baja
- Author's personal collection
Photo: Capt. Tom's Paradise
- Author's personal collection
Photo: Providence Panama Canal
- Author's personal collection
Photo: Providence Gaillard Cut
- Author's personal collection

40   Sailing Backwards
      Photo: Adventure Map
      - Author's personal collection
      WikipediA: Sailing Directions
      WikipediA: Portobelo, Colon
      Photo: Quarter Real (2 Photos)
      - Author's personal collection
      Photo: Map – Loop Currents in Gulf of Mexico
      - Author's personal collection
      Photo: Benecia Cat in Sail
      - Author's personal collection

41   Roaming No More
      WikipediA: 1989 Loma Prieta earthquake
      Photo: Leonard Matlovich
      Photo: Golden Fire Plug
      Photo: Rick Cook
      - Author's personal collection
      Photo: Randy Shilts -
      © Phyllis Christopher
      http://www.Phyllischristopher.com
      Photo: Michael Schoch
      - Author's personal collection
      Photo: Scott Smith and Harvey Milk in their Castro
      Street Camera Store circa 1974, © Marc Cohen
      Photo: Hans Von Braun
      - Author's personal collection

Epilogue
      The Dish: Two Popes, One Secretary
      February 27, 2012 @ 12:15 PM
      By Andrew Sullivan
      Huffington Post:
      Pope Benedict XVI Will Be Called 'Emeritus Pope' In Re
      tirement, Vatican Says

By Nicole Winfield – February 28, 2013 05:28 PM EST
New York Daily News:
Vanity Fair Cover: Padre Georg

Afterword
    Photo: Lou Kief & Bill Walls
    - Author's personal collection

Index

Symbols

A

C

D

E

F

G

H

N

O

P

Q

R

S

T